# MORE OF CANADA'S

# BEST CANOE
# ROUTES

# MORE OF CANADA'S

## BEST CANOE ROUTES

Edited by ALISTER THOMAS

A BOSTON MILLS PRESS BOOK

Published by Boston Mills Press 2003

First printing 2003

**Cataloguing in Publication Data**
More of Canada's best canoe routes / edited by Alister Thomas.

ISBN 1–55046–390–X

1. Canoes and canoeing — Canada.  2. Canoeists — Canada — Biography.
I. Thomas, Alister, 1953–

GV776.15.A2C66 2003    796.1'22'0971    C2002–901682–7

Publisher Cataloguing-in-Publication Data (U.S.) is available.

Published in Canada in 2003 by
Boston Mills Press
132 Main Street
Erin, Ontario N0B 1T0
Tel 519-833-2407
Fax 519-833-2195
books@bostonmillspress.com
www.bostonmillspress.com

IN CANADA:
Distributed by Firefly Books Ltd.
3680 Victoria Park Avenue
Toronto, Ontario M2H 3K1

IN THE UNITED STATES:
Distributed by Firefly Books (U.S.) Inc.
P.O. Box 1338, Ellicott Station
Buffalo, New York 14205

Jacket design: Gill Stead
Text design and page composition: PageWave Graphics Inc.

The publisher acknowledges the financial support of the
Government of Canada through the Book Publishing Industry
Development Program (BPIDP) for its publishing efforts.

Printed and bound in Canada

*To my parents, Bettie and Keith Thomas,*
*for sending me to camp, for lending me*
*enough money to buy my first canoe...*
*and for suggesting I build character*
*by paddling upstream more often.*

# Contents

## SECTION TWO: 18 Profiles of 24 Trippers

## SECTION THREE: Vital Tips for Paddling and Protecting Canada's Waterways

# Preface

LIKE ITS PREDECESSOR, *CANADA'S BEST CANOE ROUTES*, PUBLISHED IN 2000, *More of Canada's Best Canoe Routes* has three sections. In Section One you'll discover fellow paddlers regaling tales of 31 great canoe and kayak trips, from coast to coast to coast. Section Two features eighteen profiles of twenty-four proficient paddlers — young and old, male and female, First Nation and Canadian. Section Three highlights stewardship (the Grand River Conservation Authority), craftsmanship (the Canadian Canoe Museum), canoe tripping ("The Ascetic in a Canoe") . . . and a rant (Raff's Maxims).

## 31 Terrific Trips

We start on the West Coast and move east, jumping to the north on a few occasions, touching down in all ten provinces and three territories. Dunnery Best's lead story begins: "When I look at the old maps now, the idea of paddling an open cedar-strip canoe from Bella Coola to Prince Rupert, about 330 miles (530 km) north (as the seagull flies) on the British Columbia coast, doesn't seem particularly extreme. After all, most of the route followed the famed Inside Passage, sheltered from the full brunt of the Pacific Ocean." Find out whether it was dumb luck or minor miracles that allowed Dunnery and Sandy Hart to complete their journey.

Like your first love, the first river you paddle runs through the rest of your life. "You discover your definition of a river, the journey where your subconscious learns the pattern for what a journey should be. You can be years or miles away from the physical river, and suddenly its reflecting pool will bubble up to the surface of your life to remind you who you are," writes Lynn Noel in her story, entitled "The Hotfooters." "My first river was the Margaree [in Nova Scotia]."

In between, geographically, Ksenia Barton and Stephan Kesting find a perfect honeymoon destination on Manitoba's Seal River. "I won't deny the appeal of a tropical honeymoon — fun and sun in a simple package," Ksenia explains. "But seeking adventure and romance in the Canadian North was more our style. We craved true wilderness and a chance to be totally alone as newlyweds."

On the Rupert River, in Quebec, Teen Sivell finds . . . poetry. "And time yet for a hundred indecisions,/ And for a hundred visions and revisions,/ Before the taking of a toast and tea." She says, "In moments of duress, it is still that line of T. S. Eliot's that pops into my head, lightens my concern and lets me carry on clear-headed."

David F. Pelly describes how young people from around the world cope with wilderness on the Kazan River, which flows through the Northwest Territories and Nunavut. On part of a multiyear, cross-Canada trip, Max Finkelstein appreciates the mighty, muddy and majestic Peace River in Alberta.

Scott Cunningham, twice, and Kevin Redmond find turbulent water and much more on New Brunswick's Bay of Fundy and Saint John River, and in Newfoundland's Gros Morne National Park, respectively. Meanwhile, Kevin Callan goes looking for laser guns, Pi and the center of the universe in Ontario's Wabakimi Provincial Park.

Some trips are not complete without a portage or two from hell. Laurel Archer relives a trip, the Nitinat Triangle canoe route on Vancouver Island, that was more portaging than paddling. And her sister, Sheila Archer, recounts a few bruisers on Alberta's Grease River. So too does Faye Hallett on a trip on the Peel–Rat–Porcupine Rivers in the Yukon and Northwest Territories. To conquer these portages, it takes equal amounts of brute strength and humor.

There are three accounts where the canoe displays its versatility. Keith Morton describes a trip in a replica of a 33-foot-long West Coast native canoe, while Howard Heffler gives invaluable pointers for poling a mountain river in autumn. Geoff Danysk goes one further by giving an insider's report on training for the ice canoe race at Quebec City's Winter Carnival. "After getting dressed in my car, I step out into the minus 13 degree Fahrenheit (-25° C) December morning, thankful it is calm . . . no wind chill," Geoff writes. "Not exactly your typical weather for the first day of the paddling season, but this isn't your typical paddling."

Encounters with an irate carnivore and human stupidity are told by Paula Zybach, charged by a grizzly bear on the Yukon's Alsek River, and Patrick Mahaffey, faced with impatience and thoughtlessness on the Clearwater River in Saskatchewan.

Paddling can also be a vehicle for spiritual quests. John Geary finds the spirit of Grey Owl in Saskatchewan's Prince Albert National Park;

Hap Wilson learns from the lessons painted on stone on Manitoba's Bloodvein River; James Cullingham has a personal epiphany on Ontario's Winisk River; and Bert Horwood expresses his feelings for five northern rivers — Coppermine (picturesque), Nanook (raw), Ellice (tumultuous), Horton (tranquil) and Kuujjua (sublime).

Bob Henderson explains the appeal of returning year after year to the Chiniguichi River and Laura Creek Circuit. Also in Ontario, Ned Franks describes the thrill and pleasure of the Madawaska, just a half-day's travel to more than a third of Canada's population. On the Little Nahanni River in the Northwest Territories, Glenn Hodgins makes an emotional return, in memory of a friend and trip leader who disappeared mysteriously twenty years before.

Joanie McGuffin recounts a three-month circumnavigation, with husband Gary, around Lake Superior's 2,000-mile (3,200 km) shoreline, circling the lake according to its own natural counterclockwise currents. Bruce Hodgins presents a whimsical history of the No-Name Trent-Peterborough Canoe Group. "We love the anarchy of our organization and the quiet collective self-discipline and mutual help on the waterways," Bruce writes. "We have the J-strokes, the back paddles and the pries in the stern and the high braces and cross-bows in the bow. We have the overall skills with the back and front ferries. We do not need a collective rudder."

In Bluenose country, Andy Smith uncovers mystique and mystery in the Tobeatic Wilderness Area. "The Tobi is a vast hinterland — by Nova Scotia standards — of ancient Mi'kmaq migration routes, trout pools, bizarre balancing rocks deposited by retreating glaciers, bogs — lots of bogs — and mosquitoes, blackflies and other things appropriate to these dark regions," he writes. Not far away, Sheena Masson and Sue Browne take us on a water trail tour of the South Shore.

Also in Atlantic Canada, Bryon Howard finds mussels, seals and herons on Prince Edward Island's East Side, and Shawn Hodgins details a trip on the breathtaking, bodacious and buggy Notokwanon River in Labrador.

You'll find all types of trips — daylong to expedition length, Far North to close at home, serene lakes to open ocean.

## 18 Paddler Profiles

In the middle section of this book are profiles of paddlers from across Canada, representing every province and territory. They are canoe builders, whitewater fiends, visionaries, instructors, outfitters and paddlers who are just crazy about canoeing and kayaking.

Wendy Grater, owner of Black Feather Adventure Company, Canada's largest paddling outfitter, has a simple explanation for why paddling is so fulfilling. "I feel most at home in the wilderness. . . . In a small, like-minded group you can witness natural team-building," she explains. "Ultimately, a paddling trip simplifies life."

Venture north to Cambridge Bay, Nunavut and experience five-year-old Ayalik's first canoe trip. "If you ask me what the best part of the trip was, I say paddle, rapids and fish," he says. "If you come up here, I can tell you which birds we have — I know them pretty well now." You'll be impressed by Ayalik's enthusiasm.

On the East Coast, meet Scott Cunningham, who circumnavigated the 4,350 miles (7,000 km) of Nova Scotia's rugged, diverse shorelines. Not bad for a fellow who didn't start paddling until he was 29. Scott, a PhD in molecular biology, now operates Coastal Adventures.

Betty Pratt-Johnson knows all about adventure. She started scuba diving at 37 years of age, whitewater kayaking at 47, paragliding at 67 and then at 70 . . . ice climbing. Few people have paddled more British Columbia rivers.

By the time Kyle Kraiker and his brother, Brendan, were 9 and 6, respectively, they had paddled all over North America, thanks to their parents, Rolf and Debra Kraiker — the foremost experts on paddling with young ones. "Canoes are a great way to take children into the wilderness," says Debra. "Regardless of their age, kids will want to feel like they're part of the trip and parents need to be prepared to accommodate them."

A former Olympian biathlete (cross-country skiing and rifle marksmanship), Jim Boyde is a veteran northern paddler and instructor. "Students need to rediscover how traditional First Nations travelers, European explorers, prospectors and contemporary recreational paddlers discovered themselves in the wilderness of Yukon," he explains.

The paddling community lost an influential and important member on May 20, 2000. Victoria Jason, the first woman to kayak the Northwest Passage, and responsible for reintroducing the kayak to the Inuit village of Kugaaruk, formerly Pelly Bay, in the late 1990s, died from a brain tumor. She was 55.

Back in the early 1970s, select paddlers from across Canada had dream jobs. They spent the summers paddling wild and remote rivers. And best of all, they got paid for the pleasure — approximately eight dollars an hour. Harry Collins, a former Wild River surveyor, is now executive director of the Miramichi River Environment Assessment Committee.

Cathy Allooloo's first experience in a kayak was far from auspicious, but she was determined and talented, going on to represent Canada at the world championships and Olympics. Today she runs NARWAL, a Yellowknife-based outdoor adventure training school.

Very occasionally you meet someone who lives an urban life but who is also comfortable spending months paddling wilderness rivers, portaging remote forest trails and camping wherever that day ends. Meet Max Finkelstein, who happens to be in charge of communications for the Canadian Heritage Rivers System.

David Finch collects canoes, builds canoes, finds homes for canoes and supplies canoes for the film industry. He paddles and poles, year-round. As he explains, "I like to encourage people to paddle because it gives them a different way to experience the river, the landscape and . . . life."

Despite having no money and no publishing experience, Scott and Tanya MacGregor created *Rapid* magazine. It has become a great success. Then Scott and Tanya started *Adventure Kayak* magazine, and it, too, has filled a need. *Canoeroots* magazine is the latest venture from the paddling publishers.

David Mills has fostered and nurtured canoe awareness, skills development, whitewater appreciation, canoe building and power paddling on Prince Edward Island for close to 40 years. He knows how important and fulfilling it is to get out on the water.

A dream trip came true when Bill Jeffery participated in a three-week adventure with local Dene. The elders provided a living history of ancient Dene names for every aspect of the land, and around the campfire, their stories and legends infused Bill with a newfound appreciation of their culture, writes Bill's wife, Joan Jeffery.

After much experimentation, Ted Moores, who has an encyclopedic knowledge of canoes and their builders, pioneered the woodstrip-epoxy canoe construction technique. The result: a ribless canoe, satin smooth inside and out, that is strong and light. One of these was a wedding gift to Prince Charles and Princess Diana.

He is an acclaimed paddling instructor, prolific canoe and sea kayak writer and photographer. Kevin Redmond, the second person in Canada to become a Master Canoe Instructor with the CRCA, has paddled throughout most of Canada but most intimately in insular Newfoundland and Labrador and along the Eastern Atlantic coast.

Five of Canada's top-rated competitive female paddlers — Anna Levesque, Tiffany Manchester, Saskia van Mourik, Jodee Dixon and Naomi Heffler — discuss their favorite paddling trips, why paddling is special and qualities needed to be a good paddler.

Pierre Elliott Trudeau, Canada's long-standing prime minister, federalist, activist, intellectual, gunslinger and international irritant, will be remembered by a certain group of Canadians because he paddled a canoe. Not only did Trudeau take to his canoe for adventure and solitude, he made it okay to do so.

## Vital Tips for Paddling and Protecting Canada's Waterways

There are four stories in the third section of *More of Canada's Best Canoe Routes*. We begin with a pilgrimage to Peterborough, to Ontario's Canadian Canoe Museum. To let you know what to expect, Gwyneth Hoyle provides a walking tour of the CCM. "Many museums have canoes as part of their collections. In Canada, the Museum of Civilization in Ottawa, the Royal Ontario Museum in Toronto and the Glenbow in Calgary all have sizable collections of Aboriginal craft. In the northeastern United States, one of the nineteen buildings of the Adirondack Museum is devoted to portable boats, which include birchbark canoes as well as the famous Adirondack guide boats and lightweight Rushton canoes. At Clayton, New York, near the Thousand Islands, the Antique Boat Museum has a selection of carpentered canoes among its classic motor launches," she writes.

"Only one museum, the Canadian Canoe Museum . . . is devoted entirely to the collection of canoes, kayaks, allied watercraft and related artifacts. The latest extensive exhibit at this museum tells the story of the development of Canada through the medium of the canoe."

The next story in this section is about the revitalization of the Grand River in southwestern Ontario. The Grand River Conservation Authority, established in 1934, started turning neglect into concern, inaction into action, and helped bring the river back to life. The GRCA is Canada's first and the third-oldest conservation authority in the world.

"The vision of the GRCA is one of a healthy and sustaining relationship between the natural environment of the Grand River watershed and the demands on this environment by all forms of life," explains Chairman Peter Krause. "The GRCA's mission is to conserve the natural processes and resources that support a safe and healthy environment for future generations in the Grand River watershed."

The GRCA, which in 2000 was awarded the Australian Thiess River-prize, the world's most prestigious award for river management excellence, established various initiatives to reduce flood damage, improve water quality, provide adequate water supply, protect natural areas, and institute watershed planning and recreation and environmental education.

To get a proper feel for what the river has to offer, we follow Eric Thomlinson, founder of the Ancient Mariners, a paddling club for seniors, and unofficial protector of and advocate for the Grand, as he paddles from source to mouth, a distance of 185 miles (296 km).

The third story is former prime minister Pierre Elliot Trudeau's inspiringly eloquent "Exhaustion and Fulfilment: The Ascetic in a Canoe." It's a classic.

Wrapping up this section is a Joe Canadian-like rant from Jim Raffan, Canada's premier canoe writer. Here's a sample of Raff's Maxims for Happy Paddling:

Borrowed canoes bend
Nylon is not soundproof
Wet food is better than no food
PFD, Perfected Flotation Device
Duct tape can save a marriage
Wash your socks
Don't grab the gunwales
Scout before you shoot
Wet rocks are slippery
Declination is not politics
Hurrying can hurt
Clean your teeth
UV light rots nylon
Dirt repels bugs
Real women portage
Real men cook

These are the paddlers you'll meet in *More of Canada's Best Canoe Routes*. I hope you enjoy the book and become a paddler, too.

*Alister Thomas*
*Calgary, Alberta*

# Acknowledgments

Like a long portage, putting this book together required lots of grunt work, fortuitous rest spots and many hands to lighten the load. First and foremost are the good folks at Boston Mills Press. Thanks to John Denison for suggesting the project, Noel Hudson for the go-ahead and keeping me on track, and Kathy Fraser for grammatical and style assistance. Tip of the paddle to Kevin Cockburn of PageWave Graphics for the fine page composition and Gill Stead for the cover design.

Much gratitude to my wife, Gae VanSiri; my brother, Kevin Thomas, and Sue Savor, for assistance with the lift-overs.

For guidance in upstream tracking and downstream lining, merci to Morgan Fisher, Phil Hossack, Gary Norris, Allan "Vin" Norris, Bruce Hodgins, Paul Mason, Mark Scriver, Max Finkelstein, John and Pauline McAllister, David Finch, Bev Wilson, John B. Hughes, Michael Peake, David F. Pelly, Jim Raffan, the Grand River Conservation Authority's Ralph Beaumont and Barbara Veale, and the Canadian Recreational Canoeing Association's Paul Graner and Heidi Seida.

A heartfelt thanks to all the paddler-authors for their fine stories. This is your book.

To paraphrase a familiar saying: Keep your paddle in the water and always lean downstream.

# More of Canada's Best Canoe Routes

Natokwanon River

Gros Morne National Park

Margaree River

Nova Scotia's Coastal Water Trail

Offshore New Brunswick

PEI's East Side

Saint John River

Tobeatic

No-Name Trent-Peterborough Canoe Group

Rupert River

Wabakimi Provincial Park

Chiniguchi River and Laura Creek Circuit

Madawaska River

Winisk River

Bloodvein River

Lake Superior

Nanook River

Ellice River

Seal River

Kuujjua River

Coppermine River

Kazan River

Horton River

Little Nahanni

Clearwater River

Prince Albert National Park

Rat-Peel

Grease River

Ice Canoeing

Peace River

Poling

Alsek River

BC's Inside Passage

Telegraph Cove to Bella Bella

Nitinat Triangle Canoe Route

# 31 Trips From Coast to Coast to Coast and Everywhere In Between

# Paddling B.C.'s Inside Passage in a 16-Foot Canoe
## Minor Miracles or Dumb Luck?

Dunnery Best

W HEN I LOOK AT THE OLD MAPS NOW, THE IDEA OF PADDLING AN OPEN cedar-strip canoe from Bella Coola to Prince Rupert, about 330 miles (530 km) north (as the seagull flies) on the British Columbia coast, doesn't seem particularly extreme. After all, most of the route followed the famed Inside Passage, which is sheltered from the full brunt of the Pacific Ocean.

Nor did the idea seem outlandish when it was first proposed late one rainy Vancouver winter evening. The trip was the culmination of several years of dedicated exploration of British Columbia, an addictive pursuit for a couple of Eastern Canadians. By that point, my old friend Sandy Hart and I had covered much of the province, including rainy trips to Prince Rupert and the Queen Charlotte Islands, often working in the woods and on ranches. We had been through the arid Chilcotin, the back door to Bella Coola, and hiked and climbed along the interior side of the Coast Mountains.

We often made long trips in my 16-foot, cedar-strip Tremblay canoe, and spent much time discussing the adventures of earlier, more daring travelers. So there was a certain continuity and logic to the Bella Coola-to-Prince Rupert enterprise.

But months later, when we finally pushed our loaded canoe from a beach on North Bentinck Arm, a half-mile or so west of Bella Coola, the ample stupidity of the venture was obvious. To a casual observer, the water seemed relatively calm. But big, active, tidewater with lengthy fetches, when seasoned with even modest amounts of wind, becomes truly dangerous.

As we stood watching the waves lapping up to and occasionally cresting over the midship gunwales, before we even got in the canoe, the whole idea really did seem beyond normal practice. Nevertheless, to my amazement even today, we did manage to launch and we did cross North Bentinck Arm, several miles across, and we did make a start on our foolhardy journey.

To be sure, we were heavily loaded. The Tremblay is a big, capable boat — twenty-plus days of necessities such as food, not enough whisky, and fuel was a serious load. As well, we carried a full sailing rig, consisting of lee-boards and rudder, which Sandy had lovingly crafted from ¾-inch solid mahogany and brass hardware. The mast, lateen sail and sundry rigging added to the freight.

This sailing gear was heavy-duty, engineered to withstand anything the Pacific could throw at it. Alas, our first attempt to use the rig proved to be the last, as the overly powerful sail tried to drive the bow under water, even in the lightest breeze, and steering was like wrestling a bear. From that point on, the sailing stuff was just an additional burden.

The essential tone of the journey was well established on that first day, when the wind picked up, along with serious rain and mounting waves, as we made an unsuccessful attempt to round Messachie Nose. There the big water of Burke Channel mixes it up with the confluence of North and South Bentinck Arms, given salsa by the addition of Labouchere Channel; all in all, it was a confusing smorg of increasingly stormy water.

When you read "nose" on a British Columbia coastal map, think proboscis of truly epic proportions. Think danger for any open canoe if there is even the faintest sign of life from wind and waves. Survival soon dictated that we get off the water, which was clearly impossible on a windward cliff-bound coast. Then came one of the numerous minor miracles that occurred on the trip. As if by specific order, a tiny cove appeared, like a welcome eddy in a rapid, getting us out of the main wave action. We were able to find

enough footing to fend the canoe off the rocks, and hand the freight and finally the canoe up over several mossy boulders to a safety zone at the trunk of several massive firs.

The spot was safe, thanks be, but not even remotely flat. As the rain gained strength we erected our self-supporting tent and wedged it between the giant trees. The slope was something like what you'd get on a fully extended reclining chair, just the thing for tired canoeists settling in for an evening of television on an ironbound coast. Except that through the course of the evening, sleeping bag and occupant slowly, inevitably slid to the foot of the tent.

We spent two wet days at that spot, finally teaching ourselves the cardinal rule of Pacific Coast open-canoe travel: Get up really early, before the weather has a chance to rouse itself, and accomplish difficult passages long before you'd normally be having your first cup of coffee. From that point on, any additional mileage is a bonus.

Actually, we learned many things on that trip. It rarely stops raining in the rainforest, which is the whole point, I suppose. So, in order to light matches, it pays to keep a small rock in an inner pocket, where one's body heat is the best bet to ensure dryness. And, dry firewood is plentiful to anyone willing to invest a bit of effort. Simply find a piece of cedar driftwood of any size (huge is best), and chop away the top 6 inches (15 cm) or so, and lo, there is dry wood below. The saving grace for us in this wet world was that we carried an Optimus stove and lots of fuel.

## Open Water All the Way to Honolulu or Japan

Anyway, we eventually managed to clear the Nose, and work our way westward on Dean Channel, seeking Sir Alexander Mackenzie's Rock, marking his arrival on the coast. He was the first European to traverse the continent. "From Canada by land, 22 July 1793," reads the inscription. It's worth a look. Until you paddle those waters in a small wooden boat, with pipe and bannock, it's not really possible to understand the enormity of Mackenzie's achievement.

Still it rained. In those days I was acclimatized to rain. I was used to wet canoe trips. No big deal. I had just spent much of a winter in logging camps on the West Coast of Vancouver Island, where in one instance (not unusual) it didn't stop precipitating in one form or another — rain, heavy fog, snow, drizzle, whatever — for twenty-seven days. But that was winter, and wet was expected. In the summer, endless rain was a challenge, both spiritually and physically.

Contending with the ceaseless wet became a focal point of our enterprise. The rain slowed each day's progress. It demanded additional care and attention for all small tasks — keeping sleeping bags and some clothes dry, defending the tent from steady sodden encroachment, contending with wet food, whatever. The wet was cold and could have been dispiriting. Some days the sun would briefly appear as if offering a sporting gesture. On other occasions it rained through the night and continued all day, never letting up, varying only in intensity.

This is no exaggeration: Our trip took us past the entrance to Cousins Inlet, which leads north to Ocean Falls, a declining sawmill town, reputed to be the wettest place in Canada, receiving 10,000 inches (25,400 cm) of rain annually. Our policy was to travel every day, regardless, if only to burn sufficient calories to maintain body warmth.

Paddling through narrow, intricate Gunboat Passage, we eventually arrived in Bella Bella, a Native village on Campbell Island. It was very unusual for us to be paddling among ocean-going yachts, tugs and fishing boats in our open canoe. Bella Bella is noteworthy also as a location of the last licensed premises until Prince Rupert.

The crux pitch, so to speak, came soon after. The Inside Passage route links a series of fjord-like channels that run north-south, sheltered from the full might of the Pacific. Nevertheless, it is occasionally necessary to poke one's bow out into open ocean. Which is why, one rainy morning around four o'clock we were breaking camp, ready to traverse Seaforth Channel, on the way to Milbanke Sound — open water all the way to Honolulu or Japan, your choice.

This was a remarkable morning. As we loaded the canoe, a Canadian Coast Guard hovercraft suddenly appeared out of the dark and drizzle and, turning the corner, sped by, leaving only a flashing bright orange memory.

Out on Milbanke Sound, there was no wind. Belying that, 10-foot (3 m) waves rolled in from the Pacific, the product of some distant storm. Around us, the rollers crashed whitely on shoals and outcroppings as we picked our way through the mist into open ocean. In the bow, looking back, the stern towered 6 feet (1.8 m) high, and then, as the roller passed under the canoe, the vantage point was reversed.

It was a thrilling, dangerous ride, with water flowing gently over the midship gunwales with each wave. Poor visibility made navigation difficult, and we missed our intended route, continuing the open-water passage until some hours later we finally found calm behind Cecilia Island, and smoked a pipe to celebrate safe passage.

(Some months later I named the Tremblay *Milbanke Sound* in honor of its feat, and a friend painted the name on the bow in white Gothic lettering. Years passed, and when fractured planks and broken ribs finally forced a major rebuild and recanvasing, I cut the name Milbanke from the old skin. Framed, the faded green canvas with Milbanke still delights me with the memory.)

A day or so later we were paddling into a stiff headwind, in rain, into waves, against the tide, water slopping as usual over the gunwales, and making no progress. Paddling into a tide is a form of hell. After hours of brute labor, driving hard, it's easy to make the mistake of thinking you've actually accomplished something, which, of course, you haven't. You must know many, many songs to successfully engage the tide.

In this case, the sight of a small open canoe in big open water was unique enough to attract the attention of a Fisheries Canada vessel, a yacht chartered for the salmon season. Intrigued, she steamed up slowly, then paced us 50 yards to starboard. Finally, she came up closer and the captain hailed, asked after our mental health and whether we wanted a lift to Klemtu, a small Native village some miles further up Finlayson Channel. That was a reasonable guess as, other than the occasional abandoned fish packing plant, there was little else until Prince Rupert.

We answered in the affirmative, and willing hands soon helped lift us on board. Gear stowed, canoe lashed to the deck, coffee in hand, we joined the skipper on the bridge to enjoy the spectacle of what really were terrible conditions even in a modern 65-foot vessel. Dinner was fresh salmon, standard fare for the Fisheries crew. That night we stayed in the crew's aft quarters, draped deep with our drying gear. A minor miracle, indeed.

## Instant Local Heroes

Of course, the grunt work of bucking a headwind and tide in a heavy canoe is soon forgotten when the same forces are aligned in one's favor. There were days when tailwinds, waves and tides combined, and we rocketed north on narrow waters like Tolmie Channel and Graham Reach. I have no idea of our speed, but I do recall spectacular, unbelievable runs with mile after mile of sustained surfing with the bow wave cresting behind the bow seat.

The big Tremblay handled it all, thanks to its high sides and keel-less bottom. What was sacrificed in terms of leeway in a wind was more than compensated for by nice manners on waves.

The reality was — is — that open-water paddling is a dangerous pursuit. One missed paddle stroke and the canoe could be lost, as it nearly was. To this day I recall that single stroke, when a paddle slid sideways and the paddler's weight was suddenly misplaced, and we came within a heartbeat of having to try a self-rescue in cold water too far from land. But heaven watches over children and sailors, and we obviously qualified in both categories.

Another image has never left me. We were on Grenville Channel, a remarkable fjord, sometimes miles wide, sometimes narrowing to a few hundred yards between soaring granite cliffs. We were paddling far from land on glass-smooth water. Notably, it was not raining. With no warning, an orca rose 20 feet (6 m) from the starboard bow, rolling as it lifted out of the water, taking a look at us and vanishing. Silence. The whale stunned us, stuns me still, establishing the proper order of precedence on that coast.

Our final joust with eternity came late in the journey. The last piece of difficult water on the route is Chatham Sound, which leads directly into the port of Prince Rupert.

Chatham Sound is a rough piece of water. To the west, it opens to Hecate Strait. From the east, it receives the outflow of the Skeena River, a mighty river in its own right. We needed to traverse this turbulent channel or spend days working around it. As the hours passed we paddled further into open water, not realizing that the Skeena currents made a straight-line crossing impossible. Visibility was so poor, we only gradually realized our predicament.

If we had been smarter, we would have been frightened. Miles from shore, we were bucking a powerful current as the day waned, and conditions gradually deteriorated. Then, as usual, fortune shone. A fishing boat steaming back to Prince Rupert with a load of salmon spotted us, and came within hailing distance. Boys, he hailed, come aboard, come aboard. The skipper was a Native. He told us later that his own son had died on that water only a few years before.

So ended our voyage, after less than two weeks at sea, sooner than we had originally planned. We were deposited late that evening on a public wharf adjacent to the terminal for the Vancouver Island ferry. The next day, we lined up with the cars and campers, and carried our boat and gear aboard the *Queen of Prince Rupert* for the voyage south.

The captain of the ship provided a final memory. In the course of making announcements to passengers (don't smoke on car decks, control your pets, et cetera), he noted that the ship was carrying unusual passengers, a pair of canoeists who had just paddled the Inside Passage. Instant local heroes. That night we put up our tent on the steel deck. Next morning, shipboard fame notwithstanding, the crew still felt it necessary to use a hose to clean the decks. By then we were used to heavy rain, of course, and refused to budge.

# Nitinat Triangle Canoe Route
## Strain, Pain and Rain

Laurel Archer

ALWAYS ON THE LOOKOUT FOR ADVENTURE, BRAD AND I HEARD ABOUT the Nitinat Triangle canoe route soon after we moved to Vancouver Island. There was just one problem: everyone knew about it, but no one had ever paddled it. This seemed strange.

The Nitinat Triangle is located in the Pacific Rim National Park Reserve; it is an unequal triangle route. One side, 16 miles (26 km) in length, connects Nitinat Lake to Hobiton Lake to Tsusiat and Little Tsusiat Lakes by a series of long portages. Another side, 13.5 miles (22 km) long, involves paddling Nitinat Lake from the Pacific Ocean back to the first side's put-in. The bottom section is 4 miles (7 km) of ocean paddling. What did we choose? The side with the portages, of course. And not only that, we did it twice.

In my readings about the route, the words "wet, difficult portages" and "physical stamina required" did catch my attention, but so did "wild and remote" and "spectacular coastal scenery." Maybe it was the fact we couldn't find out a whole lot about this popular trip, or maybe it was the lure of the untouched rainforest, old-growth Western cedar and hemlock that finally hooked us. Or, perhaps it was the anticipation of the Dungeness crab for sale at the Nitinat Narrows ferry crossing, the likes of which we had eaten in ecstasy the year before when we hiked the West Coast Trail. I don't know. Whatever it was that possessed us to do one arm of the Nitinat Triangle canoe route, it quickly became the most unforgettable canoe trip of our lives.

It is a bright, breezy morning. Brad and I drive along Nitinat Main, an isolated logging road southwest of Port Alberni, turn right at the fish hatchery sign, cross the Little Nitinat River and head to the usual put-in for the trip, the Knob Point Recreation Site, on the northwest side of Nitinat Lake. A few miles down the stony track, we are stopped by a road closure sign. The track has been almost completely washed out and what is left is a jumble of huge boulders. But that doesn't stop us.

We get our Blazer to the other side, and as we continue on, a warning signal starts going off in my head. The creek is dry now, but what if it rains? Will we be able to get out of here after our trip? I'm too uneasy to leave the vehicle at Knob Point, so we turn around and look for another launch site.

We need one, quick. The wind on Nitinat Lake is beginning to kick up and will increase throughout the day; locals claim you can set your watch by it. It's now noon. We decide it's important to stay on the northwest side of the lake so we don't have to cross the lake to reach the Hobiton Lake portage. We scout the Little Nitinat River from the road and head to the fish hatchery (our new launch site, we hope).

Luckily, a friendly hatchery employee tells us we can park our vehicle right there at the riverbank, so we quickly unload and set off. The lower Little Nitinat is a great float as we whisk by huge dead trees in awe. We quickly reach Nitinat Lake. I start to think this trip might not be jinxed, after all.

With the wind rushing at us, trying to push us back upriver, we paddle hard to make it down the lake. The occasional wave jumps in the boat and we get our first taste of the salt waters of this 15-mile-long (24 km) tidal lake. It has my ever-increasing respect.

Eventually, we reach the Hobiton Lake portage and smirk at the Parks Canada sign at the trail. "Looks like a walk in the park," I declare. "It can't be as awful a portage as hinted at in the literature if there's a sign, can it? Besides, isn't this one of the Island's most popular canoe routes? How hard can it be?"

We were in for a *big* shock. Have you ever tried to portage a canoe across a fallen cedar tree 6.5 feet (2 m) off the ground? Have you ever done it three or four times over the slipperiest logs imaginable? We slog through mud and trip over exposed roots for one and half hours. While we still think it's kind of amusing, we take some photos. And then we remember what it was like on the West Coast Trail last year. We grit our teeth to negotiate the half-mile-long Portage of Strain.

Finally reaching Hobiton Lake, covered with green scum and black and red mud and drenched in sweat, I think to myself that was the absolute worst. I tell Brad, "That was like hiking the West Coast Trail with a canoe on my back."

Back on the water, I start to feel better and regain my appetite for adventure and the nature of Vancouver Island's west coast. On my right rises Hobiton Ridge, carpeted with old-growth cedar and hemlock. To my left a tiny island of green and gold moss pleases my eye.

We camp on a gravel bar near Hitchie Creek. The spot boasts great tent sites and a spectacular waterfall, accessed via an exciting scramble up a creek bed. The sun sets over the lake and I appreciate this beautiful place.

## Portage of Pain

We wake to a misty, overcast morning. Hobiton Ridge is shrouded in cloud, so we decide not to hike to the top. We push on to the southwest end of Hobiton Lake, to the portage to Tsusiat Lake. According to what I've read, the portage is 1 mile (1.6 km) long, with a 40-yard bog in the middle. I say to Brad, "This couldn't possibly be worse than the first portage, or why would the trip be so popular?"

As we paddle into the bay, where the trailhead is located, a spectral figure greets us. A dead hemlock points to the sky, and all around are bone-white giant cedars. I shiver in the cool air.

The portage starts with an uphill climb and deadfall is everywhere. Countless nurse logs cradle baby trees, creating tangles through which we attempt to thread two big packs and a 16-foot-long canoe. I'm doing okay with the canoe, until the bog. The trail avoids the sinking sphagnum moss, but crosses zillions of tree roots in a quicksand of black, stinking mud. As I plod through guck halfway up my shins, I remember the bog is home to insectivorous plants, called sundews. It is so unlikely the sun would ever shine on this bog, in this ever-so-wet rainforest, that I begin to laugh maniacally. "Ha! Ha! Ha!"

Then it happens. My legs are sucked down in the sulphuric quagmire and the canoe rolls me over into the bog. I lie on my back, a shell of my former self. Brad hears me yelling, dumps the packs and runs back to see if

I'm all right. I am, physically, once we maneuver me out of the sucking swamp, but my mind is beginning to wander. Maybe the bog is humanivorous?

"Is this a canoe route or a portage route?" I ask after I pull myself together.

"It gets worse after the bog," Brad replies.

"Oh," I say as I pick up the canoe and carry on.

As I look ahead, I have two options: use the huge fallen trees to cross the maze of deadfall and take the chance of falling off and breaking my legs and the canoe, or drag, push, heave and throw the canoe over and around the deadfall. Since the rotting wood is so slippery, I choose option two. A thousand scratches and bruises and two hours later, we are at the end of the Portage of Pain, the longest and most horrendous portage, ever.

Once I regain my composure, again, at the end of the trail, I joke to Brad, "Portaging on the Triangle Insane is an extreme sport." I calculate we have paddled 8.5 miles (14 km) down Little Nitinat River and Nitinat Lake, portaged half a mile (1 km) into Hobiton, paddled 4 miles (7 km) down Hobiton and portaged 1 mile (1.6 km) to Tsusiat Lake. The time ratio is even more telling: four hours of paddling to four hours portaging. And we still have a couple more portages before reaching the Pacific Ocean.

Brad says to me, as we load the canoe, "You'll have to do some pretty fancy talking to get me to go back across that portage again."

I wince for the millionth time that day. What if it's storming when we get to the Pacific? We need ideal conditions to paddle to Nitinat Narrows and then enough time to navigate the tide. Otherwise, we have to portage 4 miles (7 km) down the West Coast Trail to reach the lakeside of the narrows, or we have to go back the way we came. "Oh, please let the weather cooperate, or I'll never hear the end of it," I whisper. Hard to believe, this trip was my idea.

We paddle to the far end of Tsusiat Lake, looking forward to setting up camp and taking off our mud-and-sweat encrusted clothes. I am absolutely exhausted. After some rest and a cup of tea, we'll decide how to reach the Pacific.

With a fire going, the tarp and tent set up, tea steaming in my mug, I finally sit and appreciate Tsusiat Lake. The water and mountains are soft blue and gray, a coastal landscape of mist. This is why people take on the hardships of horrible portages: to explore such gorgeous lakes and find true wilderness and solitude. We have seen no signs of other people, nothing. Two river otters, a mink and a marten are our only visitors so far.

As if on cue, a large dark shape in the pale blue water catches my eye. It's a black bear swimming lazily across the lake. It turns and looks at me. I take a sip of tea. Not while I'm resting, please! It turns its head in answer to my plea and carries on with its original course, enters the trees and disappears. I toast the creature's consideration and sink back into my lifejacket-and-driftwood recliner, feeling quite content. I accept this is going to be one Dr. Jekyll-and-Mr. Hyde kind of trip. When the West Coast is great, it's really great. When it's bad, it's terrible.

## Portage of Rain

That night the rain is pounding so hard on the tent fly, I can't sleep. Should we push on the next day or wait for it to clear, I wonder. Round and round my thoughts whirl. I'm so tired, but I can't sleep. This is insane!

It's still raining hard at 7 A.M. We decide to push on to the ocean; it's only a carry over a logjam, one small lake and a half-mile (1 km) portage away. How bad can it be? We love the sea and camping there on the beach would be a treat, even if it's still storming. And, we reason, we'll be ready to sprint down to the narrows and back up Nitinat Lake should we have a chance.

The battle to reach the sea is a wet one. We slip on sinking, slimy logs, falling here and there. But who cares? It's still a downpour. Finally, we reach Little Tsusiat Lake and paddle to the end of it.

Just a half-mile-long (1 km) portage to Tsusiat Falls and the ocean. The trail is more dense than the others, and as we stumble and struggle along, I begin to think most people don't actually do the whole Nitinat Triangle. They just do parts of it . . . and very rarely this part. Already soaked, I laugh in the face of the army of salal bushes slapping us with their water bombs.

Brad turns and shouts, "I can hear the falls!"

We summon up our last reserves of strength and bash our way to the brink of Tsusiat Falls. Standing high above the beach, we watch the water fall away into the surging Pacific Ocean. This is the end of the Portage of Rain.

The West Coast Trail, from here to Nitinat Narrows, is at its most spectacular, and we marvel at being here again. We leave our canoe and gear on the trail, which was built to help save the lives of shipwreck victims, and climb down the three long, wooden ladders to the long beach that skirts the Graveyard of the Pacific. Huge breakers pound the shore and the wind hurls spray in our faces. If we try to launch, we'll capsize.

We walk along the sand back to Tsusiat, but before we reach the falls, we are stopped in our tracks. The skeleton of a huge Steller's sea lion is at our feet. The bones are bleached and there are only a few teeth left in the

massive jaws. Flippers are one big bone, we discover. I am breathless, struck by wonder, by the Pacific's savage beauty.

Eventually we set up camp in the shelter of a Sitka spruce, with no hope of waiting out the storm. The wind is still from the south and we know to expect at least a couple more days of rain and wind. That evening we decide that portaging the evils we know is better than learning about the ones we don't. With the vestibule door open, we lie in each other's arms watching the rollers heave and fall and the tide press in. It takes me a long time to fall asleep. I want to look at the sea, forever.

When we awake, we take comfort in the fact the rain has eased to a steady drizzle. After coffee and oatmeal, we begin the two-day journey back the way we came, paddling every once and a while in order to reach the next portage so we can hike with our canoe and gear.

To this day, when I'm feeling slightly insane, I still ask the eternal question I pondered as we returned through Rain, Pain and Strain, "What could *the most* popular canoe route on Vancouver Island possibly be like?"

# Telegraph Cove to Bella Bella
## *Vision Quest*

Keith Morton

M Y APPREHENSION INCREASED AS WE HEADED SEAWARD IN OUR REPLICA of a 33-foot-long West Coast native canoe. The wind was roaring ominously in the treetops flanking the harbor, so the weather warning to small craft was obviously well founded. Facing us was a two-week journey along the rugged coastline north of Vancouver Island, with an unfamiliar craft and an unfamiliar crew.

Beyond the shelter of the harbor, we were soon paddling into the teeth of the wind and waves. Actually, it turned out to be quite exhilarating, with the bow rising so much over the waves that at times I had to reach low to put my paddle blade in the water. Then the bow would crash down and down into a trough, and I'd wonder how far it would sink. But at the last moment, the wide sheer of the traditional bow shape always kept us from swamping, while it flung sheets of green water sideways to be torn apart and blasted astern by the wind.

And though we had been concerned about the apparent wobbliness of the craft, there appeared to be plenty of secondary stability — the resistance to actually capsizing, which is what really counts! However, given the conditions, we were still taking the precaution of sneaking along close to shore. A couple of hours of this wild ride eventually sapped our energy, and we greeted the proposal of an early camp with enthusiasm.

A short first day is a good idea on any big trip. You get a chance to rest up from the pressure of the trip preparation and the journey to the put-in; you have more time to recover from the jarring rhythms of workaday city life while settling into the more natural rhythm of the wilds. Since most of us were landlubbers, three from Calgary, three from Prince George, and one unsuspecting Aussie, we also needed time to settle into the rhythm of the sea. Only the boat's owner, from Vancouver, was a coastal resident. Although not all of us would call ourselves paddlers, we all shared a penchant for doing wild things in wild places and a connection with the renowned explorer-photographer who had assembled the motley crew. For three of us with limited time, the trip north from Telegraph Cove, near the north end of Vancouver Island, was to end after two weeks and 200 miles (320 km) at Bella Bella near the mainland coast. Substitutes would continue for another three weeks to Prince Rupert. Later in the summer, the canoe was one of two paddled back south from Hazelton to Victoria by crews of Natives and RCMP personnel, as part of the Vision Quest fundraiser for an addiction treatment center.

## Vulgar Belching, Roaring, Sparring and Defecating

The archipelago at the north end of Johnstone Strait is renowned for its fast-moving tidal currents, but until you experience these saltwater rivers, it's hard to imagine their speed and power. Our first inkling of the speed came when we saw what appeared to be the distant dorsal fin of an orca moving fast through a channel. On closer examination with binoculars, our killer whale turned out to be a cormorant perched on a log being carried rapidly along by the current.

Our route led into the current, and there we got to play at the river-paddling technique of upstream eddy-hopping along the shoreline. Approaching the first eddy line, I expected the blade-like waterline of the bow to catch the current and try to fling us sideways downstream. I braced myself ready to counteract with the bow draw stroke of my life, and then — surprise, surprise — apart from some gurgling turbulence beneath my feet, nothing happened and we held our line. This became almost fun, and we gained considerable distance as we hopped from eddy to eddy, watched with apparent interest by a sailboat under power.

But soon we had to cross to the other side of the channel, and it was time to try a strenuous upstream ferrying maneuver. As we moved out into the main current, it suddenly became clear what the sailboat had really been doing while we eddy-hopped. He wasn't just taking his time to watch us, he was going as fast as his engine would push him against the current and simply not making much headway. Eight paddlers can make a 33-foot boat move quite fast — our GPS showed 5 knots at times — but we sure lost a lot of ground — and calories — on that ferry.

The crossing brought us into the channels near the abandoned Native settlement of Mamalilaculla, where we had permission to land and view the relics. As we approached the beach, one of the caretakers — a black bear — wandered off across the tidal flats, but it was likely that the berry patches around the settlement harbored more of his kind. This sunny afternoon, wandering around the village and seeing the fallen relics of its former totem-pole glory was a pleasant, though thought-provoking interlude.

Another day, we encountered a settlement of a different kind, heavily populated and advertising its presence with a pungent smell drifting on the wind. A colony of sea lions on a rocky islet were happily engaged in their customary communal activity of vulgar belching, roaring, sparring and defecating as they piled against each other in a lardy huddle.

Our lunch stop in the sun, on a nearby island, was much more genteel. However it came to an end when the ever-sneaky marine weather produced a sudden cold squall that woke us up to the harsher realities of boating this coast.

Another reality of this coast is that good landings and campsites are not easy to find. On one occasion, we had to make do with a dark and rather uninspired little cove. Luckily the tide was out and there was enough beach space for landing, unloading and cooking, and to reduce the claustrophobic feel of the place. A scramble over a jumble of logs into the dank woods led to a couple of marginal tent spaces under the dripping trees. Another night was a spacious natural wilderness harbor, where our arrival surprised the folks on an anchored cruiser. They were eating dinner in the cockpit when we hove silently and suddenly into view, pulled in to the beach and the entire crew sprinted for the forest like rats from a sinking ship — what a

strange apparition we must have seemed. (It had been a long time since the last bathroom stop!)

The crème de la crème of our campsites was a spectacular 2.5 mile (4 km) swath of sandy beach, wide open to the Pacific. Having a healthy antipathy to surf landings in a boat like ours, we were glad to avoid the turbulence by sneaking into an estuary at one end of the beach. But in the bush behind our camp was a wrecked kayak with a note indicating the owners would return for it. I was glad to be in a warm bed back in Calgary when, months later, I read the story of the near-fatal epic that had befallen the kayaker's party. They had arrived to find heavy surf making landing risky, and unfortunately, had already overextended themselves. With insufficient time or energy to make what would have been a prudent but long retreat to a more sheltered location, they had attempted a landing. The results were disastrous and eventually required Coast Guard assistance.

I'll always remember the two days on that shore, enjoying the wild and exposed seascape, the seabirds along the waterline, the blowing spray, the mostly blue sky, the long walks along the sand and up the creek into the hinterland. It was rather like the Welsh beaches of my Atlantic childhood, but without the people and the development. Long may it stay that way, protected by the dicey landing conditions.

Of course, dicey landing conditions are also dicey launching conditions, and looming over my reverie was always the question of how we would get off the beach to continue the journey. The estuary provided the best solution, but the timing of the tides would dictate a predawn start. That was a low point for me — I'm not at my best in the early morning and don't want to eat the breakfast I know is necessary to fuel my body for a demanding day. With knots in my gut from the prospect of the forbidding-sounding Cape Caution, breakfast had even less appeal. As the dropping tide threatened to leave us stranded, we escaped the estuary in the nick of time and headed towards the Cape, which was occasionally showing itself to our bleary eyes as it poked in and out of the dawn mist. But our early start paid off — we rounded the Cape at slack tide and before the day's winds rose, and were soon into a less-exposed coastline with more coves and shelter.

That turned out to be a long day. With calm weather and advance knowledge of another superb but distant camping location, we decided to push on and paddle nearly 30 miles (50 km). Bypassing an uninspired intermediate camp would allow two nights at our next camp, and reduce the need for the tedious loading and manhandling of the 660-pound (300 kg) boat. Ha!

By arriving late and tired, would we be heading for the same sort of trap that caught the shipwrecked kayakers? No. From the chart, it was clear that the intended site offered sheltered beach landings from two opposing directions, so if the weather brewed up, one or the other would still be feasible. And if worse came to worst, we could delve deep into the nearby sheltered archipelago and be safe, though not very comfortable.

The grunt was worth it — our island site featured magnificent big-sky vistas out over the Inside Passage to the wide ocean, but with a more peaceful feel than our open wave-battered beach of the previous days. However, it was obviously not always peaceful. The enormous logs that provided such convenient camp tables and wind protectors for our tents had ridden some scary seas to arrive at their present position above the high-tide line. And the shattered massive timbers of a wooden ship were further reminders that the ocean was treating us rather well on this occasion. Actually, apart from the first day, it had treated us well for the whole trip so far, and telling our Aussie crew member that "it doesn't get much better than this" was becoming a daily ritual.

## Cruise Ship Leaning Like a Cyclist

Entering the Inside Passage meant we began to see cruise ships. I felt no jealousy as I sat on the warm sand in this exquisite place, watching one of the behemoths motor past. Maybe the passengers were being waited on hand and foot and served all sorts of delicacies, but we were seeing and experiencing so much more. Like them, we had the wide background vistas of the Coast Mountains, but we also had the intimate contact with the micro-scenery. We had the fascination of the channels and tide pools, the twisted grain patterns of the castaway logs, the changes brought by the tide, even the beach beetle viewed through a macro lens as it valiantly traveled over its boulder field of sand grains. And besides, we too were eating in a decidedly superior fashion and being totally spoiled. I'm the cook on most of my trips and hadn't argued when told that our one and only female crew member would do all the cooking, and that I only needed to bring my lunches.

Heading further into the more sheltered inside passage, where the forests were tall and thick to the water's edge and beaches were fewer, I began to miss the more open vistas of the outer coast. But a side trip up the estuary of a famed salmon-run stream to camp at a landlocked meadow was still a magical experience. There's a clearcut at the mouth of the river and the ugly ruin of a bunkhouse, though the barely visible overgrown remains of an abandoned gypsum mine reminded us that the land can heal. Whether the fish stocks heal and recover after watersheds are silted through the effects of irresponsible logging was the question in my mind as we paddled up this hitherto clear-water stream. It's a question that disturbed me again later while flying back to Vancouver and seeing the naked ground of a mountain valley, stripped right to the edges of the creek.

A day later we wandered the semi-derelict cannery at Namu. Perhaps this vast complex had also contributed to the reduction of salmon stocks — employing 600 people in its heyday, it must have trafficked in untold numbers of dead salmon. Now its plant and bunkhouses were silent, likely never to operate again. As at the gypsum mine, the wooden buildings and boardwalks of the shore facility were gradually succumbing to decay and the encroachment of the trees and bushes, and will eventually disappear. The steel sheds and machinery built out at the water's edge will be an eyesore for eons.

Although largely derelict, Namu was the first sign of civilization we'd seen in nearly two weeks. As we got even closer to Bella Bella, we were seeing more people and boats and cruise ships. While we were navigating a narrow channel, one of the monsters came up behind us, seeming to dominate the place. That would be close enough, but then another cruise ship appeared in front of us, leaning like a cyclist as it rounded the corner. However, the steep-sided channels are deep to the edges and there was plenty of room for the giants to pass.

My lack of enthusiasm for a return to civilization was not helped by the enclosed feeling and the dull weather; I was relieved as we headed back south, out of the Inside Passage towards the open ocean again, for a last fling before my trip would circle back to end at Bella Bella.

We spent a day in the village with some of the Native community; they were intrigued by our canoe, and so we took local children on paddling tours of the harbor. This was the end of the trip for me, but the rest of the crew continued on for three more weeks to Prince Rupert, without incident, I'm told.

# Alsek River
## *Awesome and Then Some*

Paula Zybach

YOU NEVER KNOW WHAT YOU'LL SEE OR HEAR WHEN HAVING A PEE IN the woods. On one occasion, on the Alsek River in the southern Yukon, I was charged by a grizzly bear.

My husband, Anton, and I had been charged by grizzlies on five different occasions before, but this time the bear acted like none I had ever seen — breaking into a full charge the moment he saw me, about 400 yards away. He didn't hesitate or test the air, and it was abundantly clear this was no bluff.

I know you never run from a bear and I pride myself in doing the right thing. But this time, I ran. I ran for my life!

I made it to our kitchen area, where most of our group were armed with pepper spray and bear bangers. Anton, who sounded the alarm, was the first to see the grizzly, so he went to get his camera but quickly realized it was charging the willow clump where I had gone to pee. Arming himself with a camera was not going to cut it, at least not for me.

Now, as we stood shoulder to shoulder in readiness, the grizzly stopped only yards away and stared. Sharon, in a state of undress in her tent, could hear it breathing right beside her. We set off a bear banger, but the grizzly, who was probably used to the cracking of glaciers and calving booms of icebergs, didn't even blink. It was a standoff. A minute later, Anton shot a flare just above the grizzly's head, with red sparks and smoke everywhere. The grizzly retreated a little, but continued to watch us for a while from various spots in the bushes. Long after the bad news bruin eventually left the area, we continued on high alert.

## Exploding Waves and Sudden Whirlpools

When we were invited by Peter to paddle the Alsek, we laughed. Portaging Turnback Canyon did not appeal to us. But wait . . . there would be a helicopter to lift us over the Tweedsmuir Glacier around Turnback, a permit for the trip was already arranged, and Fred and Richard would have a cataraft to carry the thunder boxes (all solid human waste must be carried out). The whole trip, including flight back to Whitehorse, would not exceed $1,200 (Cdn.) each. To further tempt us, Peter would order the best weather. Who could refuse?

Our group, paddlers from Colorado, South Carolina, California, Vancouver Island and Calgary, met in Whitehorse and then drove together to Haines Junction. We registered at Kluane Park headquarters, learned about the strict regulations, and arranged transportation to the river.

Starting in the St. Elias Mountains, the Alsek eventually makes its way into Alaska and the Pacific Ocean. Near its source, it flows through a broad valley with open, braided sections, which allowed for lots of channel-picking practice. There were also hiking opportunities amid fascinating rock formations. Sprinkled about were enormous white-granite erratics and clear, cold ponds.

These ponds and nearby creeks were welcome for drinking and bathing, as the Alsek itself carries the heaviest silt load I've ever seen. Like roiling mud, it picks up its burden from a multitude of glaciers. Cutting through the world's largest non-polar ice field and passing close to the Fisher, Vern Richie, Battle, Melber, Reynolds and Novatak glaciers, the river actually cuts into the Lowell, Tweedsmuir, Walker, Alsek and Grand Plateau glaciers.

After the first days, the pace picked up as the river narrowed, and we were rollicking in exploding waves and sudden whirlpools, avoiding pour-overs and holes, which were difficult to see in the brown froth. A GPS reading indicated we were floating at 10.5 miles (17 km) an hour.

Our boat choices were as diverse as our home bases. There was a big Sotar-oared cataraft, a Perception hard-shell kayak, an Aire Super Lynx inflatable kayak and four tandem SOARs (inflatable canoes). Everyone was self-contained, except Mike in his hard-shell kayak, and all could either roll or do a midstream self-rescue.

Each stop invited exploration and only once in sixteen days did we come to shore and not see wolf or bear tracks. One morning we spent an hour watching a female grizzly and her two cubs. The small dark one never ventured far from the sow's side, but the larger blond was always wandering off between romps with its sibling. The little one began to pester mom, climbing up on her and nipping playfully. Intent on her feast of soap-berries, she tolerated it just so long before batting him off like a beach ball. With a leap, she was straddling him, play biting as he flailed upwards with all four paws. Blondie heard the ruckus, of course, and came bounding back to join in. The three of them sat on their bums, in a circle, slapping at each other joyfully.

## Yee-haw . . . Iceberg Riding

Goatherd Mountain provided the chance for a full day of hiking. The view the whole way was of Lowell Glacier, Mt. Kennedy and icebergs floating in Lowell Lake. Flowers, berries and ptarmigan were underfoot on the steep climb, and the top was a seemingly endless sea of knobs interspersed with brooks and meadows. The front dropped away instantly into cliffs that hosted an amazing number of mountain goats.

There were lots of feathered creatures to keep the birdwatchers in our group amused, but my favorite were the rock ptarmigans. They seemed to take glee in rushing by the tents at night, sounding for all the world like drunken Disney ducks!

The river was very much alive, too. Whirlpools suddenly appeared and corners featured dramatic shear lines. Some landings had to be timed with powerful surges. An almost invisible hole caused a capsize, but a well-rigged boat and know-how had the paddler upright and back in control within seconds of flushing.

Lava North's 10-foot-deep (3 m) holes, numerous pour-overs and 8-foot-high (2.5 m) exploding waves made it the most challenging rapid we ran. A blown neck-gasket on a drysuit stopped one couple from running Lava North, but lining through the large, smooth boulders made for some more dicey maneuvering. At camp that evening, we managed to repair the offending equipment.

Peter came close with his promise of perfect weather. In an area famous for fog, wind and rain, we had only three miserable days. We kept our drysuits on at all times, though, as any swim could have fatal consequences. Drysuits also made it possible to try a new sport. Occasionally a small ice floe would venture close to a boat and one of the occupants would step out to try to ride it! While a bull-rider in the rodeo tries to stay on his mount for eight seconds, we were lucky to stay atop a baby berg for half that long.

Our most miserable weather fell in the middle of the trip, at Turnback Canyon, where we had planned another layover day for exploration. But with the rain, Noisy Creek was too high to ford, and we contented ourselves with hiking through thick, wet alder for glimpses of the canyon and Mt. Blackadar.

Dampened spirits turned jolly when we crowded under a tarp to feast on a potluck dessert. The fare included blueberry pudding cake, chocolate cake with Grand Marnier icing, Southern Comfort muffins, apple spice cake, cherry cheesecake, chocolate kisses and applesauce. Everything was consumed, except for the applesauce. Healthy calories can wait for sunshine!

Crawling out of our tents the next morning, we were still content despite the continuing bad weather. Boats were deflated, rolled and packed in anticipation of the helicopter shuttle. Visibility was poor through the drizzling mist, and I feared we wouldn't be able to see the canyon. But as we approached the opening, just above water level, Doug, the pilot, pointed out Last Chance Eddy, and I readied for the chopper to rise up, over the walls.

That wasn't in Doug's plans. He knows Turnback like no one else, and we dove in through the gaping entrance. Turn by turn, with rotor blades just a few feet from the cliffs, we saw every detail. Waterfalls cascaded down from above and exploding waves shot 16 feet (5 m) up from below. Huge drops, unfathomable shear lines and the legendary Double Indemnity were awesome.

It was that night, at the foot of the canyon, where I met the charging grizzly. Not to be outdone, Peter and Gerhardt took a small side channel the next morning and were chased by a sow with a cub. They nearly had their getaway foiled by an untimely sweeper.

The weather turned sunny as we approached the confluence of the Tatshenshini River. On Alsek Lake, we camped at a different spot each night for four days while we explored between magical icebergs and into every little bay. Our boats were dwarfed by the walls of tingling and rumbling blue ice. Mt. Fairweather loomed above, and from a hike up a hill, we could see all the way across the Novatak Glacier to Mt. Logan. The warm weather encouraged lots of action from both the Alsek and the Grand Plateau glaciers. At lunch, we climbed up and watched apartment block-sized chunks crashing off into the lake and then waited for the inevitable surge wave.

We were licensed for sixteen days, and two planes were rendezvousing with us at Dry Bay, Alaska, so we pulled up camp for the last time and paddled to the airstrip where we deregistered with the U.S. Park Service, and quickly packed all our filthy gear.

Just as the last of our things were stowed in the belly of the Air Van, it began to rain. Time to leave.

# Rat–Peel–Porcupine Rivers

## *Rediscovering Historical Roots and Routes*

Faye Hallett

T HE 5-MILE (8 KM) PORTAGE AROUND ABERDEEN FALLS CANYON: A TWO-
day grunt. The seldom-used trail: found following faded surveying tape. The
gear: hauled up a steep bank, through swamp, over deadfall, around hummocks
and holes, in soft oozing moss and around charred stumps of a long-ago burn.

On my final trip, the fourth, I carried two large personal packs, a shovel
and a grill strapped to an army pack frame. In the light rain, I slogged
through mud, bounced from hump to hump, swatted mosquitoes and wearily
followed the trail, now a soggy mess from so many people trampling too
many times in this fragile environment. Parched with thirst, I kneeled and
lowered my head between two hummocks and began to drink mosquito-
infested water. It was refreshingly cooled by the permafrost.

Hard to believe I was pursuing a dream. But that surreal moment, on the
shores of the Peel River, sandwiched between the Richardson and Ogilvie
Mountains, in the northern Yukon, was one of many onerous experiences.

Some canoe trips are years in the dreaming stage, waiting for the right time to happen. The Peel–Rat–Porcupine Rivers trip became a reality for me and John Vlchek and six others when we had six weeks of holiday time. We dreamed of exploring a surreal part of Canada — the tranquility of the northern wilderness camp, the novelty of continuous daylight, gentle rain on the tent, wild muskeg flowers, the close comradeship of good friends and the challenge of the physical.

Our plan was to begin in the Yukon, pass into the Northwest Territories and back to the Yukon, by following the Ogilvie River, navigating the Peel River east and north past Fort McPherson into the Mackenzie Delta. From there we would ascend the Rat River, traverse the divide, paddle the Little Bell and Bell Rivers to the Porcupine River and to the settlement of Old Crow, where we would fly out. If all went well, we would complete the 620-mile-long (1,000 km) trip in less than five weeks.

There were two main historical precedents for this trip: the Rat River was the back-door route for the Klondike gold rush of the late 1890s (there was no Chilkoot Pass), and even earlier, it was one of the routes for Hudson's Bay Company traders to establish fur-trade posts.

From the Klondike Highway, the 125-mile (200 km) journey north on the Dempster Highway, which opened in 1979, was a scenic delight. The Tombstone Mountains, entirely carpeted in tundra vegetation, loomed beside the road. Only along the rivers did we see short spruce and willow. Our trip began where the Dempster crosses the Ogilvie River. Arrangements were made for men at the road maintenance camp to drive our two vehicles back to the Dawson City airport.

The 18-foot-long, home-built, fiberglass canoes were well stocked with gear and a five-week food supply. John had designed the canoes for long-distance wilderness traveling, where greater capacity and maneuverability in rapids are important. With excitement and anticipation, we ferried out into the fast current of the Ogilvie River. We encountered continuous Class I and II rapids, several Class III sets and many ledges. After careful scouting, we paddled some ledges; some we lined and some we portaged. Where the Ogilvie joins the Blackstone River, the Peel River is born.

At the end of day seven, we were camped by the Caribou River on the Arctic Circle, with 230 miles (375 km) of paddling behind us. We had passed the mouths of the Wind, Bonnet Plume and Snake Rivers, all of which substantially added volume to the Peel. That explained the second demolished aluminum canoe we saw. A group of Germans we met on a portage told us of another group who had lost everything a week earlier in one of the first rapids of the Peel, forcing them to hike out to the Dempster Highway. We heard later they had survived the ordeal, despite extreme mosquito bites. Meanwhile, a party of twelve Natives, in two scows from Fort McPherson, stopped for tea.

Our pace had been pushed by four of our party who had less time to complete the trip. The next evening we held a farewell potlatch of beans, spaghetti, bacon and red cabbage salad, with banana cream pie for dessert, and all washed down with a cask of red wine. Afterwards, we soothed our souls and tired muscles in a sweat lodge laboriously constructed with willows and tarps. The next morning we felt a poignant sense of loss as our four friends departed camp, a heavy drizzle erasing their tracks.

For the 100 miles (160 km) before Fort McPherson, there was continual rain or drizzle, making for not-so-pleasant campsites of mud and mosquitoes. We observed three tall, white pyramid-shaped log structures. We learned later they were markers for four members of a NWMP patrol who died in 1911 in a dog-sled expedition between Dawson City and Fort McPherson. As we got closer to the Dempster Highway ferry near Fort McPherson, we saw more Native summer camps and their white canvas tents.

Fort McPherson is remembered most for its abundance of mosquitoes. The locals were accommodating and gave us precise directions for the Rat River turnoff downstream in the Mackenzie Delta. Once at the mouth of the Rat — the route to McDougall Pass, which, at 4,726 feet (1,441 m), is the lowest pass in the Rocky Mountain chain, connecting the Arctic and Pacific watersheds — we began our upstream trek.

In the 1930s, the Rat gained notoriety because of its association with Albert Johnson, the Mad Trapper of the Rat, who shot two RCMP officers and became a fugitive. It took thirty days, in the dead of winter, for a posse of police, bush pilots and Native guides to find and kill Johnson.

## Raging Rat

While the Rat River is short, it is steep and swift. A relentless, steady paddling was needed to make progress. Lining and poling were impossible due to its steep sides, muddy banks and overhanging willows. Our first camp, about 9 miles (15 km) upstream, was on a bank of sand with the river on one side and a small lake on the other. It was an island in a mosquito-infested swamp.

Day thirteen was our first rest day; it poured. The canoes, which had been tethered to the bank, needed regular emptying. By afternoon, the river was muddy, rising and increasing in speed — not exactly the right ingredients for upstream travel.

The next day welcomed us with more rain. We stayed put and kept ourselves busy trying to burn green willow, doing laundry in muddy water, drying clothes in the rain, watching a muskrat swim close to camp and making bets on how high the water would rise.

The next day found us still huddled against the rain and watching the water rise on a narrowing ridge of sand. We could only guess where our friends were further upstream and the difficulties they were encountering. We saw a lot of debris floating by and heard the plaintive cries of baby beavers as the swollen river flushed them from their homes. Our sandbank campsite was eroding away; we had to get off the river.

The next morning, with the river up about 10 feet (3 m), we broke camp. A few hours later we made it off the Rat River, heading upstream on the Husky Channel. We made good progress lining our boats and, for a while, we had sunshine, firm banks to walk on and steady movement to keep the mosquitoes at bay. A tremendous army of uprooted trees, planks, debris and a half-dozen river scows floated by. On a heavily silt-laden river, getting drinking water was a challenge.

But back on the Rat, we gave up hope of advancing further. We turned around and paddled back to the ferry crossing at Fort McPherson, where we met up with our friends who had been flushed out on a different channel of the Rat. They told horror stories of lining up a canyon in chest-deep water, clinging with one hand to willows while the other clutched a lining rope attached to a canoe bucking in surging water. With relentless determination, they had traveled about 30 miles (50 km) upstream in three and a half days — but the return downstream journey took just five hours. This had been such an unnerving experience that they ended their trip there and returned to Alberta.

## A New Plan

Disappointed but not daunted, and with enough time and food, we continued our adventure. Using the ferry telephone, we chartered a plane out of Inuvik to take us to Summit Lake, at the top of McDougall Pass. While we waited, a few locals came to our camp to share tea and tell stories of the past. One of our visitors was an elderly Native who was part of the Albert Johnson drama.

We landed at Summit Lake in light rain and heavy cloud. It was a beautiful setting, with the lake nestled at the foot of several barren peaks of the Richardson Mountains. The few stunted spruce trees, scattered willow, dwarf birch and soft moss were so welcome after our many days of mud. Shortly after our arrival, another plane landed with a foursome of German paddlers headed in our direction. Two of them had never paddled, so we gave them some lessons.

We spent three days at Summit Lake exploring, fishing and hiking. Jackfish in one tiny pond were so abundant and hungry, every cast caught a fish. We reveled in the diversity of the tundra flora: saxifrage, heather, primrose, anemone and arctic poppy. Around the nightly campfire, the never-ending twilight gave a special tranquility to our northern camp.

We finally got a day without rain, our third so far of the entire trip. We hiked to the top of a nearby mountain peak, straddling the Yukon–Northwest Territories border, and viewed the valleys of the Little Bell and Bell Rivers, whose waters eventually empty into the Bering Sea. To the east was the beginning of the Rat River and to the northeast the flat, endless expanse of the Mackenzie Delta. Life was beautiful sitting on top of the world, with a clear blue sky and warm sun, surrounded by a mountainside festival of crimson and brown and orange.

Rather than portaging to the Little Bell River, we paddled, pulled and sawed our way down the willow-choked creek that drains Summit Lake. It was entertaining, and we completed it in less than an hour. Because of the high water, we navigated the fast bends of the narrow, winding 10 miles (16 km) of the Little Bell in less than two hours. The small and quickly flowing Bell River offered no obstacles and pleasant paddling. At our first camp on the Bell, we picked huckleberries, made bannock for the next day, tried to ignore the pesky blackflies and put ourselves on alert for bears.

A highlight the next day was visiting La Pierre House, at the junction of the Bell River and a Native trail that runs through the Richardson Mountains to Fort McPherson. Fort McPherson was established in the early

1800s as a small Hudson's Bay Company depot to service all the posts in the Yukon region. Today, canoeists must be watchful so as not to miss this overgrown location and the sagging remnants of three log buildings.

Our campsite, about 3 miles (5 km) below La Pierre House, was one of the best camping spots we had this trip. But during the night, John and I were awakened by an animal snorting around the canoe and paddles. We immediately thought bear. What to do? Deciding on a surprise tactic, John exited the tent yelling and hooting. A startled moose made a flying leap over the bank and made a quick swim across the river.

The day we left the Bell and joined the Porcupine River, we paddled close to 50 miles (80 km). We caught up with our German friends from Summit Lake, and a foursome of Americans who had reached the Porcupine via the Eagle River and Dempster Highway.

After a few miles on the Porcupine, we encountered two adult caribou and five young ones swimming across the river. They were the last stragglers of the migrating 30,000-member Porcupine herd on its way to wintering grounds in the Ogilvie Mountains. Where the herd had crossed the river, their hoofs had rutted and packed the muskeg, allowing it to drain in rivulets to the river.

On our second day on the Porcupine, we observed with interest several groups of caribou, a bear and a peregrine falcon family. We explored an abandoned seismic camp on our way downstream on the wide river. By midmorning it started to pour. We stopped to share our pot of soup, made the previous evening, with an American couple who were struggling to get a fire going. Our Coleman stove came in handy.

Further on, we observed the etiquette of the North by stopping at each and every camp we saw. At one, we shared tea with a woodcutter from Old Crow, who was bucking up cordwood from a fringe of spruce that lined the river. The wood would eventually be floated down to Old Crow for use as winter fuel. That evening a group of Natives from Old Crow visited our camp to inquire if we had seen any caribou. The herd had migrated further east than usual, causing them concern about getting enough meat for winter.

We spent our final two days before reaching Old Crow battling the wind and trying to stay warm and dry in the persistent rain. The water level was high and the current swift on the half-mile-wide river. It was inspiring to watch and listen to the screeching pairs of peregrine falcons, once near extinction in North America.

It was an intriguing two days and nights we spent in Old Crow, before flying out to Dawson City. Our camp was a point of interest to the locals, who came day and night to visit and share tea. They eagerly bought our canoes, extra paddles, camping gear and anything else we would part with.

Despite the inconvenience of the inclement weather, persistent mosquitoes and blackflies, and our failed attempt to get up the Rat, our trip was all we dreamed of and more. We had rediscovered historical roots and routes.

# Little Nahanni
## *A Tale of Two Trips: 1978 and 1998*

Glenn Hodgins

Back in 1978, I was a member of a Wanapitei group — ten teenagers and two expert guides, Malcolm Thomas and Mary Ellen Ripley — that set out for a summer of fun on the Little and South Nahanni Rivers in the Northwest Territories.

After we reached Virginia Falls on the South Nahanni, Malcolm disappeared. He had gone to scout Five Mile Canyon, immediately below the falls. But he never returned to camp. Mary Ellen signaled a plane and alerted the park rangers. All of us were evacuated from the river while the RCMP conducted an intensive search on and in the river and throughout the surrounding area. His body was never found. Malcolm was presumed drowned. We were all completely and utterly devastated.

In my heart, I think Malcolm lost his balance while reaching out for the ideal photo or movie angle. In my nightmares, he falls from the top of a cliff. In a more rational frame of mind, I think he slipped at the river's edge and bumped his head. The river is cold and powerful through the canyon.

I vowed I would return. Twenty years later, I went back with friends and family. We had a physical and emotional journey to complete.

## Top of the Little Nahanni: 1978

"Where is the road to the Flat Lakes?" we asked innocently.

"You must be crazy," the locals told us. "The road is completely washed out. And don't you know the river is in flood? It's been raining non-stop for three weeks."

Such were the warnings from some of the people of Tungsten, a remote mining town about 215 miles (350 km) from Watson Lake on the Yukon–Northwest Territories border. We had left Ontario ten days earlier, destined for this idyllic put-in tucked away between the Ragged Range and the Selwyn Mountains. It was to be our trip of a lifetime. Bad weather and high water were not going to deter us. Besides, we had the whole summer.

Our boats were three wood-canvas and three ABS canoes. Fitted splash covers? I don't think so. We were equipped with sheets of plastic, extra duct tape and our Swiss army knives; the latter required to cut green saplings to make the frames for our custom-made splash covers. There was nothing high-tech about this system.

On day four, when the river rose 3 feet (1 m) in a few hours, we were forced to consider the wisdom of the locals in Tungsten. If the water level continued to rise, we would have to abort the trip. After a two-day wait, however, the level began to recede and we were able to continue. On day seven, one of the wood-canvas canoes got wrapped around a rock, but with extensive repairs, it was put back together. Fortunately, we did not have any time pressures. We had all summer.

## Top of the Little Nahanni: 1998

In 1998, three of us from the 1978 trip and other friends and family returned. It was an emotionally charged and inspirational experience. There was no choice in our minds between the Moose Ponds and the Little Nahanni as the starting point. While both routes offer exceptional whitewater challenges, we were determined to retrace and complete the original trip.

We gathered in Fort Nelson, B.C., and drove to Fort Liard, in the Northwest Territories, to pick up rented ABS canoes, complete with full splash covers, and a Twin Otter flight into the Flat Lakes. Two passengers got off the plane, looking glum and complaining about their experience on the Nahanni: they had planned to fly into the Moose Ponds but were forced to

abort mid-flight because, as they flew over the Rock Gardens, it was evident there was not enough water. Instead, they put in on the South Nahanni at Island Lake, well below the rapids, spent two days on the Nahanni and the rest of the time at Rabbit Kettle Lake hiding above a food cache for three days in fear of bears.

Because of their experience and the generally low water levels in the area, the pilot began to question our plan to fly into Flat Lakes. We considered our options and decided we would still fly to Flat Lakes to take a look at the water levels and, if necessary, fly on to Island Lake. There we could spend a lot of time hiking at Glacier Lake. This quick decision made, the pilot warned the flight would be bumpy and handed out the barf bags.

Looking at every river we flew over, we were relieved to see plenty of water. Before too long, we noticed a fairly significant river under us, which turned out to be the Flat. Since the Flat and the Little Nahanni Rivers begin in the same valley and are fed by glacial run-off rather than rain alone, this was good news. We seemed to be in luck.

Jacques, our pilot, dropped us at the end of the lake and gave us quite a thrill as he took off, heading straight for us after takeoff and then pulling up dramatically into a breathtaking vertical climb as he passed over — what a crazy man.

I was on the Little Nahanni, again.

The Little Nahanni drops 1,180 feet in its short 48-mile journey (360 m in 78 km) to the South Nahanni — a staggering 30 feet per mile (4.7 m/km). The first few miles are a gentle meander, but before long the excitement begins. Nowhere is the fast descent felt more than during the Staircase.

There is no clear beginning or end to the Staircase. It is marked on the map as a continuous series of slashes lasting over a mile (2 km) and, at its most intense, the elevation drop is 130 feet in 1 mile (20 m in 1 km). It is pointless to describe sets in detail — there are just too many to recall, and we were able to shoot everything at this water level. We stopped frequently to scout

blind corners and, towards the end of the day, to rest, since we were completely exhausted. The biggest set was midway through the day, where the river takes a sharp turn to the right and the waves are quite large. A tight maneuver at the bottom was required to miss a large rock obstructing the passage.

We had one dump, the only spill of the trip. Fortunately, the canoe immediately ended up in an eddy, so a lengthy chase was avoided and we were able to recover everything. We were all wearing wetsuits, which helped immensely in this extremely cold water.

## The Staircase: 1978

Beware of flooding mountain rivers! We learned this lesson the hard way in 1978: in the rain-swollen river, the trees were already 3 feet (1 m) into the water, eddy turns were challenging and lining almost impossible. Over one night, the water rose 3 feet and then another one and a half feet (0.5 m) the following day. The Staircase became a torrent, and for two days we sat wondering if we had taken on more than we could manage. There is an abandoned road, once used for mining exploration, that runs along the river, and we contemplated aborting our dream trip and portaging along the road back to the top of the river. However, after two days of waiting, we were able to continue when the water level began to drop. Adrenaline took over as we pulled our custom-made splash covers around our waists to paddle the remainder of the Staircase.

Those makeshift splash covers served us well. Right off the campsite, we were into waves that would have swamped us without them. On two occasions, we were forced to chop down trees that blocked the only reasonable route. On another, we came upon a tree that had fallen into the river, so we pulled the canoes up and over it, taking special care with each of the wood-canvas canoes. When the day was done, we had traveled just a mile — and it was one of the most invigorating experiences in this canoeist's memory.

## Absolute Bliss

In the gentler stretch of river, from the Staircase to First Canyon, there are four marked sets that do not offer any particular challenge, and it is possible to float along at a fairly relaxed pace. In 1998, shortly after lunch, we came upon a large grizzly bear feeding on berries at the shoreline of an island. A camera shutter startled the bear — it looked up, revealing its hefty size, and darted into the bushes.

The current is quite fast near First Canyon, where a high gravel ridge appears on the left and the river then turns sharply right into a deep gorge. First Canyon is demanding at any water level and it is normally recommended that groups portage it by bush-crashing up the steep hill on river left. We had it in our minds to explore the possibility of shooting the rapids, however, so we chose to make dinner at the riverside and then take our tents and sleeping bags to the top to make camp and scout at our leisure.

Scouting the rapids is not easy. When you are high above the river, your perspective is distorted and waves that seem small and unchallenging turn into large obstacles at the water's edge. Because the banks of the canyon are steep, eddies are rare and there are blind corners where scouting, even from the river, is impossible.

We walked along the ridge for most of the length of the canyon and were able to see all but the final set. Based on what we saw, we decided to shoot, all the while mindful of the risk that once into the canyon, it would be difficult to get out if there was any trouble. That being said, it was one of the most exhilarating days of rapids I can recall.

The next day we enjoyed a short stretch of Class II rapids as we passed Steel Creek, where the volume increases substantially; Steel Creek is essentially the same size as the Little Nahanni.

Next, we came to a set known as the Step. This is a large Class IV and it is unlikely that this could be shot in any water level. We lined the two main drops along the left shore, then ran the outwash and stopped for lunch.

To everyone's surprise, we caught a 4-pound lake trout. Not exactly the place to expect lake trout.

After a sharp bend to the right, we took a look around a blind corner at the base of a steep set of rapids, and this turned out to be Second Canyon. As we scouted, we realized we could shoot it, unlike in 1978, when we had to make a formidable cliff climb up and down. There is a ledge where the river takes a sharp left turn, so there was some maneuvering required to get to river-left and into the channel through the ledge. What a delight to be able to shoot instead of portage.

The Little Nahanni takes a sharp bend to the east after Second Canyon, and we enjoyed a relatively leisurely paddle through continuous Class II rapids. The scenery is fabulous, changing dramatically around each bend, and though we scouted several blind corners, none was particularly challenging. We stopped for a short fishing break, where I caught three grayling.

The river gets bigger around every turn as it moves towards the South Nahanni. Soon the Sapper Range, on the far side of the South Nahanni, came into view and we arrived at the much anticipated Third Canyon.

Third Canyon, a challenging Class III–IV, is located approximately 2 miles (3 km) from the end of the Little Nahanni and begins as the river takes a sharp turn to the right and then doubles back to the left. The first curve is a Class II but increases in difficulty as it plows into a steep slate wall on the left shore. Although the waves are big and the current powerful, this set was the most fun of all. We all took pictures of each other shooting the set in absolute bliss.

At the confluence, we stopped for hugs and congratulations at having completed the challenge of the Little Nahanni. We took six days. Back in 1978, with extensive delays because of flooding and having to make repairs to the wood-canvas canoes, it took us eleven.

## For Who Has Seen the Wind?

The visit to Virginia Falls, a week's paddle from the Little Nahanni, was difficult, emotionally. While the falls hadn't changed in twenty years, there was a designated campsite, a longer portage trail . . . and lots of people. We found an out-of-the-way spot and held a ceremony, with sparklers, to remember Malcolm and the way we were.

A poem, written by Malcolm's father before his disappearance, was read out loud.

### *For Who Has Seen the Wind?*

*Listen to the wind in the poplars,*
*listen to the wind in your ears,*
*listen to the wind through your senses:*
*the wind will quell your fears.*

*Feel the wind in your face, son,*
*feel the wind draw forth the tears,*
*feel the wind through your bones, son:*
*the wind will quell your fears.*

*The wind blows where he likes, son,*
*it shapes the sea and foam;*
*the wind can carve the earth, son:*
*the wind will blow you home.*

*The wind blows in our cells, son,*
*it sweeps where comets roam;*
*the wind blows through all lives, son:*
*the wind will guide you home.*

I began to feel closure for a long, unsolved ache.

We portaged around Virginia Falls and continued on. We felt the wind, navigated rapids, marveled at magnificent canyons, lounged in a hot spring . . . and completed the trip. Going back was a healing experience.

# Grease River

## *Very Hard Work, Very Beautiful, Very Scary Rapids*

Sheila Archer

EVERY NOW AND AGAIN, I HAVE TO GIVE MYSELF A PEP TALK, A PICK-ME-UP. "This is it — this is exactly what I want to be doing right now! I love this more than anything else in the whole world! Think what we paid just to be here!"

Shouting and laughing, we continued to lurch forward along the face of the steep slope. Somewhere ahead and semi-lost were our packs, sitting at the base of a tree, waiting for us to find them . . . again. Our current task was to haul Alph the canoe through the tangled aftermath of the old burn. Normally, that alone is enough to make me break a sweat, but we were traversing an incline (somewhere in that confusing gray zone between hill and cliff) high above the roaring rapids of the Grease River Canyon. Only the hip-high fallen trees kept us from sliding down into the canyon, as we pushed Alph over and through the knots of burned wood.

Those who have traveled in difficult conditions know how important it is to stay light; your sense of humor is the most important thing you pack. Fortunately, my definition of fun is quite broad and I have a laugh that has saved my life before. Don't think for a moment this was some conquer-the-river expedition. Finding out what my limits are doesn't interest me nearly as much as it used to. The challenge of enjoying all aspects of life, even the most difficult, conscious of having chosen all of it, makes a trip like this not only possible, it makes it a delight.

We were having a really great day, Craig and I. Today was the grand finale, the final chapter of our journey through the rugged country that lies along Lake Athabasca's north shore in northern Saskatchewan. Even the flight in had been rough, the single-engine Otter tossed about in the turbulence. Flying over the high, steep and deeply carved terrain, I strained to catch a glimpse of the infamous canyon of the appropriately named Grease River. Searching for a river he could travel up to reach the Arctic, the intrepid explorer Joseph Tyrrell gazed up the river's mouth and apparently exclaimed, "You've got as much chance of going upstream on that as you would climbing a grease mountain."

The Grease River drops swiftly from its headwaters at Fontaine Lake, racing through the remains of some of Earth's oldest mountains, formed by the colliding micro-continents that became the Canadian Shield. The river runs through cracks, over ledges and down spillways as it plunges to Lake Athabasca, descending over 655 feet (200 m) in only 42 miles (68 km).

All this steep terrain makes for extremely challenging travel, by land or by water. Traditionally, the Dene of the area moved through Grease River country using the lake-like portions only. Ancient portages still exist, but they do not parallel the rapids. Instead, they leave the river at right angles above obstacles to navigation, taking travelers off and out of the valley to parallel lakes and creeks, such that all major rapids are avoided. Not surprisingly, this area continues to have few visitors of any kind.

The Dene who worked at the Athabasca Lodge, where we were waiting to fly out from, were convinced we were insane. They told every client we would not be coming back. The American fishermen delighted in reporting this to us the day before our flight. It was difficult to convince them we were prepared, that we'd done our homework and knew what we were getting into. One kind-hearted older Dene fishing guide asked me to sit with him; he pored over my maps, pointing to each place where the old portages his people used could be found. He assured me we could get out of the Grease Valley if we needed to. His concern was obvious — he made sure I marked every portage precisely. His only smile came when he spoke of the moose. Pointing to a slow section of the river, he said. "There are many of them here, so I go in the fall."

Only Cliff Blackmuir, owner-operator of the lodge and pilot of the plane that took us to the headwaters of the Grease, seemed to feel we were going to be all right. "How many days will you be?" he asked as he brought us down to the surface of Fontaine Lake. "We have food for eight days, but with any luck we'll be back in six," I responded.

"Good, we'll see you soon, then," he said with a wave as he closed his door. Off flew the silver Otter into the bright sunlit sky. Cliff had warned us previously that from this point on there was only one place where a plane could reach us. We were on our own now, at the top of a mountain, a double black diamond run with only one way down.

## Water Volume Is Low, Gradient Is High and Boulders Are Many

When my husband, Craig, and I decided we would paddle the Grease during the summer of 1999, we did so knowing it would be a physically demanding route. Extremely demanding. There are numerous points along the river where difficult waterfalls make the river unnavigable and where the rapids are so nasty that descent by canoe is out of the question. Only the fabulous Hunt (Lefty) Falls, which has gradually developed a trail as a result of visits from fishermen, allows the portaging paddler to pass by without great effort. I mean *really* great effort.

Choosing to paddle the Grease automatically gives you the opportunity to enjoy bushwhacking at its best. Long ago, the Grease was a glacial meltwater channel, with a huge volume of water that pushed large boulders along its bed. Now, a low-volume, rain-fed river slips between the irregular and often steep shores, lined with these giant rocks. Walking through and over them is slow, hazardous work. The shores are covered with close-growing trees, mosses and the occasional burn — all most unforgiving walking surfaces.

Physical stamina isn't all that the Grease demands. Paddlers beware: many of the navigable rapids on this remote river are at the top end of what's possible in an open canoe, and having a spray skirt won't help one bit. It isn't the waves you have to worry about; it's the rocks. The water volume is low, the gradient is high and the boulders are many. Only those who can comfortably read and run long sections of constricted Class II+ to Class III rapids should attempt this route. Lining is hazardous and the water too cold to mess around in for long — you really don't want to be in it at all. One cold and rainy day we lined the rapids below Drop of Doom Falls. Shortly after, we had to stop and peel off all our wet clothing, replacing them with our warmest dry clothes in order to avert the hypothermia we could feel stealing into our bodies.

If you've read to this point and are thinking only the crazed and or ill-informed would want to paddle this river, you'd be close to the truth. But how can experienced wilderness trippers, with good sturdy ankles and a love for high-end whitewater, resist this wild, remote gem of a river? The handful of canoeists I know who had paddled it all said the same things: "Very hard work, very beautiful, very scary rapids." These three features made the Grease irresistible.

If you do decide to go, plan to take your time. It really doesn't look like a long trip, on the map. To figure out how long it would actually take and find out more about what we were up against, we met with an acquaintance who had been on the Grease just a few years before. He had traveled with a group of paddlers whose skill levels were similar to ours. He talked about the nature of the route, described the rapids and pointed out where to bushwhack or line. "We made about 10 kilometers [6 miles] a day," he said, "so it took seven days. You have to allow one whole day just for the canyon at the end."

The Grease River Canyon is the main reason why most paddlers don't paddle this exquisite waterway. For most of its 5 miles (8 km), it races along like a sluice through continuous boulder-choked Class III and IV rapids. Only during the last mile or so (2 km), where the river widens and slows its descent, do the rapids become manageable for a loaded tripping canoe.

We arrived at the canyon on the morning of our fifth day. We left the canoe at the top of the first rapids and walked down to have a look. Having descended through the upper reaches of the Grease in good time, running and lining many of the rapids, we were in an optimistic mood. But one look told it all: everything the old Dene fishing guide at the Athabasca Lodge said was true. The country was rough, the moose were plentiful . . . and the canyon was a place where only trippers with a death wish would paddle. We soon realized that instead of running or lining sections of the canyon, the main part of the day would be spent walking. Less than 300 yards had suit-able shore to line from, since the rapids blasted along the base of tall steep-sided boulders and low cliffs. We carried and carried and carried . . .

It was an epic journey. Every time we came back out of the bush to look downstream, we saw more trouble. By late afternoon, we were tired enough to be vulnerable to pessimistic thoughts. Standing at the water's edge and discussing whether to start paddling again, I could feel Craig's frustration flare, as though he were about to self-immolate. The trick was not to react, to keep thinking when pressure becomes great. As we walked the next 800 yards, it occurred to me we hadn't eaten for at least four hours. Plunking down beside him at the next rest point, I silently put a four-cup bag of trail mix beside his hand. He ate it all.

We walked some more. Finally, after a total of 3-plus-miles (more than 6 km) of bushwhacking, we found a reasonable put-in spot — Class II+ water that both our tired bodies agreed was not beyond our resources. The late-day sun gleamed ahead of us, low on the water, but we managed to dodge our way down the last mile or so (2 km) of rapids unscathed. As we slid out into the long, fjord-like bay leading to Lake Athabasca, we shouted our thanks out loud. It was 8:30 P.M. It had taken us almost twelve hours.

That night, we camped on an ice-smoothed granite island at the mouth of Grease Bay, 2.5 miles (4 km) from the end of the canyon. The next morning dawned clear with a mild breeze, the only kind of wind to have on Lake Athabasca. With only 5 miles (8 km) left to paddle to the fishing camp, we quickly slid between widely spaced islands over the lake towards the mouth of the Otherside River. About half a mile (1 km) from the point that guarded the bay, we saw a motorboat swing out through the deep channel and turn towards the west. As it came across our path, it slowed. In the stern, taking out his clients for a day of fishing, was the old Dene guide. He leaned forward, squinted in our direction, then sat bolt upright and gave us a thumbs-up salute. Yes, we had made it back, through the roughest of country, with a few more scratches on the canoe, some marvelous memories . . . and our sense of humor intact.

# Peace River
## *Mighty, Majestic, Muddy*

Max Finkelstein

Something *big* was heading this way. Branches snapped and leaves crunched under heavy footsteps, the sound steadily getting closer to the edge of the trees, where we were camped. I sat by the fire, stewing up a breakfast of brewis, a traditional Newfoundland meal made by soaking hard bread overnight, and waited. There was a lot of bison dung around, so perhaps the first bison of the trip was going to join us for breakfast. Perhaps it was a moose. Or a bear. I didn't have long to ponder the possibilities as a fat black bear emerged from the bush and headed straight for me. I shouted: "There's nothing but brewis for breakfast!" The big bruin ran off into the bush. Obviously, he had eaten brewis before.

This was just one of many bear encounters along the Peace River. Almost daily, we would see bears swimming across the river or walking along the banks. Paddling with bears is just one of the pleasures of the Peace.

The Peace River begins in the heart of the Rocky Mountains, but the upper reaches of the river were transformed into British Columbia's largest lake in 1968 by the W. A. C. Bennett Dam. The reservoir, known as Williston Lake, is one of the most beautiful lakes anywhere. Shaped like the letter Y, the Peace Arm (the stem of the Y), almost 75 miles (120 km) long, is like a giant fiord, with the sheer limestone walls of the Rockies rising over 3,000 feet (900 m) straight up from the water's surface. But paddling Williston Lake is another story. We traveled on the Peace River below the dam, from Hudson's Hope through Wood Buffalo National Park to the community of Fort Chipewyan on the shores of Lake Athabasca.

The first European to paddle the entire Peace River was Alexander Mackenzie. In the fall of 1792, he traveled up the Peace and established an advance post called Fort Fork. This is just upstream from the present-day town of Peace River. Mackenzie spent the winter there, in order to get an early start the next spring for a daring attempt to "crack the mountain ramparts" — to go up and over the continental divide and find a route to the Pacific Ocean.

On May 9, 1793, he set out with six voyageurs, including two — Joseph Landry and Charles Doucette — from his previous expedition (a testament to the leadership qualities of Mackenzie). Alexander McKay, a clerk of the Northwest Company, two Natives and a big dog, which Mackenzie referred to simply as Our Dog, rounded out the expedition. A 25-foot birchbark canoe with a reinforced hull was built especially for the expedition.

The crew poled and paddled against the relentless current of the Peace. They hauled up the gorges, now flooded by the Peace Canyon Dam, and hacked a 9-mile (14.5 km) portage through the Rocky Mountains to bypass a series of tumbling rapids — "the stream rushed with an astonishing but silent velocity, between perpendicular rocks," Mackenzie wrote more than 200 years ago. These rapids are now drowned under 600 feet (180 m) of water, backed up by the W. A. C. Bennett Dam. On they journeyed, up the Parsnip River, inch by inch, making their way towards the Continental Divide.

The Mighty Peace, as it is called by locals, is seldom paddled. There is a perception that prairie rivers are boring, dirty, buggy and dull. But the Peace enthralled us with its beauty, its fascinating history and the abundance of wildlife found within its valley. The river today looks much as it did in Mackenzie's time. And like Mackenzie's, ours is a journey not only through distance but through history and cultures. A rich journey. A most amazing journey.

## Paddling With Bears

The Peace can be divided into two sections: a prairie river above the town of Peace River and a boreal forest river below it. Both sections have their own distinctive majesty.

*I am paddling the Peace as part of a bigger trip — retracing the route of Alexander Mackenzie. I had done most of the route alone, but life is changing, and transitions make me nervous. I'm meeting my girlfriend, Connie Downes, and I'm really nervous. Connie, a songbird biologist for the Canadian Wildlife Service, has been in southern Saskatchewan for three weeks conducting surveys. This is her summer holiday and I feel obliged to ensure she has a good time. What if the Peace River is boring? What if the bugs are terrible? What if the weather is terrible? What if she doesn't get along with me? I've never been on a long canoe trip with her.*

*I needn't have worried.*

Our journey started at Hudson's Hope, the first community downstream of the huge W. A. C. Bennett Dam and its sister dam 14 miles (22.5 km) downstream, the Peace Canyon Dam. These two dams have changed the Peace River, not only flooding its upper reaches but also changing the flooding patterns over 600 miles (960 km) downstream on the world's largest freshwater delta, in Wood Buffalo National Park. But we won't reach the delta for another three weeks. Today, just below the Peace Canyon Dam, the Peace flows swiftly between 900-foot-high (270 m) cliffs of silt and clay. Springs of crystalline water, icy cold, spurt from the cliff sides forming delicate waterfalls and creating fairy landscapes of multi-hued mineral deposits. We clambered up into a cave behind one of the springs and admired the clear, green waters of the Peace through a veil of falling water, stalactites and strings of algae. Above the cliffs is the town of Hudson's Hope, but it was barely visible from the river. A few rickety wooden ladders led from the river up to the town, but we left climbing those to others more daring than us. A trail leads from the river into town and it's worth the hike — there's a wonderful museum, restaurants and the friendliest people in Canada.

As a prairie river, the Peace flows in wide sweeping curves, framed by steep grassy slopes, groves of poplar and sheer cliffs of ocher earth. Although the river cuts through a land transformed by farms and ranches, almost everywhere along this section, the valley appears unchanged from the time when Mackenzie traveled on it, over two centuries ago. His descriptions of the majesty and beauty of the river still hold true today: "From the place which we quitted this morning (near the present-day town of Dunvegan,

close to the B.C./Alberta border), the west side of the river displayed a succession of the most beautiful scenery I had ever beheld . . . the ground rises to
a considerable height . . . at every interval or pause in the rise, there is a very
gently-ascending space or lawn, which is alternated with abrupt precipices
to the summit of the whole . . . This magnificent theatre of nature has all
the decoration which the trees and animals of the country can afford it."

The only elements missing today are the vast herds of elk and buffalo
that Mackenzie reported, and which sustained his expedition. However, we
did see a few elk and plenty of deer, in small herds resting by the riverside, or
clambering up almost vertical cliffs with ease. The air is filled with the sweet
perfume of clover, mint and chives. Serviceberry trees are heavy with plump
blue berries. Prickly pear cactus cover the steep slopes with yellow blooms
on the north side of the river. The slopes on the south shore are forested
with spruce and poplar.

However, the beauty of this section of the Peace may be jeopardized. The
push is on for more electric power in the United States, and the power mon-
gers are greedily looking at the Peace. Plans are afoot for a new dam to be built
near the Alberta–British Columbia border, which would back the river up to
the Peace Canyon Dam above Hudson's Hope, a distance of 93 miles (150 km).
The caves, the springs, the waterfalls, the limestone islands, the prairie
benches — all would be submerged under the waters of this new reservoir.

At Fort Dunvegan, fur-trade days come to life at this restored Hudson's
Bay Company post. But even more exciting for weary, sunned-out river
travelers, deprived of fresh fruit and vegetables, are the market garden and
teahouse. We left with a bag of fresh potatoes and a basket of strawberries.
Just below Dunvegan, a provincial historic park marks the site of Fort Fork,
where Mackenzie left in early May 1793 for his final push to the Pacific.

Below the town of Peace River, the river broadens and forests of spruce,
birch and poplar cover the valley slopes. There is one unique site here that
Mackenzie did not behold. On the east bank, a few hours below the town, a
bright orange flame dances in the breeze. A spring gushes out of the ground
at the base of the flames and tumbles down the steep bank to the Peace.
The water is gray, and the rocks it flows over are covered with a white gelat-
inous goop. Shiny black patches of oil float in tiny pools and eddies. This
natural gas well was ignited years ago, after attempts to tap it failed. No one
knows how long it will burn, but it appears like a scene out of Hell. Further
downstream, beside Peace Island, gas bubbles rise from the riverbed, testifying
to more untapped sources of oil and gas. There is a wonderful campsite on

the island, where thirsty river travelers can stay and buy meals, and even beer — a pleasure Mackenzie could only dream of.

Fort Vermilion, the last community on the Peace connected by highway to the south, was born of trading posts, missions and, most recently, pioneering grain farmers. From here, the Peace flows in seemingly never-ending curves through a vast flat land. The banks are lined with spruce and poplar forest. The ever-present swimming bears are here, as are the occasional moose with one or two calves. Each evening, the setting sun paints the broad, swirling, murky waters of the Peace with the colors of flames, opals and the inside of clamshells.

## Place of Peace

A sense of serenity and timelessness enveloped us. The Peace is a gentle giant of a river. Old, wide and wise. Some say it is the oldest river in Canada. The only portage is at Vermilion Chutes, where its murky waters, the color and consistency of chocolate milk, pour over a series of limestone ledges. We picked our way down the first ledges along the south shore. The second series of ledges form a 10-foot (3 m) drop and must be portaged on the south shore. Just below the main drop is a convenient rock ledge about three feet (1 m) above the water, where the canoe can be loaded and launched. The main ledge extends completely across the river, a distance of a third of a mile (0.5 km), broken by limestone islands. The river is framed by limestone cliffs.

We pitched our tent up on top, for a wonderful view of the falls and the approaching thunderstorms. It is interesting to note that Mackenzie described these falls as being 20 feet high (6 m). Clearly, they have eroded over the past two centuries, where today they are only about half that height.

At Peace Point, where the Cree and Beaver Indians settled a long-standing dispute, is where the river derives its name. From the grassy fields on top of white and cream gypsum cliffs that frame the river, we watch the sun sink into the water, a flaming red orb colored by the smoke of distant forest fires. It's easy to image this place as a place of peace.

The final leg of the journey to Fort Chipewyan takes us upstream on the Quatre Fourches (locals pronounce it catfish) Channel. The current is strong and progress is slow. As we steered our canoe up the Quatre Fourches Channel, we bid goodbye to the Peace. For 1,240 miles (2,000 km), we have known it and ridden on its waters and watched them change from crystalline to opaque. We feel as if we are leaving an old friend.

# Poling
## *Up the Creek Without a Paddle*

Howard Heffler

M Y FRIEND PETER ERMANN CALLED ON THE LAST FRIDAY IN OCTOBER. "Bring your Rocky," he said. "And I'll meet you tomorrow morning at the Sheep River."

Normally cautious, I asked, "Won't it be too shallow? Won't there be ice on the shoreline?"

"Stop asking so many questions," he replied. "And don't forget to bring your pole."

The Sheep is a small Alberta river in the Bow River Basin that drains from the eastern slopes of the Rockies. The upper reaches have a gradient of 50 feet per mile (9 m/km) through a deep canyon with only a few access points. With normal snowmelt and spring rain, we can paddle from May until July. Ideal flows are in the range of 500 to 1,000 cubic feet per second (15–30 cms), although we have stretched the limits to as low as 350 and as high as 2,500 cfs. It is one of our favorites for open canoes, with fairly continuous Class II and II+.

With some trepidation, I met Peter as planned at the take-out and put my old Rocky (a locally made fiberglass canoe) on the truck beside his Coleman canoe. We like to extend the paddling season to its limits. In southern Alberta, the mountain streams start to lose their winter ice in March and April, but the runoff doesn't usually allow paddling until May. By September, the water in these smaller rivers has traveled all the way to Hudson Bay, so attempting the Sheep in October was definitely a stretch.

We off-loaded the boats at the usual spot beside an ice-covered Gorge Creek. During summer, we paddle, wade and drag the canoes about 300 yards down this little creek to the Sheep. From here to the take-out at Sandy McNabb Campground is about 7.5 miles (12 km) of whitewater with many playspots and a few small drops. There is no feasible way in or out of the canyon until the take-out.

On this October day Peter dressed in a drysuit; I had only a wetsuit. We dragged our canoes on Gorge Creek towards the Sheep. Generally the ice supported our weight, but a couple of times I broke through into water to

my waist. In his drysuit, Peter just laughed as I whined about cold body parts. In a few minutes we reached the Sheep River itself. I estimated the Sheep was flowing at less than 1 inch (2 cm), not nearly enough to paddle. Besides, we didn't have our paddles, only our poles. We held our boats on the beach for a last look around, partly to see if anyone was watching this idiocy and partly hoping the other guy might say, "Let's go home."

On other occasions, we poled upstream from this point and then returned downstream. This October trip was a new experiment: poling downstream (also called snubbing). We knew the rapids and the ledges would be too difficult to return back upriver, so once we entered the canyon, we were committed. I don't remember who went first. The put-in disappeared around the first bend into the canyon. As our canoes came together, we looked at each other with big grins. We could control our boats quite well.

## Poling Dates Back to B.C. (Before Cars)

I should tell you a bit about poling. As a method of moving a canoe, it dates back to B.C. (before cars), when the rivers of Canada were the Trans-Canada Highway of today. In earlier times, before you could paddle downstream, you first had to go upstream. The choices were: paddling, wading, lining, portaging or poling. If the current was too swift or too shallow to paddle, poling was a good option. Traditionally, travelers cut a 12-to-14-foot length (3.6 to 4.2 m) of a small tree, 2 inches or less in diameter. By standing near the center of the canoe, with the downstream end slightly heavier, the poler used either end of the pole on either side of the canoe to move up each riffle and across the pools. The trick was to keep the boat almost perfectly aligned with the current and to plant the pole on the river bottom just behind your feet and walk your hands up the pole to move the boat forward. Once you came to the end of the pole, it was quickly lifted from the water and moved forward to a new placement, and up you go again.

For our October trip, we used $1\frac{1}{4}$-inch (3.175 cm) diameter wooden dowel purchased at the local lumber store. To keep the end from splintering, we hammered a 2-inch (5 cm) length of iron pipe of the same outside diameter over the end of the pole. Some aficionados prefer an aluminum pole; I feel wood is warmer. Since you are standing, you want a fairly stable canoe — 16 to 18 feet long. This is not the place for your playboat!

After lots of banged shins against the thwart and a few unglamorous exits over the gunwales, we learned how to climb upstream against the current. The secret is to align the canoe in a shallow ferry angle and balance the forces of the current with the pole as you work your way up riffles and small rapids. Many times Peter watched me lose control of the angle, spin in the current and wash back down the rapid. Before I regained my balance and fought to plant the pole to stop being washed downstream, I lost much hard-won ground (and sometimes my patience). It would take about 15 seconds to lose all the upstream effort of the previous 15 minutes.

On earlier trips, we poled upstream for two or three hours, had lunch and headed back downstream to the starting point. In some instances, there was enough water to paddle back downstream, but usually the water was too shallow to effectively paddle, so we used the pole on the descent, too. This had several advantages: from the standing position, you have better visibility to pick the best line; usually the water is not deep enough for a paddle blade; and with the pole you can stop the boat dead in its tracks and even back up to find a new line. Since we invested so much energy working our way upstream, we liked to prolong the descent as much as possible.

At first, we found downstream poling difficult. But soon we could comfortably handle anything on the descent that we accomplished on the ascent. In fact, we now pole down rapids and ledges that we are not able to pole up. Several of our descents have been down sections of rivers that, during paddling season with adequate flow, are Class III.

## Quickly Dismissed as Too Sensible

That October day was our first outing with descent as the sole objective. It was memorable. We were in a deep canyon, where the sun only occasionally reached the river; the water seeping from the north-facing canyon walls was starting to form frozen waterfalls. The air was cold: our neoprene paddling boots froze to the rocks when we stood in one place too long. The water splashing into our canoes froze on the floor, so we covered the ice with sand from the beach to get traction for standing. We stopped on a gravel bar that had some sun, and boiled water for a cup of soup. I'll never forget the sense of discovery. While we had paddled this river many times in summer in the conventional way, this trip was giving us a whole new perspective — like seeing an old friend in an entirely new way.

One particular ledge was always a thrill in the summer. It was about a 4-foot (1.2 m) drop, with an awkward approach requiring a cautious back-ferry angle until you lined up for two quick paddle strokes to take you over the edge and through the boil at the bottom. Now, with about one-tenth the summer flow, we slowly worked our way around the gravel bar guarding the approach. This was not the time to lose control. We managed to get out on the rock ledge that formed the drop and hold our canoes while we discussed our strategy. One option was to lift over the ledge and carry on. This was quickly dismissed as too sensible.

During summer, the drop was normally about 10 to 12 feet (3 to 3.6 m) wide, so there was some margin for error. Now, however, the crest of the waterfall was only about 4 feet (1.2 m) wide. The next suggestion was to wade our canoes towards the ledge and, with the correct angle, give them a mighty push over the drop. We could then climb around the ledge and catch up with them in the pool below. This option, with no points for style, was defeated by a vote of 2 to 0.

There was only one option left: attempt the drop in the standing position. We had no idea what would happen. Boat angle was critical. There

was no way to get any speed, so the only technique was to slowly let the canoe through the slot and, just at the moment it overbalanced and the bow fell, plant the pole on the downstream side of the ledge and hope to keep your balance. Everything worked except the balance part.

The waterfall was vertical and about 4 feet (1.2 m) high. The bow hit the pool below and didn't plunge too far before surfacing. At that instant I tried to get the business end of my pole on the bottom of the pool, but not quickly enough. The canoe stayed upright but I didn't. It was a quick swim.

Peter came next with much the same result, except he managed to fall backwards into his boat rather than sideways into the drink. I changed into a dry shirt and we completed the trip without any further mishaps.

Since that day in October, Peter and I have poled other rivers and returned to the Sheep several times. Our skills have increased and we now consider poling an extension of the paddling season. However, nothing will erase the sense of adventure and discovery of our first descent.

# Ice Canoeing
## *Hooked on Fun*

Geoff Danysk

During the drive to the put-in, I'm both nervous and excited about the first river-day of the season. I meet up with the guys and we relive some of the great highlights of past adventures. I've been involved in this sport for eight years, but there's a certain exhilaration as we look forward to another year. I think back to some of the great people this sport has introduced me to, and the countless moments of pleasure and pain.

After getting dressed in my car, I step out into the minus 13 degrees Fahrenheit (-25° C) December morning, thankful it is calm . . . no wind chill. Not exactly your typical weather for the first day of the paddling season, but this isn't your typical paddling. We are the Calgary ice canoe team and this is our winter ritual.

I remember my first introduction to ice canoeing, in the winter of 1992–93. I knew the team captain, Bre, through Mount Royal College and the University of Calgary. When he approached me about trying out, I asked about the sport and what was involved. After hearing the list of requirements — paddling, rowing, scootering, pushing and pulling a five-person, 350-pound (160 kg) boat through water, snow, ice and slush — I knew I was out of my league. Bre assured me physical fitness was all I needed and the rest would be learned. As I had been commuting to and from the university daily on my bike, a return trip of about 25 miles (40 km), I felt good about my level of fitness, so I agreed to give it a shot.

It was minus 13 when we met at the Calgary Canoe Club and began suiting up in layers of polypropylene and fleece. On our feet, we wore neoprene socks under neoprene boots molded to the shape of each foot. The boots had large heavy plastic cleats, studded with 1-inch-long (2.5 cm) snowmobile spikes for traction. On our legs we wore a thin layer of polypropylene, covered with hockey shin pads to protect them when banging against the boat and ice floes. The upper body got another thin layer of polypropylene, along with lightweight fleece and windbreaker jackets. The rest of the warmth was to come from moving the boat. I was assured I would be working hard enough not to require so many layers, but I was apprehensive.

We were only three of the five-member team as we began the practice on the frozen Glenmore Reservoir. We were just going to push the boat across the reservoir on a 2-mile (3 km) triangular course. I had no idea what I was getting myself into. The reservoir was covered with about 2 feet (60 cm) of snow and pushing the boat was e-x-h-a-u-s-t-i-n-g. Pushing requires you to be bent over to the level of the boat, greatly decreasing the oxygen passing in and out of your lungs. Halfway to the first corner of the triangle, my lungs were about to explode and my legs were in knots. No amount of bike riding had prepared me for this.

At the first corner we took a couple of minutes to catch our breath, stretch our legs and prepare for the next leg. Bre and Barney didn't let on at the time, and I was too out of breath to realize, but they were hurting as much as me. We completed the triangle with frequent breaks, however, I couldn't cool my burning lungs. I walked away from that practice knowing ice canoeing was not for me. I said I wouldn't be back.

The call for the second practice came a couple of days later, this time to the river. The team was one man short, so I agreed to fill the empty seat. It was a sunny Saturday afternoon, about 14 F (-10 C), as we unloaded the boat at the Bow River, near Prince's Island. Off in the boat and pushing through the snow once again, memories of the previous practice's pain came back. But this time it was different, easier. Then came my first transition. Running at full speed along the snow-covered ice, we reached the edge where the ice gave way and the flowing river took over. Diving into the boat, narrowly avoiding the river's

icy grip, I took my seat and reached for my oar. Setting it into its oarlock, I got my first pull and . . . the feeling of power transferring from my body through the oar to drive the boat forward. It was tremendous. But even stronger was the feeling of camaraderie, of five people giving everything to move the boat.

There were countless transitions: hopping from water to ice and back to water, scrambling up on ice pads in the middle of the river only to hurtle towards open water on the other side. I never really knew if the ice under-foot was thick enough to support my weight, but I attacked it with reckless abandon, secure in the knowledge the team was there to help me out. It was exciting, challenging, demanding, rewarding and . . . fun. I was hooked.

## Quebec Embraces Cowboys from Calgary

Talking about ice canoeing in Western Canada is like speaking a foreign language that only a select few understand. The mention of my sport is met with raised eyebrows, statements of disbelief and one question: why?

Ice canoeing is a proud Quebec tradition, beginning out of necessity at a time when no bridges spanned the St. Lawrence River. At that time, the exchange of goods between various communities, such as the cities of Levis and Quebec, was possible only by crossing the river. In all four seasons, food, medicine, clothing and supplies were loaded into canoes and transported across the river. As more canoes became available, competition to provide the fastest and most efficient crossings increased. Today, more than twenty teams brave the challenges of the icy St. Lawrence as part of the Quebec Winter Carnival. As Quebec's sister city, Calgary has been sending a canoe team every February since 1967. As the Cowboys from Calgary, we are always met with lots of support, encouragement and enthusiasm. We usually finish in the top seven.

## Three Cardinal Rules

We all approach the ice-canoe season with a high level of physical fitness, after a summer of mountain biking, marathon canoeing, whitewater kayaking and running. We start by training two nights a week with exercise regimens such as running stairs, pushing the canoe through the snow, and practicing our rowing timing and technique in an indoor tank. As the Bow freezes, our training increases to four times a week, maintaining the two evening practices and adding two river practices on the weekend.

A crucial part of our river training is for the transition stages, from ice to water and water to ice. It is during these transitions that the canoe is

most vulnerable to capsize, necessitating smooth and coordinated movements into and out of the boat. Often the ice is too unstable to support us, a factor we always seem to find out too late. This is where the three cardinal rules of ice canoeing become critical: One, don't let go of the boat. Two, don't let go of the boat. Three, don't let go of the boat.

When you put together the excitement, adrenaline and hard work, the only time you really get cold is at the end of practice, when you might need a hot shower to remove the frozen clothing stuck to your body.

We train hard for the Quebec race, putting in countless hours of running, rowing, paddling, pushing, pulling and scootering (with one foot in the boat, the other provides propulsion) our boat across the Bow River. Yet no amount of training ever prepares us for the magnitude of the St. Lawrence, or the enormity of effort required to navigate across such a huge expanse of river. The Bow has ice that usually freezes hard and flat. The only thing consistent about the St. Lawrence ice is its inconsistency — from hard chunks rising above the river, as high as 6 to 10 feet (2–3 m), to slush that offers very little purchase for pushing or pulling.

Another tricky factor is the tidal movement of the St. Lawrence, which ranges from no current at slack tide up to 2.5 knots in high tide. The challenge is further complicated by the fact the race involves completing two complete triangles across the river, covering a distance between 3 and 7 miles (6–12 km), depending on the speed and direction of the tidal flow.

I now look forward to training for ice canoeing. But I don't tell many people about it.

# Kazan River
## The Impact of Wilderness

David F. Pelly

ABOUT A HUNDRED YEARS AGO, A MISSIONARY MET AN INDIAN ON THE edge of the barrenlands. Saltatha was Chipewyan; his people depended on the caribou for their every need, from food to clothing and shelter. Saltatha knew the barrenlands well. The missionary, no doubt a well-intentioned man, was a stranger to this land at the very edge of white man's sphere of knowledge. He was there for a reason; he proceeded to tell Saltatha of the peace and beauty that awaited them in heaven. Saltatha listened carefully. When the missionary finished, Saltatha said, "My father, you have spoken well; you have told me that heaven is very beautiful. Tell me now one thing more. Is it more beautiful than the country of the muskox in summer, when sometimes the mist blows over the lakes, and sometimes the water is blue, and the loons cry very often?"

For Abdul Hasnie from Pakistan, or Choi Siu Ping from Hong Kong, or Osama Abdeen from Jordan, or even Leslie Mack-Mumford from Toronto, a summer in the land that Saltatha forthrightly compared to heaven was bound to be a novel experience, at the very least. For twenty-four young people, aged 18 to 23, from 11 different countries, it was a challenge, an adventure, an awakening. They were members of a multi-disciplinary scientific expedition in Canada's Arctic, on the Kazan River — one of the wildest, most rugged and beautiful in the barrenlands.

In 1988, we canoed 300 miles (500 km) from Angikuni Lake to Baker Lake over forty-five days. That is not an impressive rate of travel among canoeists — but it is explained by the fact that along the way we walked about 200 miles (320 km) of transects over the tundra looking for archeological evidence of Saltatha's people, his predecessors and their Inuit neighbors. We also conducted other biological and palynological (spores and pollens) field studies. It was a busy summer of hard work and constant learning for everyone involved — much more than a canoe trip.

These young people experienced the Kazan's environment on many levels: they studied its soil, plants, birds and mammals, and its record of former human habitation, at the same time that they marveled — as Saltatha would have wished — at its isolation and natural splendor. Inevitably, this had quite an impact, right from the start, as some of their journals reveal.

"The cloud cover has cleared a little and we are having our first glimpse of the arctic tundra — it looks serene and somehow waiting for us to arrive. Snow still dots the land in places — and the tundra looks a basic brown from this far up. The yellow sun is glinting off thousands of lakes dotted about the land like puddles of water on a concrete pane," wrote Sonia Mellor of Australia.

July 1. Written in a float plane: "I will never forget my feeling of awe, stepping onto the barrenlands for the first time. . . . Instantly, I was struck by how 'unbarren' the land seems to be, how beautifully green," wrote Simon Cremer of England.

Sudden displacement into the center of the barrenlands — dropped off by a float plane — was an impressive, somewhat anxiety-provoking, but exciting experience for all twenty-four who had come there from the far corners of the world. That initial camp was on the shores of still ice-covered Angikuni Lake, right beside where the Kazan flows out in a burst of rushing whitewater. Just a few hundred yards across the tundra was an old Inuit grave, the skull staring up from beneath a pile of boulders. While we were there, in that first camp, grazing caribou ranged over the surrounding tundra, and more than once walked practically into camp. The land took only a few days to embrace the young people. Very quickly the arctic barrenlands displayed its varied moods.

"July 7. The rain and wind struck about midnight and stayed all day. The temperature dropped to about 4° C [39° F] and the wind, at 25 to 30 knots, whipped up white horses on the lake.

"July 13. Long, hot, still days with temperatures 28° C [82° F] in the shade and over 37° [99° F] in the sun. However, one must share the few shadowy spots with thousands of mosquitoes and black flies," wrote Kassie Heath of Australia.

This, quite naturally, is the first level on which people adjust to their new environment: physical comfort, or rather discomfort. It is when they become comfortable, physically, in the environment that they are then ready to move on to the next level in their relationship with the wilderness. We had a big advantage, as an encouragement of this development, in that our scientific projects forced everyone to go out and experience the environment itself, to walk on the land, to examine it carefully, document its plant growth, watch for and identify its birds, record its subtle clues of previous human occupation. All of this inevitably put each person in touch with the wilderness around him or her.

Leslie Mack-Mumford, a Canadian, wrote in her journal, "I think I'm finding the nothing in this country of miles and miles of nothing."

Looking back, Sonia Mellor of Australia said, "In my journal, I started to draw things like sunsets, wildlife, or just the land, walking on the tundra, perceptions. To me that was really interesting, because it was the first time the land itself, the environment, touched me so much."

Different participants moved, naturally, in different directions, at different speeds. Some, reveling in the scientific fieldwork, found themselves examining the world around them in unprecedented ways.

"I saw a wolf on a boulder shore. This was my first experience with the wolf because my country is a modern commercial center. I was excited and scared. The wolf stared at me with shining eyes from 10 meters [about 30 feet]. It went away after about 20 seconds but it was a very long time for the two of us. It had a den underneath the boulders. I heard the voices of the young. I will never forget this contact with the wolf," said Choi Siu Ping of Hong Kong.

For some participants, the archeological work had the most profound impact, as it transported them back through time, to an era when other peoples lived along the Kazan River. Finding stone structures and an array of artifacts on the surface led to knowing that someone — 50, 100, 300 or several thousand years ago — was responsible for making them and leaving them there, possibly undiscovered through the intervening years.

"What had been an empty landscape when we first walked on it, now became a living environment for the people who were once there. Sometimes

I would sit on a high spot and imagine all those people walking around and working and putting meat into caches and smashing the bone to extract marrow. The landscape became something more than just a beautiful place for canoeists. It became somebody's home," wrote Hillary Woodward of England.

Through this sort of experience, the expedition felt the impact of Native people who once lived there. An equally profound Native influence came to us in the form of a Dene participant. Betty Ann Betsedea came from Wrigley, a tiny village on the banks of the Mackenzie River, about one-third of the way downstream from Great Slave Lake to the Arctic Ocean. The barrenlands are not her people's traditional territory; to this day, she reflects that she felt somewhat strange in a setting without trees. But the concept of living with the rhythm of the land, the river and the sky was as natural to her as breathing. Those who traveled closely with her commented on it without exception.

## Landscape of the Imagination

By the end of the third week of the trip, midway in the process, every participant had evolved quite some distance from their earliest relationship with the barrenlands. It had become home for them, in some sense. There existed a new familiarity and understanding. Simply staying comfortable, by now, seemed incidental, natural. They had found the rhythm of the land and of their own journey through it. This heightened familiarity shows up in their journals in many ways, but not just in words. In the latter stages of the expedition, most who were keeping journals began drawing maps, sometimes simple schematics, sometimes complex works of art. Whatever their

form, these maps aided them in describing their experience and relationship with the land, suggesting a heightened sensitivity to the environment.

"Somehow the people around me have lost significance, or at least their urgency in my thoughts. The land and its rhythms have gained predominance," wrote Kassie Heath, in a telling entry from her journal.

This echoes British novelist Lawrence Durrell, who wrote: "All landscapes ask the same question in the same whisper: I am watching you — are you watching yourself in me?"

It is one thing to bring a group of young people into the wilderness — in all probability that process in itself will set them to thinking about the place, developing a landscape of the imagination. It is quite another to have them empowered by that landscape to look into themselves. Towards that end, journal keeping is at the very least a positive influence. The mere process of writing pushes the participant to appreciate the greater depths of his or her experience. Perceptions become finer. Journal writing develops eyes that can see and ears that can hear more of what is going on about the writer.

Journal keeping during a wilderness experience develops one's ability to express wonder, the inevitable response to something large and spiritual, such as the wilderness.

It is the manifest power of geography, of the land. On some level, just as the physical journey stands as a metaphor for life's quest, the writing of a journal becomes the search for meaning. That searching is most apparent in the final pages of a few of the participants' journals.

"There is such a loving, soft vulnerable part to me — but I lose it when I lead. I lose my softness to a self-disciplined monster. It's why I dropped out of university the first go-round, because I thought it would lead me to a tough, business-type character. I became frightened of that tough, lonely person."

"As this journey is drawing to a close, I am just starting to realize that as one episode closes, so many doors open up. I will carry with me, for the rest of my days, my experiences on the Kazan. Already new plans have been laid for the future, different plans to the ones I began with."

Asked afterwards to comment on what value the journal-keeping process in this wilderness setting had had for them, several responded. "I think my journals made me really aware that I was learning lessons," said one.

"I felt it was a great outlet for my emotions," said another. "Sometimes I would read back those writings and learn a little bit about myself and why I was feeling like that. It was a tool, in a way."

And a third: "There's a lot in my journal that I haven't even told my family or friends. So it was quite a step for me to actually write down what I was really feeling."

The experience of merely writing a journal added to the impact of the expedition itself, that is, to the impact the land was having on the travelers. Not only did the journal-keeper create a record of his or her journeys, both physical and spiritual, but the journals themselves became an instructive tool, as one put it. There are elements of the wilderness experience, and of the individual's personal growth, that could not have emerged had the participant not been keeping a journal. The journal is not a guarantee of success — real personal success — in a journey, but it is arguably a necessary component.

## Voyage of Discovery

"The completed journey always ends with a return, a homecoming to the ordinary world of conventional reality that was left behind," says writer Ralph Metzner in *Opening to Inner Light*. "This world has been transformed, if our journey has been successful, into a new world, seen with fresh eyes. The end of the journey is the beginning of a new, empowered way of life."

It is now many years since all these journal entries were written, since these twenty-four young people canoed down the Kazan River. They are all in their thirties now, many of them with young families of their own. The question inevitably arises: what has happened to them since? What power did the land exert upon them that has affected their lives?

It's best to answer that by citing a few examples. Jeremy Tate returned to England after the expedition, and left his job at British Telecom to enroll at university, an option he had not previously felt possible; he graduated with an Honors B.Sc. in oceanography and now works on projects around the world. Leslie Mack-Mumford from Toronto has spent the past few years variously studying environmental science at McGill University in Montreal, and learning about organic farming and shiatsu in northern British Columbia. Eddy Chong returned to his ad-copy writer's desk in Singapore, lasted a couple of years there, then decided he needed to find a more human field of endeavor; he graduated from a university in the United States with a degree in physio-therapy, and returned to a practice in Singapore working with infants.

Sonia Mellor, in Australia, wrote to me the year after the expedition, with a report of her progress: "To the trip's credit, I have become a lot more environmentally aware. My thoughts were the first things to change after my journey through the barrenlands — then followed an evaluation of what was important to me. So much that I had taken for fact, I questioned — and continue to do so. I have the self-confidence in my convictions that I lacked before. I started volunteer work for a conservation foundation, where I got heavily involved in a campaign to save some virgin eucalyptus forest in the southeast corner of New South Wales — the area has trees over 300 years old, up to 200 feet (60 m) tall and supports a huge range of wildlife and flora — and the state government can justify chopping it down and sending it as wood chips to make paper in Japan — Arghh!!"

She went on, eventually describing her plans to do graduate work in environmental science. She now has her M.Sc. and works for the National Parks Service in Australia. For Sonia and the others, this voyage was about building bridges: young people building bridges to their own future, bridges between their inner and outer selves, bridges between one human from one part of the world and another from somewhere else, between humankind and the environment. Building these bridges comprised a voyage of discovery for them all, and their vehicle was the canoe.

The Kazan River experience gave each of the participants a heightened environmental awareness and concern. It lent each one of the young people a newfound confidence in themselves; offered them, because of the trip's multi-cultural composition, a new view of their place on the planet. It allowed them to probe within themselves, enriched them with a profound respect for the value of close human contact, and gave them the courage to set their sights high. All of these phenomena emerge in the letters that have accumulated from the many corners of the globe over the years.

One line in one letter, from Kassie Heath in Australia, perhaps sums them all up: "Dreams can be made to come true — my summer taught me this."

The unspoken question at the outset was, "What impact did an expedition in the Arctic wilderness have on these people and how was it achieved?" The answer is evident in their own words. That is how it should be. The leaders did not preach or lecture. We simply gave these young people an exposure to the natural world, in its finest barrenlands glory. They decided to let it have an impact upon them — they decided how, they decided when and in what way. The barrenlands left an impression on them all — not unlike that expressed by Saltatha.

If there were lessons learned and values acquired — and I think there were — then it is the great teacher that we have to thank: the land.

# Prince Albert National Park
## Paddling With the Spirit of Grey Owl

John Geary

As we landed on the bank of the lake by the cabin, pulled the canoe ashore and secured it, the feelings washed over me — reverence, respect, wonder and a sense of tranquility. This was Beaver Lodge, the actual cabin where Grey Owl had lived, worked and produced much of his nature writing in the first third of the 20th century.

The special sense of reverence I experienced upon entering the cabin could not have been any greater if my wife, Ann, and I had passed through the Gothic archway of a monumental European cathedral. I half-expected the ghosts of Charlie the Moose or Jelly Roll and Rawhide the beavers to pop out of the woods at any moment, challenging our intrusion into the sanctity of this lonely and now-empty abode. Although we paid homage at the gravesite of the man the Ojibwa called Wa-sha-quon-asin (He Who Walks by Night), we did not need to visit the grave to feel his spirit. It had followed us the entire trip, reminding us of its presence in the trees that lined the shores of the lake, in the breeze that rustled the few remaining leaves on those trees, in the wildlife that honored us with its presence.

We began our pilgrimage to the final home of Grey Owl, born Archibald Stansfeld Belaney, knowing very little about the man other than the fact he was an Englishman who passed himself off as a North American Indian during the 1920s and 1930s. He journeyed through North America and England to preach a message of conservation, his travels made possible by the popularity of his books and magazine articles about the outdoors. His passion for this writing seemed to draw from his close relationship with adopted beavers, first McGinnis and McGinty, then later, Rawhide and Jelly Roll. The latter two shared his cabin at Ajawaan, hence the name Beaver Lodge. Belaney, who grew up loving stories like *The Song of Hiawatha* by Henry Wadsworth Longfellow and James Fenimore Cooper's *Leatherstocking Tales*, came to Canada in 1906 at the age of seventeen to try to make his urban fantasy into a frontier reality.

He hooked up with Bill Guppy and his brothers, Alex and George, in Cobalt, Ontario. At Lake Temiskaming, during the winter of 1906–1907, they taught him the wilderness skills he would use as a guide, trapper, ranger — and later, to masquerade as a half Scottish, half Apache Native.

His charade was successful until his death in 1938, when the *North Bay Nugget* newspaper revealed the hoax to the world.

Immediately following his death, many of his supporters refused, initially, to believe he was false; others wrote him off as a charlatan. Despite the revelation, both Anahareo, his wife, who helped turn him from a trapper of beaver to a protector of beaver, and their daughter, Shirley Dawn, worked tirelessly throughout their lives to promote his message of conservation and animal rights. For her tireless efforts, Anahareo — also known as Gertrude Bernard, or Pony to her friends — received the Order of Canada in 1983, three years before her death.

It could probably be argued that without his Native persona, Belaney would not have made the impact he did in raising awareness about conservation. While he cannot claim to be the father of Canadian conservation, his lectures and writings about beavers and other wildlife certainly planted the seeds of awareness. That growing awareness helped lay the foundation for the conservation movement that began thirty years after his death, as people looked past the facade and realized the importance of his message.

I never thought much about his charade; I was more interested in his writing and his love of nature. Before setting out on our trip, I read one of his stories, *The Adventures of Sajo and her Beaver People*. I enjoyed it, without much thought about the fact he had misled the world.

So it was that we came to paddle to his cabin, located in Saskatchewan's Prince Albert National Park, in a quest to find out more about this enigmatic character while enjoying the wilderness he loved so much.

Grey Owl had moved to Ajawaan to work as a park ranger for Canada's national park system in 1932. It was there he wrote many of his books, including *Pilgrims of the Wild*, *Sajo* and *Tales of an Empty Cabin*.

At Ajawaan, he solidified his magical relationship with wild animals, connecting with them in a way he never could connect with humans. In addition to his beavers — or perhaps because of them — the birds, squirrels and even the moose at the lake seemed to accept him without fear.

The morning before we arrived at Ajawaan, we put our canoe into the Kingsmere River in the northern part of the park. A short, 20-minute paddle brought us to a platform that allowed us to load the canoe onto a hand-powered railcar.

At one point, the railcar led to a dock just above a small dam that kept the water level artificially high and made for easy boat access into Kingsmere Lake. Just a month before our trip, the dam was removed as part of a renaturalization program the park management initiated to restore biodiversity to the river and its surrounding habitat.

With the dam gone, the water level in the river by the dock was too low to transport motorized boats — and for that matter, most canoes — into the lake from that point. That meant those seeking the lake had to portage their watercraft from the railcar's end to a put-in on the actual lake. While my shoulders were not particularly forgiving during the half-mile-long walk through the woods hauling a canoe, the conservationist in me applauded the move. There are many other lakes in the park that provide easy motorboat access. This one would stay — or at least be returned — to a more natural state for the future good of the ecosystem.

The spirit of Grey Owl was at work.

As it turned out, the lake's level in October was even too low near the lakeshore to paddle a fully loaded canoe into its waters. We had to roll up our pant legs and wade about half a mile (1 km) out into the icy waters before we could load ourselves back into the canoe. The water provided an even better wake-up call than the industrial-strength espresso we traditionally brew and consume early each morning on all our canoe trips.

As we paddled along, following the eastern shore, we could hear the voices of people hiking along the 12-mile (20 km) trail that followed the lakeshore to a connecting trail to Lake Ajawaan and Grey Owl's cabin.

The longer we paddled, though, the quieter it became. The calls of loons, red-necked grebes and mergansers along the lake replaced the voices of people. We welcomed the respite from humanity, losing ourselves in nature's song, accompanied by the rhythmic percussion of our paddles dipping into the water, stroke after stroke.

We had thought to paddle all the way to the Northend campsite that first day, then either hike or portage the canoe to Ajawaan, depending on our mood at the time. However, a late start combined with the early autumn twilight persuaded us to camp at Sandy Beach instead.

One other couple occupied one of the campsites; they had hiked up earlier that day. They were to be the last humans we would see until the end of our trip two days later.

While I was hauling our gear from the lakeshore to the campsite, a flash of calico caught my eye. The thought flashed through my mind: "What the heck is a cat doing out here?" My mind just as quickly dismissed the thought as I slowed my pace to avoid scaring the animal away. I gazed at it through some low brush, trying to determine what it was, my efforts hampered by the deepening twilight.

It was a fox! I've seen many foxes — red, gray, even light brown — but I had never seen a calico fox before. Of course, my camera was back at the campsite, so I had to content myself with watching him. He was checking out a firepit for any scraps inadvertently left by previous users, but he found none. I approached cautiously, trying to get a better look at him, but my movement spooked him. He darted off into the brush, stopping to glance back at me for a moment before losing himself in the dense forest.

That night, as I went down to the lake to fetch water for cleaning our supper dishes, I heard a splashing sound. An otter surfaced lazily 10 yards out from shore. He rolled around a few times as if taking his evening bath, then dove beneath the surface.

The next morning we set out to cover the final hour of paddling to the north end of the lake. Halfway there, a hawk flew past us overhead. Moments later, we enjoyed the sight of a bald eagle winging his way through the skies above.

"Far enough away to gain seclusion, yet within reach of those whose genuine interest prompts them to make the trip, Beaver Lodge extends a welcome to you if your heart is right." — Grey Owl, in *Tales of an Empty Cabin*.

We arrived at the empty Northend campsite, where we cached most of our food and gear, taking only enough to have lunch at Beaver Lodge. We decided the only really appropriate way to visit the cabin would be to paddle there, as Grey Owl would have done. We portaged the couple of miles to Ajawaan and put in at the south end of the lake.

There was a quiet stillness to this lake we had not experienced on the much larger Kingsmere. The cabin was nestled in the woods at the far end of the lake from our put-in. After the sounds and sights of the birds on Kingsmere, their absence during our paddle to the cabin on Ajawaan was eerie.

"Ajawaan; a small, deep lake that, like a splash of quicksilver, lies gleaming in its setting of the wooded hills that stretch in long, heaving undulations into the North, to the Arctic Sea." — Grey Owl, in *Tales of an Empty Cabin*.

We pulled up on shore and paid our respects in his cabin.

Then, while Ann prepared lunch, I visited the graves of Grey Owl, Anahareo and Shirley Dawn. Although I had never been here before, I felt a connection, an empathy for the man and his work, his struggles and his joys, his successes and his failures. After several moments of quiet contemplation, I walked along a path through the woods, different from the one that had led me to the graves. It took me up to a cabin Grey Owl had built for his wife when living in the same cabin as two industrious but messy beavers finally proved to be too much for her to bear.

Then, still soaking up the spirits of the past, I strolled down to the lakeshore and lunch, wondering at all the emotions running through me. After lunch, we bid farewell to Beaver Lodge and paddled back to Kingsmere to continue on to the Bagwa Lake circuit.

It was 3:30 P.M., and back on the big lake, a three-hour paddle to that night's planned campsite on Bagwa Lake awaited. The lake, dead calm, reflected the overcast sky. Rain threatened to dampen our spirits as well as everything in our canoe. With the rain came the threat of wind; this lake is renowned for its treacherous and sudden strong gusts. To reach our destination, we had to make a partial open-lake crossing where the winds usually blew strongest.

As we prepared to head out from shore, I heard an eagle's cry. Halfway across the inlet, it started to rain, so we put a little extra energy into each stroke. After forty-five minutes, we reached the far shore and started looking for the channel between Kingsmere and Bagwa Lakes. While the rain made it difficult to see, we spotted what appeared to be a channel. Or was it just an inlet? I then heard another eagle. Moments later, Ann located the marker for a campsite that told us we were indeed in the correct channel. It was not the campsite we planned to stay at that night, though, so we paddled on.

We reached another point, uncertain where to go. The eagle flew overhead. We paddled tentatively towards the point where the eagle went, and sure enough, there was a sign prohibiting the passage of any motorized boats past that point.

Our confidence buoyed, we paddled further into the marsh. Our map was not to scale, and with the marsh full of little bays and inlets, it was difficult to find the main channel. Again, though, the eagle showed up on a tree ahead. We paddled in that direction and we were again rewarded.

It happened once more. But as we paddled to where he was perched, I took out the map. After a few moments, the eagle flew back the way it had come, as if to say, "Well if you're not going to trust me, I guess I'll leave you with your map!" Or perhaps it was enough that he had taken us this far.

As it turned out, we had very little difficulty finding our way through the rest of the marsh.

As we paddled into the lake, small flocks of mallards heralded our exit from the marshy channel into the larger body of water. We landed at our campsite at the south end of Bagwa Lake, just in time to experience a glorious autumn sunset.

That night, as we drifted off to sleep, a chorus of mallards sang us a lullaby, while a nearby barred owl (or perhaps, a great gray owl?) provided a solo accompaniment.

The next morning, as we finished our breakfast, the howls of a wolf pack thrilled us from the far shore of the lake. The pack serenaded us twice

more during the next half-hour, the final chorus coming as we pulled our canoe out into the lake.

As we entered Lily Lake, through a connecting channel, we spied a lone eagle sitting on a brush pile less than 30 yards to our left. He spied us too and, as we were a little too close for his comfort, he treated us to a majestic rise from his perch into the air, across our bow.

A portage to Clare Lake, a short paddle and another portage brought us back to the southwest corner of Kingsmere Lake. Paddling towards the Southend campsite, we watched three monstrous lake trout swim by, just a few feet beneath our canoe.

All too soon, we were taking our canoe ashore for our final portage and short paddle back along the Kingsmere River to our waiting vehicle.

As we loaded our canoe and packed our gear into the van, groups of gray whiskey jacks pestered us for handouts. I felt it rather appropriate that Nature's spirit selected these birds to bid us farewell at the end of our trip, as Grey Owl often fed them at his cabin, truly enjoying their company:

"This whiskey-jack is a small bird, about the size of a blackbird, but he has more mischief in his body than there is in a whole bag of cats. He is a scamp, but a likable rascal at that. He loves human company and, at the first smoke of camp fire, he appears mysteriously from nowhere like a small, gray shadow, and perches on a limb . . . for me their friendliness and cheerful whistling have brightened many a lonesome camp fire."– Grey Owl, in *Men of the Last Frontier.*

Perhaps these birds lobbying us unsuccessfully for crumbs of food were descendants of those birds he had loved so much at Beaver Lodge. Descendants or not, their presence made it all that more difficult to bid Nature adieu and head back to civilization. But as one of Grey Owl's favorite authors, James Fenimore Cooper, wrote, "Every trail has its end, and every calamity brings its lesson."

The calamity in this case was the end of this particular trail. And the lesson it brought could be considered the mantra of Grey Owl: "Remember . . . you belong to nature, not it to you."

# Clearwater River
## *Trouble in Paradise*

Patrick Mahaffey

My paddling partner and I puffed along the indistinct trail with the canoe overhead, getting whipped in the face by willow branches. Running a rapid can be enjoyable, but running a portage? It's not going to catch on as a sport.

We had been perched on one of those wonderful lichen-covered outcroppings that thrusts out of the ground in Shield country, discussing the long and complicated Gould Rapids on the Clearwater River in Saskatchewan.

"I think we would be okay if we back paddle down the center and through that bunch of standing waves, then dodge the large boulder on its left side and side-slip to the far left to catch the safe chute."

"Sounds fine, but we'll have to check around the bend."

"Do you think we should play it safe and portage most of the gear around?"

The conversation was going just fine when suddenly someone shouted, "Who the hell is that going around the bend?"

"Hey, they're with us — what *are* they doing?"

"They're going to run the rapid — but they aren't slowing down!"

"They're going to swamp if they don't slow down — they've got all their gear!"

"Look, they're filling up!"

"There they go — they're already swimming — and right at the top of the rapids!"

"Hey — the falls aren't far downstream — we've gotta do a rescue!"

It was quickly agreed that the two of us should run our canoe over the portage and get down to help our trip mates. One minute it was a discussion about paddling through a rapid and the next it was a discussion about running around it.

After a short paddle, we found the two culprits — they were so impatient with our slow group, they decided to shoot the rapids alone — sitting on shore, looking like a couple of drowned (but uninjured) rats. As for the canoe — after a half-mile-long (0.5 km) sprint, we caught up to it bobbing in a pool just above 65-feet-high (20 m) Smoothrock Falls. In another few minutes, it would have been bye-bye boat.

Mistakes happen, but it's frustrating when they are avoidable mistakes, such as failing to communicate, poor judgment and carelessness.

On another day, we were at a shallow, rocky chute. Most of us decided to portage the short distance, however, our reckless twosome wanted to line their canoe down the chute. This was fine, but as they proceeded, the upstream painter knot came undone. In a panic, the downstream man ran upstream and suddenly the canoe was in the worst possible position. We watched in stunned disbelief as both ends of the canoe jammed on the rocky sides of the narrow channel, rolling and quickly filling with water. With heart-rending creaks and groans, it thumped down the rocky channel into the pool below. The canoe had an amazing 12-inch-long (30 cm) gash and other deep gouges in the normally tough ABS plastic hull.

A proper repair was required; this was not a job for duct tape. We had days to go to our destination below Whitemud Falls. But who brings a repair kit for ABS canoes? Only the fiberglass canoe was actually packing a repair kit, and it was for fiberglass, of course. Would fiberglass even stick to the ABS hull? Well, fortune smiled. We had brought along a friend with a Ph.D. in chemistry in case this happened. He had good advice: give it lots of time to dry. The weather was sunny and warm, and we waited and waited. After much discussion and careful work, the patch stuck and held for the remainder of the trip, to everyone's surprise — and relief.

## Historic Methye

Okay, so we had a few problems, but it wasn't the river's fault. The Clearwater, the only westward-flowing river between Winnipeg and the Rockies, is a wonderful trip. It has untouched wilderness, fine scenery, interesting vegetation, challenging rapids, spectacular waterfalls, nice camping spots and unparalleled history.

The upper reach of the river, from Lloyd Lake to the Highway 955 bridge (near the community of La Loche), flows through level Shield country and is characterized by low riverbanks, limestone outcroppings and sandy soil. The map shows many lakes and bogs surrounding the river. It's the same from an airplane: a huge landscape stretching out to the curve of the world with unending lakes and forest.

The middle reach is from the highway bridge to Whitemud Falls, at the Alberta border. It starts with waterfalls and big rapids as it leaves the Shield, and it cuts down into a deep valley with outcroppings and high-forested sides, then changes to a slow-moving and meandering river as it enters the northern interior plains. The Saskatchewan section of the Clearwater River has been protected from development, both as a Canadian Heritage River and a provincial park. The Alberta government has been refusing both designations for many years.

The lower reach continues through the northern interior plains from Whitemud Falls to its confluence with the Athabasca River at Fort McMurray. The deep valley continues, with meanders and a few rapids. The entire Clearwater is 175 miles (280 km) long.

The 100-mile-long (160 km) section we paddled, from the Virgin River to Whitemud Falls, was a bit of the upper reach and all of the middle; it was a fly-in and fly-out from La Loche. Our trip took six days and included the river's three waterfalls, most of its rapids and both of the main geographic areas.

What's in store if you go?

*Waterfalls:* We felt their power, from the safety of shore. Smoothrock Falls is a series of 10-to-16-foot (3–5 m) drops around a few bends in the river. Skull Falls, often featured on tourism brochures, is twin short drops through separate gashes in towering rock. Whitemud Falls is a complex series of short falls around a bend. A big drop overall.

*Rapids:* They go by the names of Bielby, Olson, Mackie, Warner, Gould and Simonson (Class II to IV); there are also countless unnamed ones. In addition to lots of long, glorious stretches of runnable rapids, there are classic pool-and-drop sets. All in all, a wonderful smorgasbord.

*Meanders:* Drifting south, east, south, west, north — basking in the sun and listening to the song of the white-throated sparrow: "Oh, sweet Canada Canada Canada."

*Camping:* Lots of spots to call home for a night or two — flat and open, forested and close, sand banks and grassy knolls. Swimming, fishing and watching a magnificent sunset are included.

*Methye Portage:* Hiking up part of the Methye Portage, I felt history in my bones. The 13-mile-long (21 km) Methye, or Portage La Loche, connected the Churchill River system to the east and the Clearwater-Athabasca systems to the west and north. Peter Pond of the North West Company was the first European to cross this historic route in 1778. Alexander Mackenzie crossed it ten times. Others who set foot here were David Thompson, John Franklin, George Back, Robert Hood, John Rae and Sir John Richardson. It has long been Chipewyan and southern Dene country, of course.

From the Clearwater, the Methye starts as an ordinary grassy trail at the edge of a clearing. Climbing up an escarpment, the trail is in a 6.5-foot-deep (2 m) trench. It's like an old road, not a hiking trail, and was used by pack-horses and ox-carts right up to the mid-1880s, when it was displaced by the Athabasca Landing Trail, near Fort McMurray. At the top of the escarpment, it is a different world: flat country with an open and dry spruce forest. The view of the valley must have been expansive in years past, when the trees were cleared for cooking fires and pitch-melting fires. Three miles (5 km) down the trail is Rendezvous Lake, fringed by forest. But no sign of the fur trade settlement at this transhipment point.

*Back to Reality:* We were brought out of our historical reverie abruptly when half a dozen low-flying F-15 fighter jets screeched by from the nearby Cold Lake military base. Welcome to the here and now.

Everyone in Alberta and Saskatchewan seems to go to British Columbia for summer holidays. Give me northern Saskatchewan with its great landscapes and invigorating outdoor opportunities, with no crowds. The clear water of the Clearwater is clearly the best.

# Seal River
## *Perfect Honeymoon Destination*

Ksenia Barton and Stephan Kesting

"WHERE ARE YOU GOING FOR YOUR HONEYMOON?" IT WAS A QUESTION we were asked frequently in the months leading up to our wedding.

"Hawaii?"

"No."

"Bali?"

"No."

"Niagara Falls?"

"No."

Our friends were generally dismayed by our post-nuptial plans. Let's face it, northern Manitoba has an image problem as a honeymoon destination.

I won't deny the appeal of a tropical honeymoon — fun and sun in a simple package. But seeking adventure and romance in the Canadian North was more our style. We craved true wilderness and a chance to be totally alone as newlyweds. We chose to paddle the Seal River, which flows into Hudson Bay.

In spite of the dangers of venturing into that remote location with a single canoe, we felt confident enough with our paddling skills. We were well equipped and our gear list included an ELT (Emergency Location Transmitter) in case of an emergency situation. As a couple, we already had one big canoeing trip under our belts, our Waterfound Fond-du-Lac trip in northern Saskatchewan in 1998. Stephan also had extensive solo and group canoe-tripping experience, including a 1993 solo journey from Jasper to Hudson Bay (when he first paddled the Seal River).

While I agonized over wedding details, Stephan took on the formidable task of preparing for our trip. Not only did he arrange all the trip logistics and gear checklists, he planned and prepared two weeks' worth of dehydrated meals during the frenetic month leading up to our wedding.

On August 12, 2000, we were married in Whistler, B.C., surrounded by our family and friends. The following morning, we rushed to the Vancouver airport with a monstrous amount of luggage. After convincing the airline agent to waive our excess baggage fees, we flew to Thompson, Manitoba, via Winnipeg.

It was early evening by the time we arrived in Thompson and checked into the Northern Lights Bed and Breakfast. Exhausted and hungry, we decided to treat ourselves to a nice meal on the first night of our honeymoon. At 9 P.M. on a Sunday, the best restaurant in town turned out to be the Pizza Hut.

After dinner, we headed back to the cozy Northern Lights B & B. Our hostess graciously prepared a lovely breakfast long past the normal schedule when we slept in the next morning. During the day, we made arrangements to rent a 17-foot canoe with a nylon spray deck. Afterward, we took all our gear and canoe to the Thompson airport to fly to Tadoule Lake.

The Manitoban communities that lie north of the roads are served by various tiny airlines. We flew on Skyward Aviation's Bandit, a twin-engine E-110 Bandeirante (made in Brazil). The Bandit left about two hours late, piloted by very youthful-looking men. We shared the hour-long flight to Tadoule Lake with a handful of Northerners. They seemed as amazed as our Vancouver friends at our honeymoon plans, especially given the foul weather that obscured our views during the flight.

Tadoule Lake is a tiny community of approximately 300 people. The village is home to one of the smallest Native bands in Manitoba, the Sayisi (People Under the Sun) Dene First Nation Band (approximately 600 people). The Sayisi Dene once lived semi-nomadically, following the caribou herds and returning annually to Little Duck Bay. When caribou became less plentiful, the federal government made the ill-considered decision to move the

band to the town of Churchill in 1956. The sudden change to an urban and coastal setting inevitably contributed to disastrous social and cultural problems. As a result, the band decided to return to their traditional lands, eventually choosing the site at Tadoule Lake.

After landing at Tadoule Lake and unloading our gear in a torrential downpour, we called a cab to ferry our gear down to the beach. In Tadoule Lake, calling a cab consists of approaching a pickup truck driver and offering a few bucks for the ride. Our hearts sank when we saw the whitecap-covered lake in the evening gloom — it would be a difficult start to the trip. Camping in the village was out of the question, given the many curious and rowdy dogs.

Our driver turned out to be Stephen Thorassi, a former band chief. In a gesture of typical First Nation hospitality, he arranged for us to stay at the Awasis Agency, a clean and comfortable child and family services center. Before settling in for the night, we visited with the kids who were gathered there while their parents played bingo. I managed to elicit shrieks of amusement by reading out the French portion of a candy wrapper. Their supervisor then encouraged them to demonstrate their growing grasp of the Dene language. When they left, we flopped into our sleeping bags, grateful for a quiet, warm, dry night indoors!

## River Otters and Tundra Polygons

The following morning we awoke to beautiful weather and eagerly set off in our heavily loaded canoe. In addition to survival gear and food, we had fun stuff — novels and a Scrabble game — and convenience items such as the environmental fireplace. Made by Churchill River Canoe Outfitters, the environmental fireplace is a collapsible metal box with a grill on top. It provides a steady surface for cooking, requires hardly any firewood, and shelters the flames from the wind. After cooking, the ashes can be easily doused and disposed of without marring the pristine beaches.

As we paddled across Tadoule Lake, we were reminded of my grandmother's wedding wish for us: "May the sun be on your face and the wind at your back." We had planned on about two weeks' worth of paddling on the Seal River. The lack of wind was promising: the paddling would be more relaxing and we'd have more time to hike and loaf around in camp. Even better, it was late enough in the season so there were few mosquitoes.

Eventually, we stopped for lunch. After our picnic, I surprised myself by promptly falling asleep on a rock. I was still exhausted from the excitement of the wedding and the weeks leading up to it. Stephan gently covered me up and whiled away the time with a novel. When I finally awoke in the afternoon, we set off again.

We set up camp for the night at the first beach we spied. Sand beaches provided relatively flat, scenic and bug-free sites for our temporary abodes. After setting up the tent, I was treated to the first of many delicious meals.

It rained as we slept that night, but we awoke to sunny weather the next morning. For the canoeist, the Seal River varies quite a bit. That day we did some relaxed lake paddling, some easy whitewater paddling and some intense paddling through the choppy waves on Shethani Lake. The river often broadens into long lakes, where paddling conditions are strongly affected by wind. Careful navigation is required to find the outlet of the lakes. The rapids were a guaranteed adrenaline rush for me, especially since I was often splashed by waves in the bow. Stephan's expert paddling compensated for my novice canoeing skills.

Our first campsite on the lake was so pretty that we stayed for two nights, exploring the nearby pond, esker, forests and bog. Eskers are large-scale, Ice Age relics that enliven the boreal landscape along the Seal River. The long, sinuous ridges of sand and gravel are the sediments deposited by ancient rivers flowing through tunnels in and under the melting glacial ice. Eskers can be forested, bare or vegetated with crowberries and lichens. These ridges provide nice views and an open place to hike. Apparently the animals think so too, as we often saw abundant animal signs on these highways of the north.

The forests are mostly scruffy and soggy, dominated by spruce and tamarack. Drier sites such as eskers are often covered in skinny paper birch or pine. Trembling aspen trees fringe the beaches, but they remain stunted due to the harsh climate.

As we continued along Shethani Lake, we noticed some huge smoke plumes in the distance. Forest fires are typical of the area, occasionally threatening canoeists. There is an endless cycle of succession in the boreal forest, where forest fires are followed by years of regrowth and regeneration. By exploring the banks of the river, we were able to witness the forest in each stage of the cycle.

Boggy areas sometimes yielded cloudberries, delicious orange berries that look like raspberries. Blueberries, a great dessert, are also widespread. Crowberries are bland, seed-filled black berries. Dark green crowberry plants form beautiful tapestries with coral and reindeer lichens on open esker ridges.

Our lunches were occasionally supplemented by grayling, a small,

tasty fish. One grayling we caught turned out to be two: there was a completely intact smaller grayling in its stomach. We're terrible fishermen, so catching a fish was always a triumph. We spotted bald and golden eagles and osprey fishing more successfully at the rapids. Our arrival sometimes disturbed raptors from their lookout posts, and we got close-up views of them as they flew by.

The most obvious mammals of the Seal River are black bear (seen from a distance), caribou (lots of signs), mink (often frolicking along the rapids), seals and river otters. The otters are some of the most entertaining river creatures. As we paddled out of Shethani Lake, we heard sharp alarm calls and noticed a large group of young river otters diving and fishing. They reacted strongly to our presence, approaching us, following us and growling at us breathily.

Our days took on a sort of routine. I tended to sleep in while Stephan prepared breakfast. Then we would pack up our gear and set out for a couple of hours of paddling. We would pick a scenic lunch spot and lounge about and eat for a while. Then more paddling. In the afternoon we'd keep our eyes open for a camp spot. When we stopped for the day, we'd set up the tent, anchor the canoe with rocks and make dinner.

Stephan designed our menu around home-dehydrated foods and grocery store items rather than expensive dehydrated camping food. I was delighted by his delicious meals. Wouldn't you enjoy pasta in a smoked salmon and vegetable sauce on a camping trip? How about brussel sprout ragout on rice?

How about a hearty soup with fried tortillas and coleslaw? I decided that married bliss was not as complicated as people make it out to be. After dinner we dunked ourselves in the river for a shivery bath, or went for a little walk, or chatted beside the fire, or just settled in with a novel.

In the course of our trip, we passed through a gradual climatic gradient, from northern boreal forest to the Hudson Bay lowland tundra. As the trip went on, the zone of willows along the river became broader due to the seasonal ice scouring. The forests changed from continuous to restricted to isolated pockets. Wet tundra, resembling a bog without any trees, became more widespread as we neared Hudson Bay. We started to see tundra polygons, where the ground is patterned due to permafrost processes. Surprisingly far upriver from the Bay, large seal colonies started to appear on the river.

Our final day on the river started out with lovely weather as we concentrated on the fascinating transition of ecosystems. The day's challenge began when we reached the mouth of the river, where the Seal fans out into a broad and confusing maze of whitewater, islands, rocks and too-shallow channels. We had a wild ride on Waikiki, a memorable rapid with huge rolling waves. Soon afterwards, though, we ended up in a shallow channel that forced us to wade the boat, submerged up to our hips in icy water. The weather turned cold and rainy and we finally reached Hudson Bay chilled and exhausted after eleven hours on the river.

We made our way towards a rough shack that provides protection against the Hudson Bay weather and polar bears. We hadn't seen a soul since Tadoule Lake, but we saw a tiny figure greeting us from the shore. Our fellow lodgers in the shack turned out to be David and Colette Pancoe, a brother and sister pair who were excellent company in the following days. David runs Northern Soul, a Manitoban guiding company. We passed the next day chatting, eating and playing Scrabble as rain and wind lashed the shack's flimsy plywood walls. The following day was sunny and glorious. We eagerly explored the fascinating environment of Hudson Bay, finding polar bear prints, watching snow geese and sandhill cranes, spying belugas in the distance and admiring the beauty of the red-tinged mud flats.

When our boat pickup failed to materialize, we all paddled to the Seal River Heritage Lodge, a short paddle north of the Seal River. We spent the night there, staying up late to admire the most vivid aurora borealis I've ever seen. The next day we finally chartered a Beaver float plane flight to Churchill, taking off into the howling wind with our canoes strapped to the floats. The flight gave us fabulous views of the treeless Hudson Bay coastline. In Churchill, we boarded the train for a luxurious overnight trip to Thompson. We stayed up late in the dining car with David and Colette, sharing stories of our past adventures and future dreams. The next morning, we sat by the train windows and watched the boreal panorama pass by during the final hours of our northern adventure.

Our trip on the Seal River was a wonderful balance of paddling, exploring and lounging. The river's beauty was subtle, with an ever-varying combination of weather, water, wildlife and landscape. We found the solitude and wilderness that we craved. Our honeymoon was unforgettable.

# Bloodvein River
## *Lessons on Stone*

Hap Wilson

THE BISON IMAGE REMAINS A MYSTERY, LIKE THE PAINT ITSELF, USED TO immortalize ancient thought and the transcripts of a healer-shaman. So what was the bonding agent? Fish oil? Egg albumen from gull eggs? Some sort of Neolithic acrylic? Or, was it, perhaps, the blood essence of the stone people — the memegwishiwok — proffered to the artist for some sublime ceremony, emblazoned on the rock face of granite by sheer magic? And, how is it that two, almost identical bison images, painted long before Euro-travel connected the two continents, show up on rock walls thousands of miles apart? Coincidence? Or perhaps some metaphysical soul transfer, a telepathy exchange that could transcend any boundary, any distance, any dimension?

I'm referring, of course, to the internationally renowned pictographs, or rock paintings, found along the Bloodvein River. This heritage waterway wends its way through the woodland caribou country of northwest Ontario and east-central Manitoba. There are at least twelve known pictograph sites, each one imparting a lesson, possibly a warning, to those who venture close enough, to gaze into their own soul and immortality. These rock scriptures go far beyond the whimsy of present-day, rock-cut graffiti; alive with spiritual energy, they may well be the conduit, or portal, to the spirit world itself.

Once an agnostic about such things, my rather limited view of the spirit realm blossomed after my initial ghost experience some years ago, which took place while renovating an old farmhouse in the Laurentians. My wife and I were treated to an unexpected social call by the long-departed first lady of the century-old dwelling. It was an eerie and frightening experience, at first, but the everlasting and profound effect the visitation had on the way I now view life — and beyond — was remarkably liberating. I no longer felt encumbered by doubt. My own existence and station on Mother Earth took on a new pithiness. I began studying shamanic practice and North American Native ideology, almost to the point of obsession. I was particularly fascinated by rock art, something that white anthropologists with

strong Christian persuasions seemed to dismiss as pagan renderings of little religious importance.

When my studies took me to the Ontario Coroner's Office in Toronto, while researching the more than thirty deaths that gave the Missinaibi a reputation as the River of Death, I had made the startling discovery that one-third of the drownings occurred at spiritual, or sacred sites. These were places known as points of harmonic conversion, where the shaman-teacher cum healer practiced his or her trade, where the physical world as we know it, melds easily with the spirit world. Were the deaths coincidental? I don't think so. Human error certainly played a tragic part in many deaths, but upon reading police reports and third-party testimonies, including historical references, there was an obvious spiritual force at work here. In other instances, the spiritual element became even more distinct. There were the two miners who defaced the pictographs on Tramping Lake, on Manitoba's Grass River, who had died violent deaths soon after perpetrating the deed.

Could there be an evil power at play here? Malevolence spawned from the depths of some primal religion? A vengeance? Visitations to such sacrosanct places were not allowed, at one time, unless in the accompaniment of a healer-shaman. Today, little or no respect or reverence is paid to these sites other than mild curiosity, as paddlers snap pictures, fondle the rock and even scratch their own names among the rock effigies. The practice of leaving a tobacco offering, at least, if not taking a moment for a prayer, or asking permission to pass by in safety, is not common enough.

## Strong Medicine Here

Miskowiskibi — the Bloodvein — best represents the drama of place, both geographically and spiritually. Flowing from Knox Lake in Ontario, just northwest of the town of Red Lake, the river tumbles recklessly over abrupt granite ledges on its 185-mile (300 km) journey to Lake Winnipeg, west towards the setting sun, west towards the sea of prairie grass, spilling into the geographic umbilicus of North America. Gentle current drifts between tumultuous chutes and rapids, actually making upstream travel possible — one of the prime factors that popularized the Bloodvein as a Native travel route, dating back as long as 9,000 years ago when Paleo cultures followed the retreating glaciers as the boreal-upland forests flourished. Archeological exploits along the river have literally unearthed a plethora of burial mounds, middens, entire village sites, skeletal remains, chipped stone, pottery, worked copper and, most important, the richest conglomeration of rock-art sites found in the country.

After being detained in Red Lake for three days because of interior wild-fires burning in the vicinity of the Bloodvein, I was able to work my way slowly towards the headwaters, trying not to think of the fires as some kind of prophetic caution. Since its inception as a Canadian Heritage River and because it bisected both Ontario's Woodland Caribou and Manitoba's Atikaki Parks, the Bloodvein corridor had been well documented by the bureaucrats. Much of the study material was not readily available to the public, and with good reason, too. More and more graffiti had been showing up on top of easily accessed pictographs, but since my research was purely investigative, I was privy to all archeological findings. I agreed not to give exact locations in my Manitoba guidebook of any pictographs not already publicly identified in printed material.

Gaining access to the Bloodvein demands a somewhat dogged persistence. Dealing with bugs and recent burn-overs where blow-downs littered the lengthy portage trails leaves you feeling somewhat daunted. But as with any wilderness river, the necessary grunt-work generally means that few people have trekked the upper reaches. In fact, with the Bloodvein, most paddlers opt to fly in to Artery Lake on the Ontario-Manitoba border, where it's a much easier two-week paddle to Lake Winnipeg, thereby eliminating the more than 5 miles (8 km) of ankle-wrenching portaging they would have endured had they started their trip at Red Lake. The downside to this option is that the paddler misses half of the twelve pictograph sites.

I picked up a client group at Barclay Lake, about 18 miles (30 km) east of Artery. I explained the importance of approaching the pictograph sites with caution, and that I would make a tobacco offering at each one, as I had been accustomed to doing, and that anyone wishing to leave prayers could do so. Not everyone agrees with my sentiment, or cares to share the seriousness of approaching such places with reverence, for whatever reason — religious faith being one of them. All usually agree to the practice, if only out of respect for the group dynamic.

On day two, I slipped behind the group while photographing a mink with a dead merganser duck clenched in its jaw. The others were heading down a deep bay, off the main route of the river, at the extreme northeast end of Mary's Lake, making rather good time to the base of a high cliff where I told them we would find a pictograph. It was dead calm, and I caught up to the group who were now collected below the immense rock face, and the painting of red ocher and magic was as visible as the day it had been created. It portrayed a lone shaman, a powerful image — a simple, cartoon-like figure. There was strong medicine here.

My skin prickled and I found nausea welling up in my stomach — the same feeling I had when I met my first ghost, or whenever I walk into a dwelling that has strong energy, a resident spirit milling about. A commanding southwesterly, without due warning, slammed into our little flotilla of boats, crashing gunwales together in a moment of angry mayhem. It was time to leave. It was obvious that I had allowed our group to approach the site in such a manner as to evoke the wrath of the residing entity. The reproach came in the guise of a rogue windstorm that precipitated a hasty

retreat. A quick offering of tobacco seemed to be a senseless gesture, like closing the gate after the lion had escaped.

The wind persisted. The ominous clouds that rolled in, like massive bulwarks, meant that a quick camp was required. Within fifteen minutes, one of the worst summer storms I had ever experienced fell upon us. The forces of Nature had quite outdone themselves; trees toppled around us while gale-force winds pummeled the boreal landscape like a heavy fist upon its back; lightning seared around the makeshift camp, stabbing randomly at the bent forest while the rain whipped at us in horizontal sheets. We had no protection. And as quickly as it had come, it was gone. And the evening sun probed the remnant clouds for openings through which to cast an orange patchwork glow over the drenched riverscape.

Nearby was another pictograph site; in fact, it was the most celebrated rock-art site on the Bloodvein, and the prime time to view it was under the patina of evening light just before the sun set. Everyone in the group, including the skeptical, literally jumped into their canoes after I had suggested we make some kind of amends with the river. And as a devout Christian might enter a place of worship, we approached the pictographs slowly and quietly, each canoe party ready to divulge some form of personal offering.

This was the famous bison site, and, as Selwyn Dewdney remarks, "The site is perhaps a hundred miles north of the parklands where the bison herds once roamed; but the artist shows familiarity with the animal that supports either frequent hunting excursions southward, or his own southern origin."

Halfway across the world there is a similar bison image, depicted with circled hooves, and as much an anomaly there as the painting at Artery Lake, Manitoba. Coincidence seems unlikely. Shamanism and the art of healing souls are the fundamentals of an ancient religion and practice that predates Christianity by 20,000 years. Not a black art, as branded by modern religious scholars, shamanic faith bonds itself to the rhythm of the Earth and is the basis of North American Native beliefs and healing practices. The possibility of early healers having the ability to transcend known planes of existence, to vault their spiritual selves through some kind of time-place portal, to be able to exchange wisdom with other shamans linked like some kind of spiritual Internet, is not fantasy or mythology or simple campfire story . . . at least to this writer.

The granite wall absorbed the incident light, turning ocher from pale yellow to reddish yellow. The dark waters of the Bloodvein and the thick moss and boreal crown above framed the canvas of rock and highlighted the magical, mysterious paintings. There was not a word spoken, lest the charm of the spell be broken. Our canoes drifted as if suspended between two dimensions, drifting like the ephemeral light, hovering momentarily, bathing the moment in surreal calm.

The sun dropped below the fringe of trees on the opposite shore, leaving the teaching-site in evening sameness and shadow. The magic was gone, the latch on the door once again bolted. None of us made a move to paddle back to the campsite. Our earlier transgressions against the spirit world had been purged. It was an experience all of us will remember for some time.

The Bloodvein River conveys a message understood by very few. I resign myself to that place of bewilderment, like most others who travel its waters, play in the rapids and walk the nastawgan trails, getting caught up in the waterplay and the landscape and the camaraderie, and such vain pleasures that appease the physical senses. But I hope, as I visit these places and revel in the sanctity of ancient wisdom, that I may someday understand more about what went on here, in the mind of the teacher who left us such cryptic lessons on stone.

# Five Northern Rivers
## A Wanderer in Enchanted Lands:
## Inner Responses to the Outer Landscape

Bert Horwood

> *I break the spirit's cloudy bands,*
> *A wanderer in enchanted lands…*
> — Archibald Lampman

Consecutive trips on the same river can be entirely different. In the accounts that follow, I do not mean to characterize the rivers, because they are much too changeable, but I do characterize my inner response to them as the trips I was on unfolded. It is also true that each person on a trip will have different responses, at different times. And the various sections of a river will affect us differently. But in these trips, I responded most to one dominant characteristic.

My response to five rivers, one trip on each, is best expressed in five words: picturesque, raw, tumultuous, tranquil and sublime. The rivers are the Coppermine, Nanook, Horton, Ellice and Kuujjua. This is the story of how those rivers revealed themselves.

## Picturesque Coppermine

The Coppermine rises in eastern Northwest Territories and flows north across the Arctic Circle and enters Coronation Gulf at the village of Kugluktuk (formerly Coppermine). From the start, at Rocknest Lake, I was awed by grand vistas on every bend. It is no wonder that, in the absence of the storied rich deposits of copper, outfitters have found other forms of revenue on this river. My capacity to see its stunning outlooks was enhanced by my decision to carry a small watercolor kit instead of a camera. I was an untutored and inexperienced painter. The challenges of capturing the scope of the scenes that unfolded sharpened my vision, even if the resulting pictures were mere daubs. Although I painted on only four or five occasions, I found myself recognizing paintable scenes and impossible colors around every bend.

My journal is full of visual descriptions and sketches. Low light angles emphasize the contours, I noted, "shadows give shape and color to the land." The scene could shift from harsh to soft. The high bald hills, parabolic clay banks and rolling distant hills, clouded in misty rain, contrasted with sharp cliff edges, grotesque chimneys and hoodoos, and stark silhouettes of the last tough sentinel spruces guarding the treeline.

The colors were particularly intriguing. The walls of Rocky Defile seemed to glow with memory of the fires from which they emerged. In sharp contrast, the black rocks near Muskox Rapids, with minute flecks of copper, seemed cold and chill. Flat white at midday, the clay banks could become a rosy ocher, even muted violet when the sun was skimming the horizon, contrasting with the brilliant layers of rock sweeping across the distant September Mountains.

Colors and contours combined to give the land shape and feeling. The Copper Mountains and then the September Mountains loomed, their captivating striations like a many-layered cake that had been tilted for too long and had begun to slip. There were long periods when we lived in broad sweeping vistas of the river valley, marked by riverside terraces rising to higher terraced hills. Then there would be a sharp interruption in the landscape, like the jagged entry to Rocky Defile or the cliffs at Escape Rapids. The downstream vistas made me feel the river ran forever between endless lines of shrinking hills leading, wandering, down to the invisible sea.

It is easy to focus on the large scene, the grand vista, the sweeping view; but there was also beauty in more modest scale. Occasional little waterfalls graced cliff sides, tumbling down from a wash at the top to be lost at the cliff base. One such waterfall I blame for a close call at Escape Rapids. My partner and I had shot previous rapids successfully, though not without very heavy breathing and elevated blood pressures.

Escape Rapids looked entirely manageable on scouting, and indeed every other canoe in our party negotiated it as planned. But I was intrigued with a little splash of white waterfall, a delicate tracing that graced the cliff at that place. I watched it when I should have been watching the river. We lost our line and completed the run by taking the path, which, if the accounts can be believed, must have been the same one taken by Franklin's party, who gave these rapids their name. It is a tribute to my partner's skill, my good luck and a well-fitted spray skirt that we emerged upright and dry.

The Coppermine impressed me with its capacity to inspire optical illusions. We experienced mirages of such reality that we could see waves dancing above the horizon and paddlers in the sky. On a memorable morning we actually experienced being in a kind of mirage. Every canoe tripper has surely paddled on one of those special mornings when the water is still enough to make nearly perfect reflections. One morning, we were able to paddle water so perfectly still, so free of flotsam, that the reflections were absolutely perfect. So perfect that, as I stared at the water, I experienced the illusion of being suspended between sky and earth — and having no idea which was the real and which the virtual image. Archibald Lampman noted the same experience on the Lievre in the Laurentians:

Softly as a cloud we go
Sky above and sky below . . .

There is a photograph of three canoes moving in company that day. Held one way, the canoes appear doubled but normal, trailing a wake that curves away behind each craft, and runs into its neighbor. Held the other way around, each canoe, complete with mirror image, appears to be moving across the crest of a huge rounded swell. It is an exciting view, where illusion is almost complete.

## Raw Nanook

The Nanook River rises in the center of Victoria Island in Nunavut and runs north into Hadley Bay. There were some warm days, so say my journal records, but I'm hard pressed to remember them. A frequent cold wind tearing at us created an atmospheric rawness and kept us tent-bound on several occasions — long enough to start bedsores. The upper river was mean-spirited, narrow, and alternately offering rocky shoals and deep pools scarcely longer than the canoe. I broke my well-loved paddle trying to maneuver in this section. The sudden changes, from impossible shallows to 6.5-feet-deep (2 m) holes, guaranteed wet feet. Progress was won at the cost of considerable frustration. In other sections of the river, apparently stable rocks, when stepped on, would sink into the soft clay below, leaving me floundering, muddy and swearing. Near the end of the river, we were glad of a rocky side-channel, as it had just enough water to allow us to drag, lift and float the canoes around impassable whitewater. Even a shallow passage is better than portaging.

The river dropped daily; it became a ritual for one of us to build a pebble cairn at the water's edge each evening to check the loss of water overnight. It seemed as though the river was little more than a drainage ditch, and the lakes, extended shallow ponds. In places, the land was almost flat and feature-less, making navigation difficult. Early one fine morning, breakfastless to catch the calmest water, we crossed the mouth of a wide bay, in which it would be tempting to get far downwind into the bay. The wind began to blow, driving us deeper into the blind end, but it was almost impossible to find a landmark by which to determine the correct upwind course. Several difficult hours later, we stopped to cook breakfast. Hot food and liquids were badly needed, but we were able to see that our labor had successfully kept us from a potentially nasty trap.

This part of Victoria Island has large tracts of dry tundra. Hiking one day, I crossed a huge hill where the lack of features made me unable to tell for sure whether the land was rising or falling. The plant life was sparse, not many more than two or three plants in a square yard. This apparent rawness and barren-ness matched the frequent appearance of small, noisy helicopters carrying diamond prospectors from place to place. The yellow and black choppers snarled and buzzed along the horizon like angry mechanical bumblebees.

The harshness of these experiences gave a special lift and grace to the presence of animals along the river. For several days, a buck caribou shadowed us as we paddled. He would appear and disappear as a silhouette limned against the west bank of the river. When we felt convinced he had lost interest, there he would be, trotting downstream with us, almost companionably, to my imagination. Wind camps were sometimes made interesting by the appearance of muskox — a cause for the exposure of much film by the photographers. I marveled at how well these animals make this severe place their home.

But it was strong winds from the north that dominate my impressions.

A companion described the occasional calms as the land inhaling before delivering another prolonged blast. The wind, of course, confined the bugs to the lee of our tents and boats, eagerly awaiting those lulls in order to dine. One memorable camp was made, in fine weather, beside a short gorge where there was evidence of an Inuit fish camp. Within a few hours the wind had resumed and I awoke to a most alarming sight. The high arching poles of my normally aerodynamic tent were being forced down almost into my face. I could press them up while lying flat on my back, but it was tiring and for how many hours could I continue that? At length, my partner and I struggled outside into the tearing wind and rotated the tent so that its teardrop curve faced into the wind. That brief discomfort was a wise investment, as we were there for another twenty-four hours, long enough for me to get well acquainted with Peter Mathiessen's *Snow Lion* — eminently suitable reading for such conditions.

In another wind camp, we were so tent-bound that it became easy to convince ourselves the wind had dropped and we could travel safely close to shore to the next bit of lee. We broke camp and set out. Fifteen minutes later, we had turned tail and were reversing the process for another long stretch with the *Snow Lion*. A strange kind of inertia comes with long periods in the tent. Despite being thoroughly fed up, we found it hard to summon the energy and will to move.

The rawness of the Nanook River persisted to the bitter end, to our arrival on Hadley Bay, where our pickup was arranged. At the airstrip we sat out two days of rain, wet snow and bone-chilling winds. The dark gray, sometimes almost brown, overcast made the ice floes glow all the more whitely. Long hours in our sleeping bags had wet the stuffing sufficiently to reduce insulation and it was easier to feel the cold. We eagerly anticipated the arrival of our plane, and had stripped down one canoe to accept a second nested inside. The rising tide gave cause for concern that we might lose the canoes, so we moved them well away from the water. Luckily, someone noticed the tide was even higher than our wildest expectations, lapping up to the beach airstrip itself — the canoes were gently drifting among the ice floes and seals downwind. Everyone was well warmed up by the time we recovered the boats and secured them from further misadventure.

Late the next day, the last day for our scheduled return, sitting glumly around a smoky fire of driftwood, behind a shelter of empty fuel drums, we felt convinced that no aircraft could safely manage the low ceiling. At that point, without the warning of engine sound, our Twin Otter dropped out of the clouds and swooped down to land and park almost at our feet. It was one of the few times, once loaded and on board with the heaters on full, that I felt glad to leave a river.

## Tranquil Horton

The Horton rises north of Great Bear Lake, north of the Arctic Circle, in the Northwest Territories. It flows northwest to Amundsen Gulf. The river seemed gentle and nurturing. This impression was supported by the presence of trees along the river valley, even though well beyond the official treeline. It's easy to feel nurtured when the weather is fine and the river flows swiftly through interesting terrain. When there was rain, it tended to fall as a fine, soft mist. My journal notes, "We've had series of fine days, then Scotch mist, then fine again. On the former, I'm glad to be alive, on the latter, I know I'm alive." Campsites were frequent, roomy, dry and flat. There was a ready supply of lake trout and grayling, better than any delicatessen. Near the end of the trip, we were surrounded by thousands of caribou and watched belugas in the ocean. A hospitable river.

The river itself is supplied by numerous side valleys, not often with streams, but soggy swales draining small ice masses in valleys hanging high above the river itself. Sometimes the hills were softly contoured. In other sections, there were statuesque rock columns and cliffs whose soft ruggedness gave an air of age and gentility. One great rounded hill split, like gaping jaws, into a small welcoming gorge. We easily negotiated almost all white-water by paddling or lining. I recorded only two short portages. It was truly a river well suited to my lazier impulses.

The most northerly section of the Horton traverses the Burning Hills, where a coal-like mineral spontaneously ignites to produce clouds of reeking smoke and a fine multicolor ash that washes into the river. This is a remarkable process to witness. In a certain way, it is a kind of earth-building that is going on: the materials locked into the rocks are being freed to join the soil being eroded from the banks to form deposits which, who knows when, will be lifted up as soil. There is a grand, long-term aspect to the nurturing face of this place.

The river is marked by numerous gravel shoals, which provide challenging choices. If the wrong route was chosen, we would find ourselves in a shallow cul-de-sac with no option but to wade, lift and drag to deeper water, all the while watching with envy our comrades who had made other choices and were floating freely downstream and ahead. The only satisfaction was knowing that soon, the positions would be reversed, because it was impossible to see far enough ahead to be guaranteed the ideal route selection.

We chose to paddle early one morning in a mist that grew thicker each minute. The sun was still low, dropping behind hills and reemerging, giving us repeated sunsets and sunrises. The light made the mist glow with opalescent colors, making it feel as though we were paddling inside a pearl. Here, the river was very shoaly and the mist severely limited visibility to a few yards at best. My partner and I decided to follow the bubbles of foam on the surface of the river. This proved a more effective way of finding deep water than trying to look far ahead. It gave a powerful meaning to the expression "go with the flow." For me, that characterizes my experience with this river.

## Tumultuous Ellice

The Ellice, the first major river valley east of Bathurst Inlet, Nunavut, flows almost due north to Queen Maude Gulf. It did not start out tumultuous, for the upper sections of the river were smooth, shallow and swift, marked by sunny hot days as we wound our way through sand dunes. Conditions were perfect for those with a need to unwind and hospitable to abundant biting insects. It was like an easy summer trip in southern Shield country, complete with excellent swimming on hard sand beaches. My journal notes sourly, "Had I wanted a trip in a hot desert, I'd have gone to Arizona."

But after these few idyllic days, the river revealed its tumultuous character. Gradually we moved into long series of rapids, many very rocky and almost always guarded at the end by a ridge of heaped boulders, niggardly with useful openings. Sometimes we were able to paddle long stretches of whitewater, picking our way as we went. More often, we shot part, lined part, and lifted the loaded canoes over or around the terminal ridge. Lining gave me problems, as early on I slipped and fell sufficiently to fill one boot. In a few minutes, a second fall filled the other boot. Before the day was done, I'd slipped into a hole up to my armpits. Luckily the water was not cold. The ease with which I lost my footing gave me concern and I consoled myself that it was due not to simple ineptness but to the reduction in equilibrium that goes with aging. It was only small comfort that others fell, too. Whatever the cause, the endless strings of rocky jumbled rapids generated a kind of internal churning to match that of the water.

There were huge falls that made the land shake and took my breath away as I gazed, entranced, at this extraordinary evidence of gravitational power. Our camps were often placed strategically at such places so that camping and portaging were efficiently parlayed into one set of moves. At one place, orange-red granite slabs, galleon-shaped, rose out of slick black water sliding down into a torrent below. Staring at them created the illusion they were bravely breasting the current and forging upstream to safety. Sleeping in sight and sound of roaring water night after night reinforced the feeling of living in a state of perpetual turbulence.

The hard carving effect of this river was evident in rampart piles of boulders lined like windrows along the shore. The tangled channels between islands hinted at the ravages of a mighty stream in millennia past. The islands posed a dangerous trap — one we were warned of by a wise navigator. There were temptingly easy whitewater sections as far as we could see down along an island. At first, seeking to avoid the harder way, I hoped to cross the river and use the inviting route. It made sense. But suppose the water was not negotiable below the island, then what? How long did I plan to spend stuck there, I was asked. And I saw the point. Several miles downstream on the harder path, I observed that had I followed my path, we might have been trapped for a long time indeed.

Away from the river, the land was gentler. Wolves, muskox and caribou appeared. We had signed on with the Canadian Wildlife Service to contribute to the Northwest Territories breeding bird survey and devoted some time each day, when the pressing demands of the river permitted, to recording all bird sightings. One embarrassing day the absence of usual standards for judging size led us to count geese, silhouetted on the high skyline, as caribou. After supper, I would often walk out to see the world over the lip of the Ellice Valley. One evening I came to the end of a high ridge and looked down into a lush swale of wetland where a pair of muskox cows idly stood, fetlock deep, entirely at peace, scarcely within sound of the roaring river. Beyond them, a pair of sandhill cranes, humped and unlovely, stalked along. I felt a surge of familiar wild. This must be much like the scene my hunter ancestors looked on 10,000 years ago.

The wildness of the Ellice, once started, continued to the end. At Queen Maude Gulf, we were met by the customary bitter cold north wind, quicksand and a navigation dilemma. According to the map, and more to the point, according to the land, we were at the strip of hard beach where our plane could land. The pilot had said we couldn't miss numerous tracks his wheels had left over the years of fetching canoeists from the river. Everything looked right, except there were no tracks to be seen. There was no evidence, bar a couple of ubiquitous fuel drums, that aircraft had ever landed here.

Tumultuous to the end, the Ellice was not about to let us go without a couple of wild days and nights in the tents. We would emerge only to take on food and to dump its remnants. The cold wind probed gleefully into every gap in my clothing, hot tea nearly congealed between the time it was scooped into the mug and conveyed to my mouth. While walking to shake out the kinks in my back and to confirm for myself there was no better place along that ravished coast where a plane might land, I flushed a tern off her nest, on the gravel near the top of the tide. There it sat, eggs intact, open to the tearing wind, serenely domestic, home, despite my impressions of the harshness of this river.

## Sublime Kuujjua

The Kuujjua rises in north-central Victoria Island and flows south and west to Minto Sound on the Northwest Territories side of Victoria Island. There I experienced what Thoreau and Emerson must have meant when they used the word sublime. All along that river there was a grandeur and power whose spirit seeped into my soul. The river rises in the Shaler Mountains, which gird the north-central part of the island. Here the shallow swift stream carried us smoothly from the low hills in transparent water over rainbow-hued gravel. The first day, my expectations were shattered by the appearance of sandhill cranes, which all my books say are never found this far north. But there they are, beyond any possibility of a mistake.

Grandeur was found in other animals, too. We met our first muskox at camp after supper on the second day. On the hike for a closer look, rare Peary caribou intercepted us, two elegant adults who cautiously kept their distance and two calves who acted as interested in us as we were in them. With such charming distractions, it was hard to remember we were stalking muskox. We soon learned muskox would be a daily event and realized their passive defensive circle cannot always be relied on. Much later, there would be arctic char in the thousands, enough to feast on, to fill the take-home limit and surplus to offer a helpful Inuk for his family.

As the Kuujjua gains water and power from its tributaries, the surrounding land also changes. The river drops more steeply, and rapids and falls appear. There are black rounded hills, breast-shaped, that seemed to me icons of the generous Earth Mother. Back from the river, tall cliffs, their towers and turrets resembling giant castles and palaces, march along the length of the valley. I found it easy to understand why my Nordic ancestors imagined trolls and goblins, for their profiles were to be seen, frozen into rocky immobility by the circling sun, on every bend. One bank of rock resembled nothing so much as a cluster of troll children naked and mooning us as we passed. The images of the gods building their noble halls reaching into the clouds became a near reality here. I was enthralled.

Grandeur goes with risks. Our flirtations with muskox resulted in a close call with a solitary bull who was none too happy to be approached. The powerful river was a challenge along many long miles of unremitting whitewater. As my partner said, when calling for camp to be made, "I've had enough terror for one day." The river rose suddenly after heavy rain over the watershed, all but carrying our canoes away overnight. I found the portages between huge boulders especially challenging. There was no right solution to the dilemma of whether to hop from rock to rock, the over-the-top method, or to snake my way blindly on the sand below, the follow-the-swearing method. But either way was better than lining down rapids hopping and hugging spray-damp ledges on a cliff just too high for the length of the lining ropes.

When our descent of the Kuujjua ended among the gleaming ice floes of Minto Sound, and we had reveled in an exuberant excess of char, I felt strongly reluctant to leave this sublime enchantment. And now, years later, when I idly stroke my canoe across the narrow waters of Desert Lake, here in Eastern Ontario, I realize the enchanted lands are infectious. Their power filtered into me through the sights of majestic vistas, eye contact with muskox, the vision of delicate louseworts. The magic crept in through my ears in the thunder of mighty waters, the whine of mosquitoes, the high, thin cries of fishing ospreys. With each breath, I absorbed the essence of the place, musty animal smells, high-flung river spray, itchy willow pollen. My body, shaking with cold, aching with labor, or stiff from long storm-bound hours, soaked up the spirit of all these rivers. The lessons of balance and oneness in the land last for life. It feels good and right to be so captivated.

# Lake Superior
## World's Largest Expanse of Freshwater

Joanie McGuffin

W E ALL STORE FLAT MAPS IN OUR MINDS OF THE PLACES WE KNOW, THE places we've been and the places where we live. Road maps are most familiar, but there are topographic maps that describe contours in 50-foot intervals and waterways in threads and puddles of blue. These maps ignite journey dreams as we picture the landscape and see ourselves following these original highways for weeks, sometimes months. Journeys turn maps into three-dimensional realities of place and time. The physical exertion of self-propelled travel, combined with our sharpened senses, creates indelible memories by experience.

Take a map of North America and zero in towards the center and you'll find the Great Lakes. At the top of these lakes is the largest expanse of freshwater on earth, aptly named Superior. This inland freshwater sea is the hub at the center of river spokes, waterways that form a myriad of ways in which to reach the four oceans surrounding the continent.

One morning, in the middle of a five-month traverse of Canada by bicycle, we rested at a spectacular lookout over Lake Superior's Nipigon Bay islands. Gary spread our map out on a flat rock. He pulled a string from his pocket and anchored one end where we stood and proceeded to kink the string in and around all the nooks and crannies of the lake's bays until the circle was complete. He cut the string at this point, sealed its end to prevent fraying and handed it to me. The string and the folded map became a dream to fulfill. I tucked them carefully into my trip diary. We climbed back on our bicycles and headed east for two more months.

Two years later, in 1989, we set off on our three-month circumnavigation around Lake Superior's 2,000-mile (3,200 km) shoreline. Planning the route had been simple. Begin where the dream was born on the lake's most northerly point, Kama Bay, and circle the lake according to its own natural counterclockwise currents. We would paddle in solo sea canoes, letting Superior dictate the schedule of our days.

A half-day's paddle from Kama Bay brought us to the mouth of Lake Superior's largest tributary, the Nipigon River. A fine sand, brought south by this river from Lake Nipigon, hangs in suspension behind the screen of north shore islands coloring the waters an opaque turquoise-green. On the east side of the Nipigon River mouth, where a rock wall drops straight into the lake, twisted, gnarled cedars grow from cracks and crevices. Nearby, a small frog swam listlessly. I scooped it up and placed it on a warm ledge of rock to recuperate. It was the first of many small creatures — from bumble-bees to butterflies — that I rescued from Superior's frigid waters over the course of the summer.

Suddenly we were aware of straight lines and arches painted on the rocks above. Long ago this ocher had been bonded to the rock with natural oils. Over time dissolved minerals seeping down the cliff varnished and pre-served them. We interpreted the paintings as people, canoes and caribou. Most intriguing was the little frog-like man, arms and legs outstretched in a dance across the rock. Maymaygwaysiwuk, we whispered, thinking of the bewhiskered little men who paddled stone canoes, stole fish from nets and followed tunnel channels between Lake Nipigon and Superior. These are touchstones with those of our own species who were aware of many things we no longer perceive.

Early on, our voyage around Superior's lakeshore became a discovery of its watershed. Each day we passed river mouths; some were small creeks, others, major rivers. We paddled through the north shore islands from St. Ignace to the Black Bay peninsula, discovering flowing currents right

within the lake itself. These seiches are Superior's tides, caused not by the moon's gravitational pull, but rather by the sloshing of water back and forth across the lake's enormous surface.

Beneath the great hulking landform of the Sleeping Giant, we paddled towards the little hamlet of Silver Islet on a sunny evening. The silver mining shafts, located near an offshore island, are no more than two dark eyes staring up from underwater. Long ago they flooded, losing the battle with the lake's November storms.

We hiked and climbed to the top of the sheer bluffs of the Sleeping Giant's feet and gazed 800 feet (240 m) below to the gray-green combers rolling in towards Pie Island and Thunder Bay. On top of the peninsula, we found jasper taconite tooled by hunters into weapons for hunting caribou 11,000 years ago. The Ice Age was drawing to a close, and as the ice melted, the Great Lakes of today were uncovered. The land rebounded from the weight of ice, something that it is still doing today. Rivers flowed in different places and in different directions. Superior, only partly uncovered, flowed southward through St. Louis to the Mississippi and the Gulf. Nothing reminds us more of the ever-changing nature of the landscape than the flow of water.

We investigated each bay, large and small. Sometimes we paddled from dawn to dark, taking advantage of fine, calm weather. We traversed Thunder Bay at Caribou Island, the smell of gulls reaching us long before the birds. Then a blizzard of wings arose from the rock and windswept nests. Swirling and diving, they appeared to us as pink kites in the sunset's afterglow.

## International Border Crossing

Thunder Bay, the lakehead city, was, in smells and sounds, a sharp contrast to the wildness of the lake we had been traveling. Instead of forest to our right, it was an avenue of commerce complete with the railway, granaries, harbors and ships. We paddled into the city, by way of the Kaministiquia River, to visit the recreated fur trade post, Old Fort William. For twenty-five years the Northwest Company maintained a fur trading rendezvous in the early 1800s. Now costumed voyageurs and traders breathe life, albeit somewhat romanticized, into the French voyageurs who paddled in from Montreal with trade goods and supplies to exchange with those coming down from northwestern Canada with a rich supply of furs. Further upstream, the Kam's spectacular gorge and wonderful whitewater rapids have been preserved by the tenacious efforts of local paddlers who fought long and hard against further damming of the river.

Paddling south from Thunder Bay, with the ocean of freshwater always to our left, we reached a bay familiar to us from a journey several years before. (We were, at that time, on our way to the Arctic Ocean from the Atlantic, having paddled 2,000 miles (3,200 km) inland with 4,000 miles (6,400 km) left to go. A 9-mile (14 km) portage around the Pigeon River's waterfalls and gorges set the precedent for an upstream challenge 50 miles (80 km) to the Continental Divide. We were following a route used for centuries by travelers before us heading west from Lake Superior.) Now, however, we were heading south, and knowing the whereabouts of the Pigeon River was significant for the practical purpose of making an international border crossing from Canada to the United States.

Producing citizenship at a river mouth reminded us of the artificial nature of political boundaries. Manmade divisions of provinces, states and countries are irrelevant to the natural flow of water. It courses through our bodies, from the Great Lakes to the sea, from the clouds through the forests and into the deepest reaches of Superior itself.

Our route southwest, along the Minnesota shoreline of Lake Superior, was almost arrow-straight. Sparsely scattered islands and only a light peppering of shoals provided refuge from winds on the stretches where we could not get ashore. A gull perched on the cliff at Palisade Head reminded us of our vulnerability to the lake's temperamental winds. We scanned the horizon, often searching for the indicator stripe of deep blue telling of approaching winds. We can't take flight like the gull, but in small canoes we can find shelter at the river mouths where larger boats cannot. The Manitou, Cascade, Temperance and Split Rock are among a handful of exquisite wild rivers pouring from the glacial-scoured Sawtooth Mountains. The volcanic rock of this magic world is full of caves and archways that sometimes lead us into quiet bays, where rivers tumble straight into the lake warming the water for swimming.

At the Duluth harbor, we turn east where the St. Louis River flows in from the southwest. We picture yet another avenue to the oceans. Resting on the long sand spit of Minnesota Point, we contemplate our map. Paddle and portage up the gorges of the St. Louis River and we could reach the Mississippi and paddle all the way to the Gulf of Mexico. The thought was satisfying. That feeling of turning a corner, following a river, just paddling on and on is a universal sentiment echoed in some of the early journals we read from fur traders, mapmakers and missionaries. But the people we think about even more were here long before them. They were the traders of copper, obsidian and pearl who paddled canoes great distances between the peoples of a continent thousands of years ago. River routes were as unending as the flow of water. Even on our journey around Superior paddling past the river mouths of several different rivers a day, we were appreciating them as more than single threads with put-in and take-out points.

## Mounding Cumulus Clouds

Reverberating deep within the recesses of a cave came the belch and grumble of waves. We followed the sound, enjoying the play of light off the green waters on the passageways of red sandstone. In the Apostle Islands, off the Bayfield Peninsula, the geology is different from anywhere else on the lake. We imagined Superior as having a giant tongue that shaped the soft rock in the way we lick ice-cream cones.

While pitching our tent between the East and West Sleeping Bay Rivers, we watched a pair of bald eagles circling and swooping low over a huge white pine. The thick limbs supported an enormous nest, and beside it, perched the eagle pair's full-grown offspring. Out over the lake, a storm was brewing. Mounding cumulus clouds thundered towards us like buffalo across the open plain of blue-black waters. The darkening sky swallowed a squashed red sun in the west, while lightning darts jabbed the horizon to the east. Two storms were converging on us. The eaglet did not move. It was as much a part of this storm as the drift logs and the stones. Although only a few big drops struck us as the storm galloped past, the deluge over the Porcupine Mountains reached us the next day by way of rising rivers.

So many rivers, each with a different character: the Brûlé, a lovely river trip in the southwestern part of Superior; the Ontonagon, where the Chippewa once harvested sturgeon in great numbers; the whitewater Montreal, dividing Wisconsin and Michigan. The shipping channel across the Keweenaw Peninsula had the feel of a river, although it is not. During one of Superior's windy weeks, this channel gave us a rest from the concerns of big-lake travel. Tailwinds filled the strong golf umbrellas we carried. We held them out in front of us and traveled for miles past the reminders of this region's copper history: the black stamp sand beaches of Freda and the crumbling copper mills at Houghton and Hancock.

Beyond the Keweenaw Peninsula, tucked in beyond the sand dunes almost out of sight, we caught a glimpse of the driftwood gray log cabins. A couple of people were meandering down a beachfront boardwalk made from slats of cedar. They carried carved walking sticks and wore starched khaki clothing, as if they were on a safari. They waved. Smelling an intriguing history, we turned into the switchback river mouth, carved through the beach, and discovered more multistory log cabins, log boathouses, early 19th-century cedar-strip rowboats and a birchbark canoe. Later we hiked through a dark hemlock grove where whitetail deer disappeared behind huge tree trunks and white birch appeared like ghosts with their fallen limbs lying like bleached bones on the empty forest floor. By chance, we met the local historian who explained the history of this privately owned watershed in the Huron Mountains. It began with the likes of Henry Ford and others who wanted to preserve the trout streams and forests for their hunting and fishing pleasure. Generations later, the offspring of these original families still preserve this oasis of rivers and forests to the great benefit of bird, animal, insect and fish life of Superior's south shore.

Eastwards from the Huron Mountains, the height of land dividing the rivers flowing north to Superior and south to Lake Michigan lies very near Superior's shoreline. And then the surprise of the Grand Sable Banks, near Grand Marais, which are not sand dunes at all but the result of a huge crevasse in the glacial ice. When the ice melted, it left this 300-foot-high (90 m) river of sand curving along the Lake Superior shore. We discovered rivers like the Two Hearted by simply walking inland a short distance. The Two Hearted flows eastwards, paralleling the lakeshore for 2 miles (3.2 km) before cutting through the beach and spilling into Superior. Nearer Whitefish Point, the watershed divide drops south again. The golden brown waters of the Taquamenon and its tributaries flow eastwards across this triangle of land to Whitefish Bay. Hearing of the curtain falls and a river looping past steep banks of ancient hemlock, we mark our map with yet another promise for a future river adventure.

## Scalloped Shoreline

The picture we held in our heads of Lake Superior, up until Whitefish Bay, was of a basin into which all rivers flowed. But then we saw the Whitefish Rapids of the St. Mary's flowing out of Lake Superior and thought of the lake as a great big pool in the middle of a much longer river system flowing to the sea. The St. Mary's River has the distinction of being the only natural outflow from Superior. Because Lake Superior is so deep, it takes 250 years to completely replace the water system in the lake. So as we meet the rivers flowing into Superior, we are meeting the waters that can stay in Lake Superior for ten generations. A special map of Superior's lake currents was given to us before our journey, and we thought often of this counterclockwise flow as we followed it. Just like a river, it forms huge eddies in the huge bays of the lake. Just north of Whitefish Bay, the currents encircle a small island called Caribou, near the place where the legendary iron-ore ship the *Edmund Fitzgerald* sank in a November gale.

We watched an upbound, ocean-going freighter pass en route to Thunder Bay, Duluth or Marquette and a downbound freighter heading south for the lower Great Lakes. We knew their destination and what lay in between.

The two deep bays lying north of Whitefish Bay, on Superior's east shore, are Goulais and Batchawana. The large rivers flowing into them are similarly named. They, along with the Chippewa, Montreal and Aubinadong, flow from a rare and special top-of-the-watershed ancient forest. The Algoma Highlands, east of Lake Superior, is one of the finest pieces of Great Lakes–St. Lawrence forest remaining on the map of North America today. The rivers flowing from the heart of this forest, fed from the wetlands, springs and small lakes, carve avenues through old-growth red and white pine forest. They are unique now, but were once commonplace from the Maritimes to the Mississippi from Connecticut to Lake Superior.

On the tip of Batchawana Island, we camp facing west. The sky flames and the rocks and trees reflect it. The Earth turns slowly away from the sun, an orange ball squeezed flat with step-like edges. Far out beyond the horizon is a shore we have paddled on this same journey, on this same lake. With darkness, the distance grows upwards as well as outwards across the watery expanse.

Spectacular beaches at the mouth of the Sand and Agawa Rivers sweep north with the natural counterclockwise flow of lake currents. Sculpted by ice and high water, both these river mouths are constantly evolving. The Sand's original name was Pinguisibi, meaning river of fine white sand. Our map shows both these rivers as being accessible by rail. We'll return to them and paddle from their headwaters down to the lake one day soon. (Or perhaps we'll even try to paddle up them.) The shoreline here is part of Lake Superior Provincial Park, boreal scenery with a fringe of arctic landscape at the lakeshore. Rivers like the Baldhead, Old Woman and Gargantua entice us inland for half-day hikes wherever the park trails allow. Orange and green lichens color the volcanic rock of Gargantua, and on bare rock, where the bellflowers and arctic saxifrages grow, ancient cedars survive. In several places, at the river mouths, we discover these thick gray trunks spiraling upwards. Some have survived here along the lakeshore for four centuries. They are living timelines that provide a link with our own past. We imagine the travelers before us leaving offerings of tobacco, asking for safe passage on the lake. Tradition, belief and faith. We, too, leave tobacco and a little of our own life story in our passing.

A great sweep of sand beach reaches south from the Michipicoten River. We camped here after a long day's paddle from Old Woman Bay and Bushy Bay. The next morning, we bucked the wind-piled waves against the

outflowing river and managed to get within the safety of the river mouth. (This was often the way on Superior. The river mouths could be treacherous if it was shallow and the wind blew onshore.) The North-west Company voyageurs, heading for Grand Portage or Old Fort William, often took a chance making a 20-mile (32 km) crossing to avoid Michipicoten Bay altogether. On a day like today, the choice could have cost them their lives.

A scalloped shoreline leads us westwards from the Michipicoten Bay lighthouse, past Point Isacor and on towards the Pukaskwa coast. Dozens of beautiful rivers, coves, beaches and cobble shoreline exist along this section of Superior. Fifteen miles (24 km) from Michipicoten, we left Superior and paddled up the Dog River in search of Denison Falls. We found the trail but decided to paddle and pole upstream instead. Near the base of the falls we left the canoes and hiked in. We discovered a rugged portage around the falls that requires paddlers to lower their canoe on a rope down a rock face. This portage begins at a benign-looking bend in the upper river. It is portage you don't want to miss. From shore, we followed the river's path as it turned sharply right then dropped over a ledge. We imagined a canoe surviving this and proceeding upright down the alley of rock walls. At the next bend, the rock walls end and the river plunges over the lip of an incredible falls.

We paddled the stretch of river from the base of the falls back out to the lake, glad we had made the effort to paddle upstream earlier that day.

Lying between the Pukaskwa River, to the south and east, and the Pic River, to the north and west, is Pukaskwa National Park, a 48-mile-long (77 km) stretch of Lake Superior shoreline with ancient rock headlands and rivers that come cascading down, often sneaking unnoticed into Superior. The Pukaskwa River, the park's southeast boundary, was formed by a massive fissure along a fault valley where the Earth's crust split. We paddle in from the lake and fish for trout at the base of the falls. The Cascade River provided a day's hike inland following the tracks of wolf and moose. Again, we cast for trout in the deep pools. Wind-bound here for a couple of days, we had a chance to explore the coast and the Pukaskwa pits. Speculation as to who made these impressions in the cobble beaches, and why, is best contemplated in one's personal search for them. They vary in size and shape and placement, giving rise to explanations of purpose — were they for hunting or food storage or shelter or vision-questing sites?

At Oiseau Bay, we followed fresh black bear tracks around the shore to the river mouth. A plain of sand, with trees anchored on strange angles, was an intriguing mystery to solve. We hiked upstream a long way following what appeared to be a recent and catastrophic flood. We later learned a beaver dam had burst and the resultant deluge had washed the banks down a great depth, leaving an intriguing cross-section of sediments, a sandwich of history.

On our last day, from Rossport to Kama Bay, we marked off the miles between river mouths, the Gravel and Jack Pine being two of the last. A circle of string had become the thread of a real journey through the seasons.

In a sixty-year-old wooden pencil box marked with my mother's initials, J.M., I keep the piece of string and the map that became a journey. Pressed flowers from the Sturgeon River's wild banks, a blue jay feather from Rainbow Falls, and various rocks, including pieces of red sandstone, quartz, taconite, gneiss, slate and more were all collected from the mouths of Lake Superior's rivers.

These various treasures are magic keys that unlock memories, which in turn become dreams for new journeys.

# Winisk River
## Learning About the Land, History and the Human Spirit

James Cullingham

IN JULY 1980, I WAS TWENTY-SIX YEARS OLD. MY DAUGHTER, JESSICA, WAS born that March and I had just graduated from Trent University in Peterborough, Ontario, with a degree in Native Studies and French. I was awaiting the beginning of law school at Queen's University in Kingston that autumn. As a canoeist, cross-country skier and shinny hockey enthusiast, a not-too-well-defined future awaited: an unusual combination of law, outdoor education and parenthood.

I was looking for summer work when Bruce Hodgins, director of Camp Wanapitei in Temagami, invited me to lead a group of adult canoeists down the Winisk River in northwestern Ontario to Hudson Bay. I was pleased but also somewhat startled by Bruce's offer. I had led teenagers on two-week trips out of Wanapitei for some years, however, I had never done a Bay trip. Furthermore, I had little experience as an adult trip leader.

The prospect of paddling the 270-mile-long (435 km) Winisk was appealing. The river flows north then turns hard to the east to the subarctic zone along the Hudson Bay coast. The Winisk is north of most commercial timber and mining activities and the people who live on its banks, Ojibwa to the south and Cree closer to the Bay, were, in 1980, engaged in trapping, fishing, guiding and the hunt of migratory caribou. Wildlife is rich: many sorts of fur bearers, large northern birds, fish, including pike, pickerel, whitefish, sturgeon, and most famously, brook trout. But the polar bear is the most celebrated and feared denizen. The proclivity of the great white bears led the Ontario government to proclaim most of the river and the adjacent Hudson Bay coastline Polar Bear Provincial Park.

The weather is mercurial at best, even at the height of summer, and the rapids and falls are varied and challenging. During any two-to-three-week trip from Webequie on Lake Winisk to the village of Winisk at Hudson Bay, one can expect extremely high headwinds, voracious insects and plenty of cold and wet.

On the other hand, the landscape is virtually untouched by industry, the river is full of navigable rapids, there are sixteen hours of daylight in July, and large, open skies are inviting.

Our group — Jamie, a law professor from Ottawa; Bill Sr., a medical doctor, and his son, Bill Jr., an Ottawa high-school student; John J., a professor of history at Trent University; Ted and John B., both instructors at the community college in Lindsay; and James G., a retired industrialist, originally from England — met at Pickle Lake, a makeshift mining town a few hundred miles north of the Trans-Canada Highway, west of Thunder Bay.

We had our last taste of civilization in the local diners and convenience stores before taking our DC-3 charter north to Webequie on Lake Winisk, headwaters of the Winisk River. Webequie was a tidy, distinctly northern Ojibwa village. Chainsaws, sturdy freighter canoes, fishing nets, traps, snowmobile parts and the like were readily apparent. It was clear we had not descended into a destination resort, nor were we among people dependent primarily on tourism.

Some of our group had bought beautifully beaded moccasins and mitts made by Webequie villagers. The sky was gray and the winds light as we paddled among the islands of Lake Winisk, thick with the distinctive tufts of black spruce.

Our first campsite, on a crescent-shaped beach, was on a smaller island just north of Webequie. It seemed an ideal choice. After tents were set up and dinner was underway, I went exploring. The island, much to my dismay, was actually full of garbage — plastic, glass, rubber and tin from Webequie. The image rather dulled my idyllic notion of the village.

The next morning we made it to the Winisk River proper, and almost immediately, we were in our first rapids. While not overly challenging, they were a pleasant introduction. At the bottom, we watched in awe as a Webequie resident, standing in the stern, expertly piloted his motorized wooden canoe upstream.

## Dumbfounded Gratitude

Our four-canoe brigade was experienced and at ease. I remember a sense of relief in recognizing that, while there were some kinks to be worked out, there would be no need for remedial, novice whitewater instruction.

James G., my sexagenarian bowman, was a particular revelation. In addition to being strong, swift and possessed of an uncanny ability to read the river, he had a passion and sensibility for river travel unrivaled by anyone of

my generation. Paddling with him was an education in canoe tripping and humility. His experience tempered my own arrogance of youth and brute physicality. I admired how he let the wind and current work for him, how he paced himself paddling and portaging, and how his demeanor and campsite etiquette always provided maximum comfort for himself and consideration for others. Besides that, he was funny. His wry, bent, British perspective was endlessly amusing.

The river soon got wilder, especially at Bear Head rapids. At the top, we had a spill and a large dent soon adorned an aluminum canoe. Ted and John B. were shaken but unhurt. One of their paddles disappeared in the current. We found it, unscathed, two days later.

The next week was a privileged cruise to the northern edge of the Canadian Shield. The weather was warm, and the fish, with the exception of the elusive brook trout, were plentiful. On a few broad flat stretches of the river, we lashed our canoes together and raised a large tarp to sail. We camped at Native campsites, when we could find them. They were hard to spot from the water. There would be a gap in the spruce trees with a trail leading into a circular clearing with a fire pit and plenty of room for tents. Sheltered from the wind or any storm, these sites were tiny oases. On other occasions, we stayed in sturdy cabins where villagers from Webequie or Winisk maintained fishing and hunting camps. Unlocked and in good condition, the cabins were a testament to a trusting culture.

Of all the spectacular waterfalls on the Winisk, Baskineig is the grandest. As we approached, a clutch of rare, seemingly primeval, sandhill cranes took off from shore and flew right across our bows. We camped for the night, with the 75-foot-tall (22.5 m) falls as a backdrop. At about midnight, James G. prepared tea as firelight flickered on a nearby canoe hull. A photograph of him, in silhouette, placing a teabag in his cup, still hangs in my living room.

Shortly after Baskineig Falls, the Winisk makes its dramatic turn to the east, out of the Shield and into the flatlands approaching Hudson Bay. Canoe-threatening boulders were now replaced by tricky limestone ledges, which appeared, at times, out of nowhere. James G. and I happened upon one such ledge in a lax moment. We were drifting lazily when suddenly we found ourselves on the lip of a 5-foot-high (1.5 m) ledge that cut a 100-foot-wide (30 m) slash in the middle of the river. Some furious back-paddling helped avoid what would have been a chilly spill.

The next 12 miles (20 km), filled with runnable swifts and rapids, are legendary. However, our fun was dampened by heavy-duty headwinds. It was the first and only time in my canoeing life when I had to paddle fiercely to keep going downstream in a set of rapids.

Two days from Hudson Bay, we had successfully completed the most challenging part of the Winisk. As a trip leader, I began to awaken to the realization that Bruce Hodgins' confidence in me had been well placed. I realized I had the canoeing skills and the organizational and leadership qualities such a trip demanded. But it would be far from the first time I would wonder how skills learned from this trip might apply to the rest of my life.

Just a few miles shy of Hudson Bay, we saw a collection of cabins, shacks and tents, mounds of conifer firewood leaning together in a tepee shape, and a few more permanent establishments on the north shore. Across the river, concealed by alders and scrub bush, a military air base, a relic of the Cold War, lay in disrepair. Reconnaissance planes and fighter-bombers used to head north from Winisk towards Soviet territory. Winisk villagers had constructed the base for the United States military in the 1950s. In 1980, the landing strip, surrounded by hangars and housing for military personnel long since returned to the south, was still used by civilians. A few of the Winisk Cree villagers lived on that side of the river — drying caribou and bear skins lent a surreal dissonance.

While our group was generally upbeat, one of our members was uneasy. He took me aside and said, "We must speak to the chief. It's very important to speak to the chief in these places." His suggestion came more from worry than from courtesy. Eventually, a band member greeted us. He said we'd be welcome to bunk in the large, white wooden framed structure near the shore until we made flight arrangements back to Pickle Lake. We straggled up to the house, which was baking in the August sun.

Inside, it was littered with garbage and broken furniture. The toilets were backed up with human waste. What had apparently been a residence for nurses and teachers had been trashed. We retreated and set our tents up in a meadow between the house and the river. There was no clear explanation for its condition. Most of us were just as happy to continue tenting. There was tension in the group, and the experience elicited some very unflattering remarks about Natives and the state of their reserves from the agitated member of our group. Perhaps sensing just how unwelcome his words were, our unhappy camper began to keep his own counsel.

Some of us took advantage of the good weather and ample time in Winisk to learn more about the village and its inhabitants. I began regular wanderings about the village. With the heat, a number of residents had summer lodgings beside their houses. Tents, wigwams and tepees provided cooler shelter, and smudge fires kept clouds of mosquitoes at bay.

Under a tarp, pitched expertly to provide both shade and a path for a cooling breeze, a woman in long flower print, cotton skirt, gumboots and a kerchief sat on a stump frying bannock and pickerel on an open fire. Her husband invited me to join them. Daniel Koostachin introduced himself and his wife, Susan. The food was delicious. Daniel asked me where I was from and how the river had been. He had a keen interest in and knowledge of water levels, animals, campsites and fishing.

I asked him about the papoose-like apparatus that was leaning against the woodpile beside their house. Daniel explained it was a tikinagan, a cradle board, that he and his wife had used to carry each of their five children in the bush. It was a simple, elegant bit of technology with a tamarack frame and plywood backing. Our visit was brief but warm. I remember being struck with how utterly at ease and satisfied the couple seemed with their surroundings. They asked if I had a family, and I told them my girlfriend and I had had our first child earlier that year.

Over at the air strip, I arranged for a split charter back to Pickle Lake. In two days, a DC-3 would bring a load of gasoline to Winisk. Seats would be put in the plane and we would pay for the return flight.

On our last full day in Winisk, we arranged a trip out into Hudson Bay. Our two guides piloted 20-foot wooden canoes, with transoms and outboard motors, to the river mouth and out onto the bay. We had indeed paddled to the sea. The coastline was indistinct, however, and after an hour or so, the point of the journey seemed elusive. As we approached an island offshore, the pilots shut down the boats and lit cigarettes. Almost on cue, seals and beluga whales began to surface around the canoes. We traveled back to Winisk as close to shore as possible in hopes of seeing a polar bear. Not on this day.

The next morning we prepared to paddle across the river and get our gear to the landing strip. As I packed my knapsack, Daniel Koostachin came by and asked if we were getting a flight out that day. When I told him of our plans, he asked me to wait. He returned holding his tikinagan, freshly painted and adorned with caribou hide and a tartan cloth cover. He offered it to me, saying he and his wife wouldn't be having more children and perhaps my wife and I could use it for our baby. I accepted the gift in dumbfounded gratitude.

The tikinagan was put to good use carrying my three daughters cross-country skiing and on canoeing daytrips. It, too, adorns my living-room wall, a warm reminder of a voyage that opened doors to the land, history and the human spirit. A canoe trip that marked me as a man, storyteller, parent and canoeist. I didn't become a lawyer.

## Postscript

The village of Winisk was devastated by flood during spring breakup in 1986. I returned to the Winisk River that summer to videotape the construction of a new village, Peawanuck, on higher ground about 12 miles (20 km) upstream. *Peawanuck: The Promised Land*, a documentary film about the relocation of the Winisk Cree, was broadcast in March 1987.

# Wabakimi Provincial Park
## *Laser Guns, Pi and the Center of the Universe*

Kevin Callan

IT WAS NANCY SCOTT, A PARK PLANNER FOR ONTARIO, WHO FIRST GOT me intrigued with the idea of paddling in Wabakimi Provincial Park, located 185 miles (300 km) north of Thunder Bay. The fact that the park measures almost 2.47 million acres (1 million hectares) in size and contains over 1,240 miles (2,000 km) of canoe trails was enough to catch my interest. But it was Nancy's story of eccentric inventor Wendell Beckwith, who lived alone for twenty years on Wabakimi's Whitewater Lake to devote his life to "pure" research, that finally convinced me to give this massive chunk of solitude a try.

Joining me on the pilgrimage to the Beckwith site was film producer Kip Spidell. It was our first trip together, but he was convinced that if he followed a bumbling canoehead like me through the wilderness for eight days, he'd get enough good film footage to make the trip worth his while.

Mercifully, Nancy also agreed to tag along as guide. Not only did she know the exact whereabouts of Wendell's hermitage on Whitewater Lake, she also knew the locations of all the unmarked portages and campsites along the way — a bonus for any group traveling in such a remote park, where woodland caribou far outnumber the canoeists.

The three possible ways to access the park are road, rail and float plane. The road is obviously the cheapest, but not necessarily the best overall. It's a relatively easy drive to the launch on Caribou Lake, 7.5 miles (12 km) north of Armstrong via the Armstrong Road (Highway 527) and then Caribou Lake Road. But the full day's paddle across the expanse of Caribou Lake to the actual park boundary can be a real bore, not to mention extremely hazardous should the wind pick up.

However, keeping to the train schedule can be a pain at times, and the flights in and out can be very costly. So, after looking over all the options, our group finally decided on a combination plan. We would access the south section by train (check Via Rail Canada for updated schedules and fees), fly out of Mattice Lake Outfitters on Whitewater Lake by way of Don Elliot's

Wabakimi Air Service, and then have Don shuttle us back to the train station in Armstrong.

Since Kip and I live in the Toronto area, we planned to take the Via Rail service directly out of Union Station. Then, if all went well, we would meet up with Nancy twenty-four hours later at the Armstrong station and continue east for another 24 miles (39 km), where we'd be dropped off at the designated access point — Shultz's Trail — at the south end of Onamakawash Lake.

Thinking back, our multi-part plan went surprisingly well. Kip and I managed to bump into only a handful of not-so-polite commuters while portaging down Front Street during rush hour. I managed to break only one overhead light while carrying the canoe through the main foyer of Union Station (which, for some reason, caused a power surge throughout the entire building). And because of a broken axle on the train, we were a mere six hours late to meet Nancy in Armstrong.

Under the watchful eyes of the tourists we had befriended in the Bud car along the way, the three of us waved our goodbyes, dragged our gear down a steep gravel embankment, and then paddled off into the Wabakimi wilderness.

## Narrowly Escaped Death

An hour and a half later, we had paddled to the northeast bay of Onamakawash Lake and flushed ourselves down the first rapid of the Lookout River (a 150-yard portage is marked to the left), all the time being pursued by a massive black cloud.

Nancy had warned us about the severity of the storms in Wabakimi. But Kip and I thought we could get in at least the first day of paddling before having to deal with one. Suddenly, the black squall caught up to us. There was no buildup, no prelude, just a smack of hard rain, strong wind, and a lather of whitecaps. We pushed for the second stretch of rapids, hastily made camp at the take-out for the 50-yard portage marked along the left bank, and then watched from under a sagging rain tarp as the storm moved across the sky.

For our second day out, we pushed off from camp early, attempting to film our own version of the Bob Izumi fishing show at the base of the rapids, with no luck, of course. And by 8 A.M. we were heading off downriver.

The Lookout River was the first of three rivers we had planned to travel to reach Whitewater Lake. And thinking back, it also happened to be my favorite. Of the series of five rapids between our first night's camp and

Spring Lake, only the fourth could be safely run. But all the portages were extremely short (100 yards on the left, 100 yards and 40 yards on the right, a possible lift-over on the left, and 150 yards on the left), and the scenery along the intimate little stream was absolutely breathtaking. Even the last portage of the day — a 900-yard trail connecting Spring Lake with Smoothrock Lake — was a pleasure to walk. Aptly named Fantasia Portage for its fairyland appearance, and rumored to be the most scenic portage in the north, the trail led us through a stand of pine, spruce and birch, all rooted in a thick carpet of caribou moss, bunchberries and knuckle-size blueberries.

Smoothrock Lake (named for its cluster of islands, scoured smooth by passing glaciers) was a different story, however. Almost the entire 18 miles (30 km) of shoreline had been affected by fire that went through the area in the early 1980s. Since wildfires play an integral part in the lifecycle of the boreal forest, they are not always suppressed here. This management practice ensures a vital habitat for the park's scattered herds of woodland caribou as well as all other boreal species. For canoeists looking for a place to camp, however, the landscape can seem inhospitable. We finally found a suitable spot on a tiny knob of rock, situated in the center of the lake, around 6 P.M., just minutes before the nightly storm moved in.

It was amazingly calm the next day as we began our six-hour crossing of Smoothrock Lake. On such a large lake, we were grateful for the lack of wind. But the payback was an intense heat, reaching 90 degrees (30° C) by 8 A.M. We kept close to the shoreline most of the day, searching for a bit of shade.

The previous fire had scarred most of the trees along the shore, however, and escaping the direct sun soon became a lost cause. To make matters worse, we could smell smoke from a distant fire, probably lit by a lightning strike from the previous night's storm. Soon, a thin veil of haze hung low over the lake, and breathing became more difficult throughout the day.

By late afternoon, as we entered Smoothrock's Outlet Bay (the second of three channels that lead northward out of the lake), a soft breeze was helping to cleanse the air and we were finally free of the smoke. But the quick shift in the wind also indicated to us that another evening storm was brewing. In the distance, we spotted anvil-shaped clouds moving our way. This time they had a green hue to them, something Nancy seemed quite concerned about, so we immediately headed for shore.

Of course, as luck would have it, we were quickly chased off by thousands of biting red ants (it was like some kind of horror flick) and we made haste toward the next rocky point. The second we pulled up on shore, the storm hit. And what a storm it was! The temperature dropped 45 degrees (15° C) in a matter of minutes; hail the size of marbles smacked down hard, leaving dimple marks on the overturned canoes; and a gale-force wind brought trees down all around us.

It was a horrifying experience. But it lasted a mere five minutes. And as we crept out to the water's edge to check the damage done to our two canoes, we realized how lucky we were to make it through the storm without serious injury. The original point we had pulled up on was now a jumbled mess, littered with uprooted trees. It was obvious that if we had stayed there, all three of us might have been crushed to death. It was a humbling experience, to say the least.

The next morning we had only an hour's paddling left on Smoothrock Lake before we reached the portage leading to the Berg River. The trail was only 500 yards long, but this section of forest had been recently burned over and it took us another hour to haul our gear and canoes through the charred debris. Once on the Berg, however, we made quick progress. We easily ran the first set of rapids, even though a short 70-yard portage was marked on the left. The second set, Island Rapids, had to be portaged. But the 80-yard trail along the left bank was an easy carry. Once we reached the third set, we decided to call it an early day and camped along the 400-yard portage, also marked to the left.

Here Kip spent some quality time shooting some whitewater scenes for his film by having me paddle down the Class II–III rapids over half a dozen times. I didn't mind the job, however. The water levels were up and most of the dangerous rocks were well covered. The only thing I had to watch out for was billowing waves at the beginning and end of the run, which became a problem after Kip duct-taped his camera and tripod to the back end of my canoe. With the extra weight strapped to the stern, each maneuver became a balancing act. And since Kip forgot the waterproof casing for the camera, he constantly reminded me that a dump in the rapid would be a costly mistake.

The morning of day five saw us finishing the remainder of the Berg River, and before noon we had entered the Ogoki River. This was the last of the three rivers en route and also happened to be the largest and least exciting to paddle. It's slow and meandering in this section, with only one section of quick water, and that can be easily run or lined down. We also began seeing fishermen from the neighboring lodges. (Wabakimi Provincial Park has seven main lodges and forty fly-in outpost camps). So, rather than taking the regular 650-yard portage marked to the right of where the main section of the Ogoki empties into Whitewater Lake, we made a sharp left turn a half-mile up from the take-out and navigated a small side stream instead.

There were no portages, and we had to wade, line and blindly run down a series of rock-strewn rapids. But in a way, the narrow outlet was a far better introduction to Whitewater Lake. And there to greet us at the entranceway to Wendell's "Center of the Universe" was our first woodland caribou. The encounter lasted only a couple of seconds, but even the brief glimpse we had was well worth it. Throughout Wabakimi, the second-largest park in the province, only 300 of these elusive creatures remain.

## Too Few Woodland Caribou and Too Many Lodges

Caribou once ranged as far south as Lake Nipissing, but they were eventually pushed further north by settlement and logging. Because they are an extremely vulnerable species that depends greatly on isolation for its survival, their future viability lies in part here in Wabakimi. The park, established in 1983, was expanded six-fold in 1997, primarily to provide for the protection of the caribou. But is this enough? According to the Ministry of Natural Resources Regional Planning Biologist for Northwestern Ontario, Glen Hooper, it's not even close enough. Hooper admits that the park provides a vast and very significant chunk of habitat for this important population but is not large enough to sustain the caribou on its own.

However, the park superintendent, John McGrath, is continuing to promote the many hunting and fishing lodges developed throughout its expansion area. Most canoeists traveling in the park feel ambivalent about the camps. In one way they seem intrusive — they don't seem to fit the "wilderness experience." On the other hand, they can be extremely handy as a link to the outside world. Occasionally, trippers use them as a meeting place for float planes or to pick up extra supplies. Others have had to use them in severe emergency situations.

Our group was no different. Before our trip to Wabakimi, John McGrath offered to have Walter, the interior park warden, meet us at the lodge situated at the mouth of the Ogoki River. From here he would give us a tow across to the Wendell Beckwith site on Best Island, situated on the far southeast bay of Whitewater Lake — a distance of approximately 12 miles (20 km).

In a way, it was a bit of a cop-out to accept the free ride. But Walter was also a member of the small group of aboriginal people who lived on White-water Lake during Wendell Beckwith's time here, and Kip thought that an interview with him would help his film a great deal. So early the next morning, our group gathered on the lodge's dock and waited for Walter to show. The following day we were still waiting. At 3 A.M. of the second day, the same day we had scheduled a plane to pick us up at another lodge just south of Best Island, we were forced to find our own way across. Of course, when we finally arrived, good old Walter was there to greet us.

After many years of traveling in the north, I've come to realize that schedules are not the same up here as they are down south. I also believe that far too many of us "visitors" have failed to see the importance of not being in such a hurry, and that we should not enter the bush without a good understanding of this. Knowing it, however, didn't seem to help curb my anger towards Walter, and it took some time before we could excuse his tardiness.

## Cleansing Mind of Mental Paraphernalia

To help ease the situation, we went off to explore the splendor of the Beck-with site. Walter gave us a tour of the three cabins and a couple of storage sheds that still remain on the island, all connected by a flagstone walkway and surrounded by a decorative cedar-rail fence. Each structure was perfectly designed, with every roof shingle and floorboard precisely cut to the same size and shape. Elaborate carvings adorned all three entranceways, and pieces of the inventor's scientific contraptions and scores of Ojibwa artifacts were scattered about. Walter even pointed out parts of a homemade telescope he had found down by the beach, and sections of Wendell's "lunar gun" (a device constructed to compute and predict lunar cycles and eclipses) resting beside one of the storage sheds.

The cabins didn't actually belong to Wendell. Harry Wirth, a San Francisco architect and developer, used the island site as a retreat and hired Wendell as a caretaker. In 1955, after producing at least fourteen patents — most of them for the Parker Pen Company — Wendell left behind a wife and five children in Wisconsin and began his solitary life on White-water Lake.

Wendell wasn't the only one to choose Wabakimi as a wilderness retreat. From 1977 to 1982, Joel and Mary Crookham trapped and homesteaded on the nearby Wabakimi Lake and raised their two young children, Sarah and Jason. And in the spring of 1994, Les Stroud and Sue Jamison lived "on what the bush provided" on Goldsborough Lake to work on their film *Snowshoes and Solitude*. Even Zabe, a graduate of Lakehead University's Outdoor Recreation program, attempted to overwinter at Wendell's place. After a close encounter with a pack of wolves, however, she decided to walk back out to Armstrong in February, just five months after she began her sojourn.

But Wendell Beckwith was surely unique. During his time here the eccentric inventor worked on various theories, ranging from the idea that the mathematical term "Pi" was constantly reoccurring in nature to the idea that Whitewater Lake was in complete triangulation with the Great Pyramids and Stonehenge (hence the "Center of the Universe" premise).

Obviously, this was no simple hermitage built by a man trying to escape the civilized world; it was a laboratory, observation post and research station.

The first cabin Walter showed us was a split-level building known as the guesthouse, or Rose's Cabin. The modest structure was thought to be the living quarters for Rose Chaltry while she visited Wendell Beckwith. Rose was Harry Wirth's secretary, who came to know Wendell through his letters to Mr. Wirth. Eventually she befriended Wendell and supported him financially after he had a major dispute with Wirth in 1975.

The main cabin, the only structure not completely designed by Beckwith, came with its own ice-box that was lowered underground to keep food from spoiling, and a sizable homemade birchbark canoe lashed to the south wall. This was where Wendell stayed at first, but he soon found it far too showy and impractical. The massive stone fireplace was especially ineffective at heating the cabin during the long winter months, and he soon became concerned about his reduced hours of research.

By 1978, he had completed construction on the "snail," a circular cabin built directly into the side of a hill. The structure was far more heat-efficient, especially with a skylight centered above a sunken stove, equipped with rotating conical shield to direct the heat and a pivoting chimney to allow for maximum draft. It was an environmental masterpiece, and touring through the unconventional earth-cabin was the highlight of the trip for me.

To end our visit to Best Island, Walter walked us down to the small beach near the Snail and showed us where Wendell died of a heart attack back in 1980, alone but content. It was then that we noticed yet another storm brewing overhead. Since the lodge where we had planned for Don Elliot's air service to pick us up was another 2.5 miles (4 km) south of Best Island, we made the call to leave immediately.

On cue, good old Walter took off, never offering us a tow, and we hastily went in all directions to complete our different tasks. Nancy prepared the boats, Kip finished filming the interior of the cabins, and I went off to sign our names in the registry book resting on the table inside the Snail. It was here that I saw an entry from Wendell's daughter, Laura, dated August 6, 1997: "Very proud to be the daughter of such a man. Wish everyone could have seen his 'domain' as it was while he was alive. By all accounts he was an exceptional and extraordinary man whose ideas and theories we may never comprehend — but we can all admire what he built here and the life he fashioned for himself. I last hugged him on the beach here — and I feel his presence still. Goodbye again, Dad."

Nothing could better have described this charismatic person. Wendell Beckwith's "vision" — to have a community of researchers living on the island in their own Snails, "cleansing their minds of the mental paraphernalia in the outside world" — may not have been a bad idea. Truly, he was not some mad scientist, something that Kip and I constantly joked about before our trip here, but a pure Renaissance man who designed a perfect life for himself in this wild place called Wabakimi.

# Chiniguichi River and Laura Creek Circuit
## A Celebration of the Familiar

Bob Henderson

THERE ARE SOME CANOE ROUTES THAT YOU DARE DO ONLY ONCE, ROUTES etched in your memory, when everything was just right and could not be repeated again. Such routes are best preserved in glowing memories and stories.

There are other routes that are valued, or rather become valued, because of a particular set of associations developed from repeated visits. For some, the year is not quite right without that annual sojourn to those special particular vistas, campsites, and storehouses of memories and expectations.

There is a tendency to write about the grandness of the novel and take for granted the specialness of the familiar, of daily and annual events. There is a different type and quality of learning to be derived from annual travels to a familiar canoe route.

Northeast of Sudbury, Ontario, in a backwater of sorts, between the Temagami canoe routes and the Biscotasing area and between the pattern of north-south-flowing river systems of the Sturgeon, Wanapitei and others, lies Lake Maskinonge on the Chiniguichi River and Laura Creek circuit. Every September, for twenty years, with thirty to forty university students (divided into four or five tripping groups), I have headed north from Southern Ontario

to this region for a five-day standard blue-lake-and-rocky-shore Canadian Shield canoe trip. It is standard in that, like so many Shield circuit trips from Saskatchewan to Labrador, there is a rich variety of terrain and sites. There are lakes big and small. There are creeks, swamps and mysterious bogs on portages that just might be a paddle — or perhaps a walk. Too bad there is nothing between these two forms of movement. There are notable features such as old trappers' cabins, evidence of logging chutes, a Native rock art pictograph site, an old mine site. There are beaches, old-growth white and red pines, significant hill climbs, and swifts and waterfalls. And, of course, there are stories from the past inhabitants.

What makes this route special for me is a personal, long-developed association with these lakes, bogs, beaches, hills, waterfalls, cabins and stories. It is a wonderful thing for a canoe tripper to have one pilgrimage route, where the yearly return takes on significance as a touchstone for the year ahead, where a specific site opens a floodgate of memories of situations and groups past, where major life lessons have been learned and revisited, where that once-a-year anticipated event is played out anew each time.

When I'm at the Lake Maskinonge base camp helping students prepare for the trip, and on the trip with each new group, I understand Jean-Jacques Rousseau's philosophy. Rousseau, like many of the 18th-century Romantics reacting against industrial growth, urged humanity to maintain fundamental ties to the Earth as a tonic for the soul. Each September, while on this familiar route, I am reminded of Rousseau's statement: "The closer to his natural condition man has stayed, the smaller is the difference between his faculties and his desires and consequently the less removed he is from being happy." There is a joy in sharing of this happiness, often a newfound happiness for newcomers.

A recent e-mail conversation with fellow outdoor educator and canoe tripper Bert Horwood allows me to examine this romantic blissful life. Bert tried his hand at providing characteristics of the Romantic movement:

- close to the earth; earthy, even raunchy
- innocent and simple in its material culture; minimal in contrivance, artifice and elaboration
- respectful of the powers and virtues of the common person; without an elite; welcoming and egalitarian
- exploring and accepting the world as it is
- balancing communal and individual development

He adds, "I've probably left some things out." But I find the list complete and compelling.

Now, after twenty years of starting each university school year on this route, and another ten years of off-and-on summer camp guiding — all those years of revisiting this place since I was a fourteen-year-old wide-eyed camper — I have some small understanding of the Australian Aborigine notion of songlines.

The indigenous peoples of Australia believe their homeland is "a narrative landscape," featuring knolls, rivers, depressions and ridges. All tell creation stories of their first ancestors in the Dreamtime. These land features and related stories are joined together into a complex web of a master story. Land and story are connected into travel routes. A saying, recorded in Bruce Chatwin's book *Songlines*, is worthy of contemplation:

*Sing the land or it dies.*
*Travel the land or it does not live in you.*
*And you do not live in it.*
*Give away your goods, or they are no good to you.*

I am fascinated by the songline idea. It offers an intriguing contemplative energy while on the trail. A celebration with the familiar can give us a glimpse into the sacredness of place and the deep relationships we can develop with place. The human and natural history stories we tell of the place, and the stories we generate, are our singing of the land. I do believe that places can get under your skin so as to live in you.

When people receive so joyously of an experience, the resulting swells of energy surprise all. The goods we possess, our usual wants, are easily forgotten in the stripped-down, back-to-basics lifestyle of simply traveling to new settings on the land each evening. Just being there is good. How did Pierre Trudeau put it in 1944? "You return not so much a man who reasons more, but a more reasonable man."

## Songs Along the Trail

I remember the first time I thought a ceremony with chocolate (and later a shot of rum) would be the right end to a portage celebration following a height-of-land watershed crossing. Now we repeat this each year with all groups at this spot. One inspired moment has generated many more.

Because of repeated reminders, I readily retain the magic of watching a black bear from a hilltop with a group who were seeing their first bear in the wilds. We tell the story to groups now and, for all, the place is a bit wilder.

I remember a magical night: a group huddled under a tarp for a long evening rain repeatedly singing Tracy Chapman's new song at the time, *Fast Car*. I remember another rainy night huddled in a now-demolished trapper's camp listening to a young man speak of his satisfaction in teaching a disabled boy to ride a bicycle at a special-needs summer camp. I was moved to tears.

I remember learning of a close call on another of our trips on a difficult catwalk portage (logs laid down over a boggy trail), where a young girl slipped with the wanigan in such a way that the tumpline was strangling her. Her guide arrived and revived her in the nick of time. She had been transporting the wanigan (a rectangular wooden box) improperly. It was a somber lesson, recalled each time I cross that catwalk, and retold again and again as a safety lesson

These memories become songs along the trail.

There are other songs along the trail, songs that sing out stories of the past. Comb the beach of our outpost base camp in an idle moment and you may find an arrowhead. This south-facing site would have been a choice camping spot for generations. We are following the land's traditions, as we are when we visit the area's pictograph site, seek out a late-season berry patch and climb the hill for the joys of a new perspective.

From indigenous peoples to surveyors (here in 1901, in this case), to trappers, loggers, tourists and canoe trippers — this landscape can tell tales of them all. One story involves a now caved-in cabin (perhaps the cabin in question, perhaps not — it matters little). Here on Wolf Lake, a young Donald "Curly" Phillips was cutting his teeth as a trapper woodsman. In April 1907, his trapping partner was found with two bullet holes in his body and a shotgun blast to his head. The rattled Phillips soon purchased a Colt revolver in Biscotasing. He continued to trap along the Chiniguichi watershed, but a year later left the Ontario north woods for a new life in the west. Perhaps he was spooked into leaving. Phillips would later go on to fame as a mountain guide in the Jasper, Alberta, area, and was involved in early climbs of Mount Robson in 1909. Each year, students stare in excitement and wonder as I retell this story at a long-abandoned Wolf Lake cabin.

We do the same at a Native pictograph site, at old trappers' cabins and at decaying logging chutes. Each of these places tells a story of the land through time.

I always revisit the pictograph site, where for years Bruce Murphy would take his group by evening candlelight for an on-the-water explanation and storytelling session. Linda Leckie rose before sunrise to organize her groups for a paddle and hilltop climb to celebrate the dawn. I would meet Zabe MacEachren's group each year at a beach campsite. In the evening, we would have a folk dance, voyageur style, with Zabe calling, as it were, and me playing guitar.

Certain experiences have come to live long as life lessons that I am grateful to remember with yearly visits. Stopping before a long portage, I had thought that a quiet relax, out of the wind and rain, with a Sigurd Olson reading passage, would serve the moment well. The group had other ideas. Finding the coincidence of all members donning bright yellow rainwear amusing, they proceeded in a giggly manner to prance about down to the beach rest-spot. Not the time for reflective Sigurd Olson. Somewhere in that moment, my teacher-driven leader tendency shifted, and I learned not to force an experience on a group who had equally worthwhile energies in another direction. I can vividly picture those dancing yellow raincoats, with me sitting dejected with soggy reading behind some shelter. The lesson here is to allow the group the space to follow their own positive energy. Not a bad lesson for a travel guide, teacher, friend and parent to hold on to, revisit and learn.

Another lesson to hold on to is how I now connect to a particular campsite and person. The weather on this trip had been very challenging. Repeated rain showers that soaked you to the bone were a daily and, at times, hourly experience. Between the blasts were calm, clear conditions. By the evening of day two, as a guide with many newcomers, I was stretched out mentally and emotionally. While setting up camp, yet another rain blast arrived. As we were rushing to secure a tarp shelter to salvage anything dry and eke out some comfort, I showed my frustration. An experienced student came up to me and offered a word of encouragement. "Akunamatata," he whispered in my ear. From *The Lion King*, popular at that time. It was what I needed. And, of course, the sky eventually cleared anyway. Yes, the weather was not to be feared, but I had missed a stroke or two that day and the friendly reminder is now embedded in my psyche, and connected to that campsite and fellow tripper. Thanks, Courtney! I pass the site each year now. Always there is a smile and reminder. Lessons learned and unwanted ways "unlearned."

Over time, as the landscape becomes familiar, there is the obvious and subtle evidence of changes. Seasonally, I delight in the changes brought on by changing water levels each year. High waters make that bog portage more difficult, but that swift runnable in canoes. Some years we feast on late August blueberries. Other years we catch the autumn colors.

Also, changes caused by human activities are evident. The extended road brings in more campers and changes forever a portage trail. This same road, over time, causes off-shoot roads to lead to shoreline campsites. A naturalist club wisely added thunder boxes to sites of increased use. An old mine site is reopened, later abandoned and left a junk heap and later still, cleaned up; all over a ten-year period. The odd new trail is cut by a snowmobile club. The affects of acid rain seem, with time, less pronounced with the south wind now than in the late 1970s.

So, this particular canoe-tripping backwater, typical of many Canadian Shield routes, has become a celebration of the familiar for me. Certainly I am not familiar with it in the everyday sense that others in the area know. It is a traveler's celebration: now, with time, a pilgrimage of sorts. Part of the excitement is sharing the places anew with each new group of people. And part of the excitement is a personal touchstone of one's life moving gracefully, one hopes, through time in an enduring landscape that allows a vision of past, present and future to come together for a time.

Songlines! Without the respect, care and love for a familiar place, how do we find our own personal contemplations? The take-home message, so to speak, is this: seek out and establish your own celebration of the familiar with family, friends and students; learn and create the stories of the place; sing, travel, give away the goods and energies of your soul.

# Madawaska River
## *Mad About Southern Ontario's Rapid-Filled Gem*

C. E. S. Franks

If I HAD TO CHOOSE ONE RIVER THAT IS FUN TO CANOE IN ALL SEASONS, from April to November, one that is easily accessible by car for canoeists in southern Ontario and Quebec, that always has enough water to be runnable, and that at all but lowest water levels has some rapids that are at least fun if not a challenge for the canoeist, it would be the Madawaska. Specifically, I would pick the stretch from Palmer Rapids to Griffith, usually called the Lower Madawaska.

I have canoed this piece of river more times than I can remember. The most recent was an early spring trip, when it was still in flood. My neighbors, two parents and three daughters, and I found that with three busy adults and three even busier teenagers we had to limit our time for the trip to two days, so this time we made it a comfortable, non-camping event. On Saturday morning we drove up from Kingston to Palmer Rapids, about a three-hour drive, and reached our put-in at the rapids above the town. Not our first river of the year, because canoeing begins on the Salmon and Moira Rivers

near Kingston in late March, but by May these rivers nearer home are drying up. The Madawaska is our first semi-wilderness river, and the beginning of another stage in the canoeing year.

The water was high, higher than most years in early May. There's a hydro dam, for water storage above these rapids, that controls the Madawaska's flow. Signs beside the parking place said the flow was deliberately being kept high to allow pickerel to spawn, and instructed us to avoid canoeing or embarking along much of the shore because that was favorite pickerel spawning habitat.

There's a vigorous chute at the top of the rapids, with a huge pool below. Here we practiced our eddy turns and front ferrying, trying to get some of the rust out of our system after a long winter off the water. No matter how many years I've been canoeing, I still get a rush at that first standing wave hitting the bow, the surge of the canoe as the draw pulls the bow around, the bounce of the canoe over the long series of waves, cold spray in the face, the coordination of two paddlers leaning, bracing with their knees, trying to get body and mind together and remember how to work with the water, not against it.

Success. Nobody dumps. Heather, in the bow of my canoe, does an immaculate cross-draw and we spin into the tongue of fast water. The canoe bucks on the waves as though it is being tossed about by a huge, writhing sea serpent. The instructor of a nearby group on the river nods his head in acknowledgment of Heather's paddling as he watches many of his group practicing rescue techniques after involuntary dumps in the same powerful tongue of rushing water. We work on these eddy turns from both sides of the tongue for a while, and then start into the more difficult front ferries. The waves are big enough and the water fast enough that we can race across the tongue, surfing on the waves.

One university group camped on the south bank isn't even up yet. They must have been celebrating the end of the school year. We do one run of the bottom rapids before lunch. This bottom piece runs in a huge horseshoe shape around the peninsula where we've parked the cars. There's a pool as big as a small lake at the bottom, and an easy take-out in the quiet lake-water that marks the start of the short portage back up to the top. This time we take a break near the cars and have lunch. The sun shines on us. A few lazy bugs wander around, but this early in the year, no mosquitoes and no blackflies. Two weeks later, the blackflies will be horrendous. But now it's bliss.

Back on the water. It's easy to run this horseshoe rapids down the middle, where there's a clear line, and all the canoeist needs to do is avoid the rocks and keep out of the huge hole at the bottom — I've seen that hole swallow a canoe and spit it out into the lake a hundred feet further on. And I've seen a brand-new Kevlar break in two on the rocks. But we don't have any problems.

In fact, it's almost too easy. The high water has drowned out much of the rapids and covered most of the biggest rocks so that there's no eddy to tuck into behind them. I like to work on whitewater skills in this sort of rapid, going across the river from eddy to eddy, moving upstream in an eddy to try and hit a different one behind a rock upstream from where we began, doing some stretches backwards, some forwards, seeing how many eddies we can hit in a stretch.

Today that sort of fun is limited. We don't go near the north shore because of spawning pickerel. Most of the middle of the river and even the south shore are drowned out into one fast-flowing sheet of black water. But we do find enough to keep us busy. Down to the bottom of the rapids. Portage back up. Try it again, and this time try to hit the tops of the eddies we were sloppy at the time before, try to find new eddies, look for waves to surf on, keep moving, keep changing our patterns. By now many other groups are running the rapids. We take sadistic glee in watching some of them miss their brace or lean the wrong way and take an icy swim. Oh well, a dump in cold spring water makes a great cure for a hangover! And it provides lots of opportunities for working on rescue techniques.

One poor bunch of neophytes has been sitting in their canoes at the top of the rapids being lectured by their instructor for hours. Perhaps he'll allow them to try and run something before it gets dark, but we won't be around to find out. It's five o'clock and time for us to get off the river.

## I Did Something Stupid . . . Like Lean the Wrong Way

Now this is where my narrative departs from the usual wilderness canoeing epic. We don't find a campsite and pitch our tents, brace ourselves with a skinny dip in the frigid river and cook a great wilderness meal. No, we return to our cars, put the canoes on the racks and drive back to Denbigh, about 20 miles (32 km) away, where we've reserved rooms at the Swiss Inn. Once there we have hot showers, change our clothes and go down to have an excellent meal in the Inn's restaurant. Some of us have Volaille Jurassienne, a Swiss version of fried chicken, some have steak, some ham. We all have homemade strawberry and rhubarb pie. I have several beers. We go to bed clean, comfortable, well-exercised and well-fed.

Bright and early Sunday morning we have a full breakfast of bacon and eggs, toast, coffee and juice. Two of the girls have pancakes, with the local maple syrup slathered on top. This is going to be a good, full day of canoeing. We need our energy. Into the cars and up Highway 41 to Griffith. Turn left on the dirt logging road that will take us to the put-in at Aumonds Bay. But 5 miles (8 km) along, we reach an impasse. The road has been washed out in the spring floods and a steep cut 3 feet deep (1 m) and 10 feet (3 m) across blocks our way. We can't do anything about this today, so we backtrack to the Swiss Inn, retrace yesterday's route to Palmer Rapids and then head east to Quadeville and the other way in to Aumonds Bay. By the time we've finished our shuttle and parked one car at the take-out at Buck Bay, we're nearly two hours later getting on the water than I had intended, but that's life. Still lots of time to have some fun.

Lord love a duck, the water's lovely! One lone and very accomplished kayaker accompanies us to the first rapid, where he revels in the holes while waiting for his companions. We'd heard him tell his buddies at Aumonds Bay that he'd come here to kayak, not to drive, and he had taken off with us while they made their car shuttle. Not having much sympathy with this sort of charm and subtlety, we ignore the chap and leave him alone. He gets bored enough in his solitary splendor that he pulls into shore as we carry on downstream.

In full flow, the stretches of Snake Rapids succeed one another. We run them all except Rifle Chute, which is as high as I've ever seen it in May. It's not hard to run, but if anything goes wrong it can be difficult to perform a rescue, and I'm not convinced our crew is yet strong enough to do a proper rescue. Besides, Rifle Chute is easy to carry around. When I first started canoeing the Madawaska more than thirty years ago, the blade of a paddle was nailed to a tree here, just in from the rapids. Written on it was someone's name and the date of his drowning in Rifle Chute. The paddle is long gone, probably a souvenir in someone's den. Another piece of the river's history disappeared.

Catherine and I dump in Racquette Rapids, the last of the Snake Rapids. It's my fault. Catherine is a competent canoeist. I try a different way of running this piece that looks good because the water's so high, but it's still too shallow on this route, we hit a rock, my paddle gets caught between some submerged rocks and I do something stupid, like lean the wrong way. Oh well, this is a learning and skill-honing trip. If you don't dump at least once in a while, you aren't discovering the limits of hand, paddle, eye, canoe and good sense. No problem with the rescue. There's a huge, pointed rock at the bottom of the usual channel down this rapid. For many years it had an aluminum canoe wrapped around it, but that's gone now, too.

We pull out at Buck Bay, haul our canoes up the slippery slope and portage to the car. Still no bugs. Some patches of snow left in the woods. Get back to the other car at Aumonds Bay, and then the long route back to Kingston via Quadeville and Palmer's Rapids. At Griffith, we go into the store and make a donation towards the upkeep of the forestry road into Aumonds Bay. Once again we stop at the Swiss Inn for dinner. It's the best food on the route. Heather, a learning driver, drives my car part of the way home. On the way, we stop at a place I will not identify and find that the fiddleheads won't be ready for another week or so.

## Should Be a Heritage River

We could have canoed other parts of the Madawaska. A few miles upstream from Palmer's Rapids is the Middle Madawaska, or Bell's Rapids, where the Madawaska Kanu Centre (MKC) is located. They have marvelous rapids at their front door and run training courses from spring to fall. My neighbors intend to take a weeklong course there this summer. I took a course more than twenty-five years ago, and I date the real beginning of my learning about running whitewater to that experience.

Even above MKC, from Whitney, just outside the border of Algonquin Park, to the even smaller village of Madawaska, there's another wonderful piece of river, the Upper Madawaska. That is usually runnable as a daytrip from mid-May to mid-June.

Below Buck Bay, the Madawaska is still good canoeing all the way to Griffith. It used to be good canoeing along the next stretch as well, but it got drowned out by a hydro dam in 1967, creating Centennial Lake. Centennial Lake, in turn, has been developed into a cottager's and motorboater's heaven. Canoeists beware. But the 15-mile (24 km) stretch from Aumonds Bay to Griffith remains an ideal piece of river for a leisurely summer paddle, with a night or two of camping among the fragrant white pines. I have run the entire distance with a powerful companion — Brian Osborne, a geographer who in his younger days was a first-class rugby player — all the way from Aumonds Bay to Griffith in less than five hours, but that was rushing things. This piece of river responds better to being run slowly and lovingly. But remember, between 13,000 and 15,000 canoeists a year paddle this stretch, so get on the river early and camp early.

A couple of years back, when the Parkers, who were very experienced flat-water canoeists, were learning whitewater skills so they could paddle the South Nahanni River in the Northwest Territories the following summer, we made a three-day, two-night trip out of the Aumonds Bay to Griffith route. We had time to savor each rapid, to watch the birds (one great horned owl, two osprey, many herons, a pileated woodpecker) and a family of otters, to camp early at Rifle Chute and watch the canoeists dump — one of the great spectator events in Ontario canoeing — and to take the time to swim, read, reminisce. The Parkers had a great trip, with no problems, on the Nahanni. Alison, the youngest, was only twelve years old when they did that trip.

Slate Falls, the only real portage on the stretch from Aumonds Bay to Griffith, and a short and easy one at that, has a new portage trail on the north side of the river. On the old portage, on the south, I showed the Parkers the names of lumberjacks carved in the hard granite bedrock above the river at the portage's end. I have often wondered whether these lumberjacks put their names there as something to do to amuse themselves while they were waiting in one of the innumerable delays that came along with driving logs down a river, or whether the names commemorate comrades who drowned at the falls. We'll probably never know.

I do know that David Thompson, the great explorer and mapmaker of the Canadian West, canoed the entire Madawaska River in 1837. He was making a survey for the government of Upper Canada to determine whether the route from Georgian Bay up the Muskoka River, across what is now

Algonquin Park and down the Madawaska to the Ottawa would make a good route for a canal. Even that early there were lumberjacks along this piece of river, and not far below Thompson bought some potatoes from a settler. He and his crew were very hungry by then. It was late October, and the fishing and hunting had been poor in the barren hostile wilderness along his route. They were cold, wet and exhausted as well as hungry. Sketches in his diary show exactly the same huge rocks standing upright below Slate Falls that a canoeist can see today.

Fortunately and wisely, the government decided not to attempt to construct the canal. It would not have been possible or economic then, and it wouldn't be now. But by now most of the Madawaska has been harnessed for hydro power. Twenty years ago Ontario Hydro had plans for another dam, at Slate Falls. That would have destroyed the river from a canoeist's perspective, though Ontario Hydro touted the increased (and largely mythical) opportunities for recreation from the Slate Falls dam.

Only the few stretches I have mentioned are in a near-pristine state. The forest along the river is still being lumbered. Canoeists should avoid the river in deer hunting season. Each year there are more cottages. The Ontario government has made a wild river park out of the section from Aumonds Bay to Griffith and out of the Upper Madawaska stretch from Whitney to the boundary of Algonquin Park. This means that the river itself, and the adjacent 200 yards of land where it is owned by the Crown, are protected from development and commercial logging. I would like to see the entire Madawaska River protected by the Canadian Heritage Rivers System. In fact, I would like to see David Thompson's entire route from Georgian Bay to the Ottawa River be designated a Heritage River. It certainly has enough history and beauty to justify the designation.

There are few beautiful, pristine, exciting and rapid-filled rivers in Southern Ontario accessible in less than a half-day's travel by more than a third of Canada's population. The Madawaska is the best of these few. Heritage not only means a historic past — which the Madawaska has — but also that we leave a heritage of something we treasure for future generations. This the Madawaska can and should be.

# No-Name Trent-Peterborough Canoe Group
## A Whimsical History: 1966 to 2001

Bruce W. Hodgins

A SUGGESTION WAS MADE THAT OUR ILLUSTRIOUS CANOE GROUP NEEDED *a written record. This is an attempt. It is based on oral tradition, memory and no documentation. It is autobiographical and subjective, as it must be. It borders on myth.*

## Origins

The Group emerged in the spring of 1966. The founder and first leader was Alan Wilson; he was the originator and first leader of many things at Trent University. I was the junior co-founder and second member. Our two families had moved to Peterborough the previous summer, when Alan and I took over Trent's History program in the second year of the university's operation. Our first local canoe run took place immediately after breakup,

on the Indian River, from Highway 7 down past Lang to Keene — the river only canoeable for about a month.

Alan and I first met in 1957, while he was teaching at Acadia (Wolfville, Nova Scotia) and I was at Prince of Wales, Charlottetown (Prince Edward Island). Alan had canoe-raced at Dartmouth-Halifax as a youth and was a Maritime champion. He had also canoe-fished with his father and brother. I had done a lot of canoeing and canoe-trip leading at Wabanaki on Beausoleil Island from 1944 to 1955 and at Wanapitei on Lake Temagami since 1956, but had not done much spring paddling in the south. We hit it off immediately, with Canadian history, regionalism and canoeing as the vital topics.

In the mid to late 1960s, besides the annual, reinitiating run on the Indian River, we began to engage in other jaunts. They soon included a run from above Lakefield (sometimes at Young's Point) down the Otonabee past what became Champlain College and the Bata Library to Little Lake in Peterborough. At first we followed the canal route from Nassau, using the Trent Canal locks when available. We once even had the lift lock put just the two of us, in one canoe, through the system.

Our early companions were recruited rather casually. They sometimes included Roy Bowles. Alf Cole (the registrar) went once or twice, as did Walter Pitman (ex-MP, associate registrar, Trent and soon MPP, on the flooded Indian River in his dress shoes), David Cameron (soon to be dean) and John Earnshaw. There were also a few students, including Romeyn Stevenson, Jamie Benidickson and the occasional Wanapitei summer staff person passing through town or studying at Trent. At this stage, the Group was primarily male — with my wife, Carol, helping with the shuttles or lifts, the two kids (Shawn and Geoff) in tow.

Alan and I continued with the spring canoe-fishing extended weekend to Wanapitei until 1976. Alan's brother, my cousin Daryl, Ivan Bateman, Ian Sandeman and Dale Standen were often with us. When I ran for Parliament in June 1968, Ivan and I campaigned for a few days from a canoe.

## The Seventies

In the spring of 1970, I was in Canberra, Australia, and therefore not involved at all in the spring paddling. That autumn, however, I went with Marcus Bruce, Michael Jenkins and Tony Lovink on a student-run overnight from Haultain down Eels Creek, across Stoney and down the Otonabee to Champlain.

By this time, Carol and I had started family spring daytripping with two or three other families, or alone, with Shawn and Geoff. We traveled Long Lake–Deer Bay Creek and Eels Creek down from Haultain — all four of us and Prince, our collie, in one wood-canvas canoe. Other families often with us included Cyril and Jenny Carter, the Scarths, the Batemans and the Standens.

During the mid-1970s, with the arrival of John Jennings to the Trent History department and with the involvement of several women, especially Carol Hodgins and Bernice Standen, as well as an impetus from Wanapitei's expansion into an adult tripping program, the Group really found its stride.

Our runs kept expanding to include the Mississauga from Catchacoma to Highway 36, the Salmon from Roblin to below Lonsdale, and the middle Moira River from southeast of Tweed. Alan was not always present, but he remained a key figure in the annual York River run, which by then included Paul Goddard of Sir Sandford Fleming College.

John Jennings and Keith Walden had joined Trent History at the same time. Alan wanted both as instant, active members of the Group. John, who had lots of tripping experience behind him, including the Nahanni, fitted in. Keith, however, did not take to the canoe. In their first spring on the York, during a Good Friday snowstorm, Keith was without long underwear, gloves or winter clothes and almost expired of hypothermia. He also had two tips with John on the Otonabee. Soon after this, Alan, Jamie Benidickson (now a colleague) and John Jennings ran the upper Beaver — in flood and snow — a trip that became a forced overnight, one that lives on in legend.

Harvey McCue (Native Studies) and Roy Bowles (Sociology, and a devout Quaker) were active for several years. Alan Wilson, together with Roy, the then-dean George Hamilton, and John Earnshaw, attempted a too-early York River run. Sliding fast down a portage hill in the wet snow, Roy, George and John aboard the same canoe, they submerged totally on entry. "Oh, dear," said Roy, as he briefly sank out of sight.

By then and until at least the mid-1980s our sons, Shawn and Geoff, were regular participants and their cousins, Glenn and Eric Hodgins, frequent occasionals. So were, over time, several Trent students, especially Marcus Bruce (from 1971), Tom Roach, Debbie Hutchins (Baldwin), Claudette Languedoc (Kohut), Mary Ann Haney and, after 1979, Nicole Jarvis — all of them also long-serving Wanapitei tripping staff.

Sometime in the late 1970s, the Wilsons and Goddards were on an extended joint family trip down the usual route on the York. Alan had just purchased (not with my advice) a very lightweight, cedar-strip, clear fiber-glass but ribless canoe in South River. He filled up in the last rapid, the canoe nosedived and hit deep rocks. Alan held onto the painter which neatly pulled out the bow deck. The canoe totally opened up into a slab and was abandoned. The next weekend he and I retrieved it and took it back to the manufacturer, crowded by throngs of prospective buyers. We were served tea in the kitchen and promised a rebuilding in only three days. That was done, but Alan retired his boat to his haunt in Nova Scotia. It was never seen again. By now, most of us were speedily converting, for spring canoeing and whitewater trips, from wood-canvas and fiberglass to ABS "rubber," or at least strong Kevlar.

During the early 1980s, our activities became more sophisticated and the membership of the Group much clearer and broader. John Jennings and Nicola Jarvis became a couple and were married in 1983 in Calgary, returning from leading an adult Far Northern Wanapitei trip on the Blackstone-Peel. Gwyneth Hoyle, the librarian at Peter Robinson College, and Shelagh Grant, later an adjunct professor and expert on Nunavut, both became major contributing members of the Group. They were soon joined by Jon Grant (Quaker Oats). Occasionally we were joined by Sandra Gillis (from Ottawa), Ned Franks (Queen's), and Peter Milliken (now House of Commons Speaker).

Our eastern runs included the Salmon, often the lower Moira, occasion-ally the Black and Skootamatta, and at least once the middle Mississippi. The runs to the north usually included the Irondale down from Gooderham.

In 1981, I had been asked by Trent's president to work with the mar-velous Kirk Wipper in an attempt to have his Kanawa Canoe Museum — now the Canadian Canoe Museum — moved from Kandalore to Peter-borough. Soon many members of the Group as well as Fred Helleiner (Geography) were all officially involved in that tumultuous long-term project. Also during this time, Marg Hobbs and I, along with several members of the Group, including Gwyneth Hoyle, John Wadland and John Jennings, worked together to produce *Nastawgan*, a 1985 book on historic journeys by canoe.

Around 1984, the Group had a large gang attempt on the Big East (in the area between Dwight and Huntsville). It was a psychological disaster; cold, snow and floodwaters necessitated an almost impossible portage up a steep hill. Alan, at the top, thought he was dead, but on hearing me realized he was clearly not in heaven — and told me so!

In 1987, Alan and Budge Wilson retired to Nova Scotia. In the spring of 1988, I was very sick with pulmonary emboli and could not participate. In 1989, I was weak but recovering from the operation, so paddled, but took it easy. For the Group, the fun and fellowship continued. The Jennings and the Grants were central in the late 1980s, and then Carol and I, and the Standens, returned to play crucial roles.

Around 1990, Bill Cormode, an engineer from Peterborough, began to participate regularly in most of the Group's spring runs. He became a very active member. Around the same time, Cathy Fretz, Patti Sharpe and Heather Dunlop joined in. As women who were not spouses of other members, they brought new dimensions to the fun and nature of the club.

## 1992–2001

During these years, the activities of the Group flourished, with the Jennings running and hosting the annual reinitiating Indian River run and the family-oriented Eels Creek jaunt. We continued to return to the Salmon, the lower Moira and the Irondale each year, and for eight years now have paddled the wonderful Opeongo, east of Algonquin Park.

In 1994, we explored the middle Moira from Highway 7. In 1995, as suggested by Shawn Hodgins and Dr. Glenn Brown (ex-Trent, Wanapitei, and now of Queen's), we ran the lower Beaver with great joy and feeling. We revisited the challenging and exciting mid-lower Madawaska, having not run it collectively for several years. Dr. Barry Campbell from Tamworth and Kingston was with us several times. Cousin Daryl Hodgins usually rejoined us at least once each year; so did my brother Larry. Also, Dave Goslin and Dr. Barry Diceman have for some time paddled as an integral part of the Group, usually two or times each year.

The Group's activities and membership and that of the Canadian Canoe Museum often interfaced, intermixed and even competed. Five members of the Group were on the CCM board. After the Trent-linked committee took over the old canoe museum board, Jamie Benidickson (who had co-authored with me *The Temagami Experience* and by then was a professor of law at Ottawa) became for several year its president. In 1997, he published *Idleness, Water, and a Canoe: Reflections on Paddling for Pleasure*. John Jennings soon became executive vice president of the CCM and, on leave from Trent, served full-time for several years. Many in the Group still go on Wanapitei Far Northern trips or have been on its staff, and many members attend and contribute to the Wilderness Canoeing Association's January Colloquium at Monarch Park in Toronto.

In 1995, Cathryn Rees, an active canoeist from Bradford and now partner of Bill Cormode, became a most valued addition. Carol Hodgins was described by the *Toronto Star* in May 1995 as "Canada's undisputed queen of the campfire kitchen" with her 1982 *Wanapitei Canoe Tripping Cookbook*, which has sold 10,000 copies, and her second volume, *Wanapitei Canoe Trippers' Cookbook: Wilderness Cooking, the Environment and You*, was published in 1999. Gwyneth Hoyle co-authored with me in 1994 *Canoeing North into the Unknown: A Record of Travel: 1874 to 1974*.

The Group is never exclusive nor exclusionary, just very important. Alan Law, a young Australian sociology professor at Trent, and his partner, Hanna, became significantly involved in 1998, and he is now one of our top whitewater experts. Dale Minor (outdoor activist and researcher) and Jean Manore (historian) met on our canoe jaunts, married, and have become two of our most active participants; Dale is also a whitewater expert. Sharon and Larry Pearson (Larry is director of outdoor education at Crestwood Secondary School in Peterborough, a program which usually involves a week-long trip in Temagami country) are also quite active; they live by the Indian River, just downstream from the Jennings.

In 1999, John Jennings, Doreen Small and I edited *The Canoe in Canadian Cultures*. It flowed out of the Canexus II conference on canoe cultures held at Trent in 1996, and included articles by me, John, Doreen and by leading canoeing writers such as James Raffan, Timothy Kent, Bob Henderson, Toni Harting, Gwyneth Hoyle, Kirk Wipper and Becky Mason. In 2000, Bernice Standen took over the coordination and communications for the Group, leaving me happily as only the honorary chief.

The full active list of participants (notified of all prospective runs) probably now stands a little above twenty: Bill Cormode and Cathryn Rees, Barry Diceman, Heather Dunlop, Cathy Fretz, Dave Goslin, Shelagh and Jon Grant, who are now only occasional participants (Jon is president of the Canadian Canoe Museum), Bruce and Carol Hodgins, Alan Law, Gwyneth Hoyle, John and Nicole Jennings, Dale and Bernice Standen, Larry and Sharon Pearson, Jean Manore and Dale Minor, and Patti Sharp.

Occasionals include Bev Winny and John Moss, Robin and Rosemary Maughan, Hilary Heath and Bob Boutilier. Shawn Hodgins remains an important river advisor.

In 2001, we made the usual river runs, at least one day every weekend through April and May and two days on the Victoria holiday. During the weekend before the holiday, we ran, for the first time as the Group, the upper Madawaska (four canoes only) from below Whitney; this was in exciting but rather low water. The Victoria holiday runs were on the Opeongo and the lower Madawaska (Snake Rapids complex) in a secondary, rather high flow. We again stayed one, two or three overnights at the Cormode-Rees cottage below the middle Madawaska.

In 2001, we had thirteen canoes on the Irondale; we therefore split into two groups, meeting only at lunch and at the finish. There were even more on the multi-generational family-oriented run on Eel's Creek. Carol and I had with us son Shawn and his wife, Liz, our son Geoff (his wife, Pat Bowles, was with us on other occasions) and our daughter Gillian, and her husband, Grant Nesbitt, plus all five of our grandchildren, with thirteen-year-old Holly in a stern position. Hilary and Bob had their kids, Lisa and Andrew, with them (as they had per usual on the Irondale). The Jennings were there, with daughter Julia almost a regular participant (son Michael had been on the Opeongo). On the Eel's Creek run we had plenty of time to play at High Falls and to cut fiddleheads.

As a Group, we seem no longer to be "pushing the envelope" — that is, upgrading the difficulty of the rapids that we shoot or the height of the water of the rivers that we run. I turned seventy in early 2001. Our top skilled whitewater participants are now probably Dale Minor and Alan Law, and they with others are happily still increasing their challenge on other excursions. Most of us look for mood, sensation, reflection, wilderness, collective experience and fellowship, together with measured adventure. We do find all of this, but it all must be renewed and rediscovered yearly. Of eleven people on an August 2001 trip on the Soper in Nunavut, six were from the Group and four were other Peterborough friends.

Several *après canot* dinners each season have now become very important. They help to hold the friendships together. They facilitate the myriad number of diverse canoeing tales — both those of the Group and of our usually separate longer and Far Northern canoe trips — all of which make up a collective heritage and growing number of myths.

Alan Law, who studies the culture of outdoor adventure recreation (first of surf-boarding in Australia and then downhill skiing and skydiving in Canada), is in the process of analyzing our canoeing Group's importance and longevity in comparison to more institutionalized canoe clubs. Ironically, he thinks it is our looseness and lack of any real membership, dues, officers, and so on that have kept it going and so important to our lives.

The looseness does help keep internal politics at bay. We love the anarchy of our organization and the quiet collective self-discipline and mutual help on the waterways. We have the J-strokes, the back paddles and the pries in the stern and the high braces and cross-draws in the bow. We have the overall skills with the back and front ferries. We do not need a collective rudder.

*A somewhat different version of the pre-1995 portion of this article appeared in the* Peterborough Review, *I, 4 (1995).*

# Rupert River
## *Profound Portages . . . and Poetry*

Teen Sivell

With a dreadful sinking feeling, I realized we were in the wrong place in a very large river — the Rupert in northern Quebec. My two canoe mates and I, already on our knees, didn't have time to pray. We capsized in a flash.

Tumbling and swimming in the numbingly cold water, I was gasping for breath when out of the corner of my eye I saw the flash of a paddle. We were being rescued by our friends from lunch.

On a gravel bar, with a fire blazing, we tried to decide on what to do next: stay put, move on, dry gear here or at a better site. From the depths of a sleeping bag, beside the fire, came this cheering voice: "And time yet for a hundred indecisions,/ And for a hundred visions and revisions,/ Before the taking of a toast and tea."

I was co-leader of this eighteen-day trip, back in 1974. Among other things, it was an opportunity to see the land and water threatened by a proposed mammoth hydroelectric development. This trip was also my first real exposure to poetry. In moments of duress, it is still that line of T. S. Eliot's that pops into my head, lightens my concern and lets me carry on clear headed.

Among the professionals entrusted to my care, all of whom were at least a decade older than me, was Nick Lary, an English and Russian literature professor from York University, in Toronto. He and the other bowperson, Marg, a nurse, would spell each other off and when not paddling rested in the middle of the canoe. I've never forgotten swinging my paddle day after day while listening to the poetry of the Romantics and the Beats. I also learned about Charles Dickens and Fyodor Dostoevsky and heard everything from Robert Service to Lord Tennyson, but it's the T. S. Eliot I remember the most.

> *"For I have known them all already, known them all: –*
> *Have known the evenings, mornings, afternoons,*
> *I have measured out my life with coffee spoons."*

We started this canoe trip near Lake Matagami, paddled upstream to the height of land into the Arctic watershed, across the Rupert Carry, from the Broadback system to the Rupert River, and down the Rupert to James Bay.

On a big lake like Matagami, headlands in the distance fade and merge, shades of blue and gray also shift and change. The next point grows no nearer for the longest while, and muscles ache and clothing chafes. But I was aching only with happiness. We were out! The lake was calm. My paddle slipped in and out of the cool gray water and the shore slid by ever so slowly, scenting our way with rushes and grasses, clay banks and poplar.

I was off roaming, "head gone one place, arms still here," as an Ojibwa grandmother in Temagami used to say. I thought of intrepid paddlers like Sigurd Olsen, Eric Morse and my cousin, Alec Hall, then back, as always, to aboriginal people and the land.

When I came out of my reverie, I realized Nick was tired. "Nick," I said, "switch sides whenever you want. It'll rest your arms."

"Oh, thank you," he replied. "But I think I'd really rather lie down."

And he did. Flopped back on the packs behind the bow seat; he lay like he was dead. I remember no concern, just surprise. How could a 10-mile (16 km) jaunt down a calm lake make him tired? That night, as we sat around the campfire, I noticed Nick's hands were blistered, his eyes bleary and the back of his neck raised in welts from blackflies. I told him about Father Charles Albanel, a Jesuit, reaching Lake Mistassini in 1678 despite thinking he would die of weariness and exposure. In retrospect, it probably didn't have the cheering effect I intended.

The days rolled on and the sky remained one color, soon dubbed James Bay gray. The big lakes stretched ahead and gray waters sloshed about. Rain swept over in bands most days. When the sun did break through, it was not a moment to be taken for granted. And we soaked in all the rays we could. Still, it seemed most of the trip was undertaken in cold, wet, stiff clothing.

Wading upstream, against the swift currents of the Waswanipi and Chensagi Rivers, we were wet to the waist. But it was fun, hauling the canoe like a recalcitrant horse against the current, reading the rapids in reverse and working the bow and stern painters to make the canoe dance up the eddies.

Where we couldn't line or pull up, we portaged. Most were long and hard — overgrown tangles of windfalls and muskeg, steep clay banks and rock-strewn mud. While cool, gray days meant few bugs, there were no swims after a long, hard carry; no leisurely basks in the sun and few nights admiring the stars.

A week into the trip, we reached the height of land, an unprepossessing puddle of a lake. We pulled over a beaver dam and instantly we were in the Arctic watershed. While it was just one bug bite further, it was a turning point — we were pointed downstream. The rains continued, the skies stayed gray and the shorelines of ragged spruce and desolate sandbanks went on and on. Nick's paddle now swung in a steady rhythm on the lakes or pulled us hard into back eddies of big rapids.

With trip participants so much older than me, conversation was fascinating. I heard principles of physics and tales of collecting camel urine in Africa. Most of all, though, I heard poetry.

When I teased Nick about his ill-fated endeavors to keep his feet dry, he murmured:

"I grow old . . . I grow old . . .
I shall wear the bottoms of my trousers rolled."

## Worse Than One Mosquito in Your Ear All Night

On our tenth day out, I got sick . . . miserably sick. Being ill on a trip is awful, and worse, makes the workload even harder for everyone else. In the middle of my co-leader's canoe, I lay in a codeine-induced stupor with the hood of my semi-porous raincoat pulled over my head as the water pooled beneath me and crept up my back.

Three days later, I still wasn't up to carrying my canoe, and so, carrying only paddles and a light pack, enjoyed a walk of rare beauty. We were portaging across Long Point on Lake Evans. Beginning on a spectacular and vast white-sand beach, the one-and-half-mile (2.5 km) carry saved us a 20-mile (32 km) paddle. The day was sunny and I enjoyed the warmth radiating on my neck and back. The trail was reasonably clear, and where it crossed an open section, I feasted on blueberries and cloudberries. I'll never forget the taste of those delicious, delicate berries.

A bit further, I came upon a bear skull mounted on a stake about 4 feet (1.2 m) high. The skull still had daubs of blue paint on its forehead; I rested a while in front of it. Cree hunters had left the skull — a gesture of reverence, thanking the bear for giving its life for theirs. I rested a while in front of it, comfortable, like I was visiting in someone's backyard.

"Men/ must be born/ and reborn/ to belong/ Their bodies must be formed/ of the dust/ of their forefather's/ bones." — From Luther Standing Bear's *Land of the Spotted Eagle*.

Between us and the fast-flowing Rupert lay one last long, rugged portage. The Rupert Carry is 3.5 miles (5.5 km) of overgrown trail, followed by a 2-mile (3 km) trip across Wettigo Lake (we sailed; it felt great) and finishing with a 1,000-yard portage.

On the Rupert at last, and under a sunny sky, we paddled to our food cache, delivered by plane a few days before in the abandoned village of Nemiscau. Nemiscau, set high on bluffs overlooking lake and river, was one of the most beautiful places I've ever seen. Its people had been told to leave by Hydro Quebec; the village and land awaited flooding (the proposed dam would make this whole area one big lake).

Canoes heavily loaded once again, we pushed on down the river. Over the next few days there were miles of shootable rapids, and despite headwinds and the cool weather, it was great fun. The shores sped by and the river raced ahead calling us to follow. The current made my paddle hum in my hands.

One day, just as we finished lunch, two solo paddlers, in green canoes, pulled in. The centuries dropped away and, apart from the fiberglass canoes, we were looking into the faces of coureurs de bois. Big men, black-bearded and eyes full of humor, they stood barefoot in ankle-deep water while having tea with us. In French and a bit of English, we learned they'd been out for a month, each carrying a fishing rod, rifle, tea and a little food.

After lunch, our friends led and we followed until my canoe capsized. When our friends saw we were all right, they paddled away and soon disappeared from sight. We never saw them again.

We repacked and returned to the river, through miles of swifts punctu-ated by bigger sets. We portaged around the magnificent Oatmeal Falls, depressed by the sights and sounds of heavy equipment crossing the bridge high over the river.

That night, the road somewhere behind us, I tossed and turned for hours; the distant whine on the highway worse than one mosquito in your ear all night. The next morning, gathered around the breakfast fire, I grumbled about my poor night's rest. "Ahh," said Nick, looking up over the rim of his coffee mug. "The muttering retreats/ Of restless nights in one-night cheap hotels."

We were nearing the end of the trip.

Approaching the Fours, a series of thundering falls where the Rupert has its last major drop before the Bay, we were apprehensive, knowing a whole day of portaging was ahead. We began with a 1,000-yard portage, fol-lowed by a hairy-scary paddle directly across to the far shore. Below, the falls plunged into a veil of mist — the home of Missipishew, the great lynx water-spirit. Portaged 900 yards. We rode the turbulent, foamy water a few hundred yards to the top of the third falls. Portaged 1,300 yards through windfalls and tangle. Scratched, mud-spattered and with shoulders aching, we arrived at a road and carried along its dusty gravel for a quarter mile (400 m) of relief. Then it was just 200 yards more.

Finally, we pitched tents, collapsed and lay in exhausted heaps. Only Chigascatagemi Falls to carry around next day. Trip is ending. Only a couple more days to Rupert's House.

In Inuit, the word to make poetry is the same as the word to breathe, and both derive from the word for the soul. A poem then, is words that have been infused with the breath of spirit. "Let me breathe of it," said an Inuit poet, "I have put my poem in order on the threshold of my tongue."

And T. S. Eliot:

*"Do I dare*
*Disturb the universe?*
*In a minute there is time*
*For decisions and revisions which a minute will reverse."*

## Epilogue

Hydro Quebec's plans to silence the Rupert were shelved in the early 1990s, and the people evicted from old Nemiscau return each summer.

My youngest son's name is Eliot.

# Offshore New Brunswick
## *The Tides of Fundy*

Scott Cunningham

THE WIND DESCENDED FROM THE NORTHEAST, AS IF ATTEMPTING TO stall the currents, but this only made the turbulent waters leap farther into the sky and curl into white foam that raced towards the horizon. Head Harbour Passage, so passive only minutes before, now surged and seethed.

Several harbor porpoises crossed my bow, but I made no attempt to remove my camera from its protective covering. What normally would have been cause for excitement scarcely turned my head. I kept my course for East Quoddy, alone on the cold, capricious currents of the bay.

Finally, I found shelter in the tiny cove below the lighthouse. Cold and drenched, I waited out the squall. I'd pushed my limits and had no desire to challenge the Fundy again that day.

The Bay of Fundy is one of the world's great natural wonders. Twice each day this funnel-shaped basin rises and falls with a tidal range of almost mythical proportions. The record of 52 feet (15.5 m) has been claimed by the upper reaches, but even at the mouth the tide often exceeds 20 feet (6 m). Its vast influence even escapes the bay proper where it runs into Maine and around onto Nova Scotia's southern shore.

At the head of the bay, the relentless tidal currents carve soft sedimentary rock, releasing sand and mud that color the water and create seemingly endless flats and marshes. At the other end, resistant bastions of volcanic rock have created the Fundy Isles. Continual upwelling distributes nutrients and a biological productivity that has no equal in Eastern Canada. The prolific food chain ranges from microscopic plankton to the largest animals on Earth, the baleen whales. Large resident seabird populations, including the parrot-like Atlantic puffin, partake of this bounty, along with migrants traveling to and from northern nesting grounds. Particularly noteworthy are the flocks of semipalmated sandpipers that descend on the flats to gorge on the mud shrimp in preparation for their non-stop flight to South America. A kaleidoscope of rockweed, dulse, sea lettuce and maiden's hair fringes the bottom of an emptying bay. This is indeed an exquisite paddling destination.

## The Inner Islands —
## Seductive Juxtaposition of Land and Sea

The Fundy Isles are located in New Brunswick, at the entrance to the bay. However, they are even closer to the United States than to the Canadian mainland and the ownership of one, Machais Seal, is still disputed. They have long been neglected by the outdoor enthusiasts, who often follow the tourist throngs to more familiar (and better marketed) regional destinations. This is unfortunate; the experienced sea kayaker will find here a seductive juxtaposition of land and sea, of quaint coastal village, struggling coastal forests and a littoral zone that can stretch out hundreds of feet.

Deer Island is the smallest of the three major islands and the least visited. Its modest ferry carries you back in time to a quieter world where ornate homesteads with peaked gables and sculpted shingles reflect an earlier affluence. A ragged shoreline mingles with the indecisive water level and Old Sow, one of the largest whirlpools on Earth. Nearby, Campobello Island is joined to the United States by both a bridge and the Roosevelt connection (former U.S. President Roosevelt had a summer home here).

Of particular interest to the kayaker are the West Isles, a collection of sand and rock, seaweed and woods, that dot the waters between Deer and Campobello. Some of these isles scarcely breathe air at high water, while others are igneous outcrops that reach over 100 yards and cover several hundred acres. Except for the bald eagles, herons and seabirds, all are uninhabited.

This wasn't always the case, and on Adams Island, crumbling shacks now overlook disintegrating wharf pilings where boats once docked to load copper ore. Mounds of waste rock glistening with iridescent minerals surround the former pithead. On other islands, apple trees and lilac bushes betray a more pastoral past.

This area supports a thriving fishery that, far from detracting from, adds a human context, to the paddling experience. Here, the fishermen tend their traps, salmon cages and especially the weirs. These are ingenious devices of poles and nets that trick the herring into entering, then disorient them so that they can't escape. These waters have the largest concentration of such structures in the country. Abandoned weirs lurk below the floodwaters, waiting to skewer unsuspecting vessels.

The currents are often two to three knots, and sometimes stronger over shoals and through narrow channels where they are constricted and accelerated into ever-changing and confusing eddies. And they are cold! This is no place for the unguided novice, but with proper skills and experience it can be a safe and exhilarating destination.

## Grand Manan — Best Dulse in the East

Grand Manan, the largest of the islands in the Bay of Fundy, is a two-hour ferry ride from Blacks Harbour, New Brunswick. This isolated gem retains its historic maritime aura. The eastern side, where the population has settled, has a low, ragged relief and several sheltered harbors. It overlooks its own archipelago of twenty islands, and the largest, White Head, still supports a small community. The Wood Island settlement, on the other hand, has been abandoned since 1975.

Kent Island was purchased by Nelson Rockefeller as a sanctuary for eider ducks in the 1930s, and it has a summer research center run by Bowdoin College, Maine. All the other islands are now deserted year-round, including Gannet Rock, the last remaining manned light station in the Maritimes, until it was also automated in 1997.

On the western shore of Grand Manan, surrounded by 400-foot-high (120 m) cliffs of columnar basalt, is Dark Harbour, once a bustling summer community but now the site of a few shanties, a salmon pen and the best dulse (an edible seaweed) in the East. A plateau of gnarled, stunted spruce overlooks the strait and the coast of Maine, 10 miles (16 km) away.

Sea life flourishes in the rich waters. Humpback, fin and the endangered right whale feed offshore from early summer into fall. Seals are common, and the porpoises and dolphins make regular appearances. Minke whales occasionally become trapped in the weirs and have to be helped out before they destroy them (a weir can cost over $50,000 Cdn.).

The island is exposed to both the open ocean and strong currents; what seems a tranquil seascape can be rapidly transformed into an environment that requires experience and caution. Fog is common, and summers have passed when the sun hasn't made an appearance until Labour Day. However, even when storm-bound, you can hike, cycle and visit the local museum. Accommodations are varied and the food is often excellent.

## Mainland Coast — Wilderness Melange of Cliff, Incised Valley, Salt Marsh and Beach

The Fundy coast of New Brunswick extends from the St. Croix River, on the Maine border, to the Missaugash River and Nova Scotia. Partially sheltered by the Fundy Isles, an irregular coastline extends to the Saint John and is accessible by road. At the other end of the bay, vast plains of mud and marsh are not particularly appealing to the prudent paddler. However, sandwiched between these two areas is a wilderness melange of cliff, incised valley, salt marsh and beach that is well worth a visit.

This rugged section between St. Martin's and Fundy National Park is an extension of the Appalachian Mountains and remains the least accessible ocean shoreline south of Newfoundland. Only a few back roads and trails

lead to idyllic, hidden valleys where decaying wharf pilings persist on the site of some of the largest shipbuilding operations in the country, over a century ago. At Little Salmon River, a corduroy road several feet deep skirts the valley floor, and at Martin Head the floodplain is scattered with huge mounds of sawdust and posts that once carried the wharves, sheds, and machinery of the mill. By 1873, the migration out of the area had begun, and this remote shore returned to obscurity.

The sea cuts into the cliffs, littering the beaches with ancient granite, basalt, jasper and porphyry. Suspended particles from soft sandstones and shales create a rusty-brown murkiness (in stark contrast to the deep blues and blacks at the entrance to the bay). The tidal currents are slowed close to this relatively linear shoreline where, barring storms, you can expect easy sailing. A major exception is Martin Head, where a portage may be called for. And, as in the case of the Fundy Isles, be prepared for fog and chilly water early in the season.

A three-to-four-day journey is needed for the 37-plus-mile (60 km) stretch from St. Martin's to Alma. The weather will determine your actual progress; if you become storm-stayed, there is no coastal highway to exit on. Camping is free for the taking, but beware of that beckoning patch of grass (especially after a full moon), or you may be in for a wet surprise in the early morning hours.

On my trip, the squall passed. As the waters calmed around East Quoddy, in the Fundy Isles, and I could contemplate in my silent haven, I realized I had found another valuable paddling area. Behind me lay the intimate seclusion of the woods. Beside me were the mussels I had gathered earlier, steaming in their oven of seaweed. And in the distance, a seal divided his attention between my movements and those of the fishermen across the cove. The tide was dropping and it was time to empty the weir.

# Saint John River
*The Flooded Forest*

Scott Cunningham

THE SAINT JOHN RIVER BEGINS ITS JOURNEY IN THE REMOTE FORESTS OF
northern Maine, where it is fast, narrow and strewn with boulders — the
quintessential wilderness river familiar to many East Coast canoeists. But soon
after entering New Brunswick, the Saint John widens and lags. By the time it
reaches Fredericton, the provincial capital, over a hundred miles later (160+ km),
it has become a maze of intertwining channels capturing low-lying islands and
creeping onto expansive flood plain and marshland. In the summer, its current scarcely moves and paddling progress is influenced more by the winds,
which usually blow up the valley from the bay, than by the currents.

The river empties into the Bay of Fundy at the city of Saint John. At
low water, it flows unobstructed into the ocean, but during the flood tide a
surge of seawater backs the river up 50 miles (80 km). These Reversing Falls
are popular with whitewater kayakers who have the skill — and nostrils —
to stomach the odors from the huge pulp mill overlooking the gorge.

The Saint John is the largest river in the Maritime provinces and is navigable past Fredericton to Mactaquac, where a hydroelectric dam blocks boats and the salmon that once blessed the river. This was the main transportation route for the Natives and the European settlers, whose large paddlewheel steamers plied the river until the early 1900s. Today, it is the realm of the pleasure boater and the cottage crowd seeking to escape the incessant Fundy fog.

In spring, when a raw Atlantic is scarcely warmer than the Arctic, this is a welcome waterway. Of particular interest is the stretch between Burton and Hampstead, where the freshet (spring melt) invades the floodplains, opening up a tangle of tree trunks and canals — an environment that is unique in Canada and reminiscent of the mangrove swamps of the southern United States.

The rising river carves the banks and inundates the islands, depositing mud and silt to nourish the red maple. Fiddleheads, the delectable young sprouts of the ostrich fern, poke up through the water, the first sight of green in an otherwise dull decor of muted colors. Barren branches sound a cacophony of warblers, pausing on their way further north, and the tapping of woodpeckers into widespread deadwood. Osprey have also moved onto the bleached trunks of the dead American elms that once lined the valley.

Paddlers seeking the pristine might want to avoid this waterway in summer, but when October chills the coastal world, and the motorboats are in hibernation, visit once more. The huge maples will put on a spectacular color show. Camp on the islands, uninhabited except for the cattle, or stay at a relic from the days of the paddle steamer. The Steamerstop Inn, 46 miles (75 km) upstream of Saint John, has been renovated and you can paddle right up to the back door.

# P.E.I.'s East Side
## A Daytrip Full of Mussels, Seals and Herons

Bryon Howard

PRINCE EDWARD ISLAND MAY BE CANADA'S SMALLEST PROVINCE, BUT ITS paddling possibilities are huge.

A 12-mile-long (20 km) daytrip on the southeast corner of Northumberland Straight is a splendid mix of leisurely sea kayaking, pleasant birding, delightful scenery, lots of ocean delicacies . . . and old cars.

Our starting point is the community of Murray River, 34 miles (55 km) east of Charlottetown, where the Murray River empties into the Northumberland Strait. Protected from the wind and waves, Murray River is an excellent launch site. (For example, longer trips such as a 25-mile (40 km) paddle north to Newport and a 19-mile (30 km) adventure to Northumberland Provincial Park begin here.)

Cross the Murray River and paddle about 2 miles (3 km) along the north shore until we pass rows of mussel buoys and perhaps see some mussel farmers pulling lines. Our first stop is at the Murray River mussel farm to purchase some mussels — you were expecting something else? — at the big, blue building up the small hill and behind the trees. Across the river, in the trees, is Kings Castle Provincial Park. Until the Disney Corporation asked that the name be changed a few years ago, it was called Fantasyland.

Back on the water and around Finlayson's Point, we enter Log Cove. A little ways inside is Point Pleasant, where we find a cleared piece of land, complete with firepit. A short walk on the grown-over road takes us to a woodland area where we marvel at how old cars can grow in among the trees.

After examining a fine example of P.E.I. waste disposal from thirty years ago, our paddling brings us back to the present and to the north tip of Reynold's Island, home to at least eighty gray and harbor seals. At low tide, they wander out on this point where they have a good view of all approaching dangers. We approach the tip slowly, cautiously and as far out as possible in order to lessen our impact. Kayakers can cause more disturbance than Gary's Seal Watch Cruiser, a 40-foot-long reconditioned fishing boat.

My theory is this: seals live their entire lives with the hum of the big fishing boats, which have been traveling the Murray River for years, so they see and hear them all the time. Kayaks, on the other hand, approach quietly and are not highly visible.

Seeing these seals is a great bonus, but we keep our distance as we make our way to Herring Island, which is owned by the Island Nature Trust. Not only is this a roosting site for great blue herons and terns, it has at least one fox den. Across from Herring Island is Cherry Island, where cormorants and common and arctic terns nest in the dead trees (dead from too much acidic bird guano). Any of these islands make for good camping, but since we are on a daytrip, we push on.

It takes just twenty-five minutes to walk the circumference of nearby Thomas Island, once owned by Colonel Wotten, but now bequeathed to the Island Nature Trust. Since we are halfway through our trip, we have lunch. If we wanted, we could turn around and paddle back to Murray River.

Leaving Thomas Island, we head northeast past Cherry Island, making sure we don't get grounded on the nearby sand spit. (I have yet to see a map or chart which shows this spit as it is today; this is not surprising since the strong winds and currents cause much erosion and shifting of sand.) There is a fairly deep channel halfway down the spit, and we are careful to keep to the left of the sandbars. I nearly always get through, even on low tide. After many trips with lots of people, I think we have only had to pull our boats over the flats once.

We keep our group together as we approach the opening in the barrier sand dune chain. While this channel is another favorite for seals, there is less chance of causing a disturbance than at Reynold's Island. We are also ready for a push — 3 knots of current, when the tide is running.

## Saved from the Bell

As we round the point, there is a foul smell, and in the shallow water we can see stains or markings on the ocean floor. Biologists say the local back eddies and surface current don't allow oxygenated water to reach the bottom to help clean it. (This theory seems unlikely to me, but I like the thought of unoxygenated water, not raw sewage, which is being fed directly into the sea from nearby communities, as the culprit. Funny how these same stains and accompanying bad smells can be found on the east coast of Boughton Island.)

With old barns, marram grass, a bracken pond behind the beautiful crescent-shaped beach, scattered with Indian paintbrushes and other wildflowers, Poverty Beach is a local favorite. It is possible to take out here, however, we want to go further north to visit some of the Island's famous high, red cliffs.

Graham Pond, our take-out spot, is a proud fishing village with a large fish factory. We are lucky not to enter this port at the beginning of the workday, at 10 A.M., 3 P.M. or the end of the workday. Why? The fish plant uses a *loud* bell to tell employees when their day starts, breaks and finishes.

We run into the harbor on the incoming tide, and as we enter the narrow channel we keep paddling to reach the nice slip on harbor-left.

We are in time to amble up to the fish factory and buy fresh lobster, clam, mussels, haddock and other ocean delicacies. It's a fine finish to a day's paddle on the east side of Prince Edward Island.

# Nova Scotia's Coastal Water Trail

*A Great Way to Explore the South Shore*

Sheena Masson and Sue Browne

AFTER TWO YEARS OF RESEARCH AND PLANNING, THE BIG DAY HAD FINALLY arrived. On Canada Day 2000, we launched and paddled the first official water trail in Atlantic Canada. About fifty people gathered early that morning in Lunenburg on Nova Scotia's South Shore to celebrate the trail and send off a small flotilla on a nine-day cruise. The flotilla included ten kayaks, a small sailboat and a few canoes that joined us for the first day. Our destination was Halifax, 80 miles (130 km) away, which could be reached in a few days, but we had planned a leisurely trip.

A coastal water trail is not, as some first think, a hiking trail by the sea. Our goal is to develop a route around Nova Scotia for recreational boaters, with a focus on continued access for launching and camping as the coast becomes more developed. As with other water trail groups in North America, stewardship of the land is key as is community involvement. To get started, we chose a pilot project covering the coastline from Lunenburg to Halifax. This project is run as a non-profit environmental group, called the Ecology Action Centre.

The water trail required months of fundraising, meetings, office work and computer time, so the chance to paddle for nine days was a welcome change. It also gave us an opportunity to test the product.

We invited some kayaking friends and anyone else to join us. With road support from our data base manager Caroline Cameron, paddlers were able to skip sections where they weren't comfortable. Our group was always changing, with new people coming along to join us for a day or two. Most were experienced paddlers and campers.

After a few short speeches, a toast by the mayor and a round of champagne, we set off for Blue Rocks, a small fishing village east of Lunenburg. Blue Rocks is protected by a maze of jagged, slate blue islands popular with kayakers. We spent a fine day exploring hidden channels and watching seals swim and bask on rocky ledges.

Several water trail issues surfaced that first day. Despite a temptation to get close to the seals, we gave them a respectful distance since getting too close can cause parents to abandon their pups. After this, we headed out to camp on a nearby island. For this trip, we got permission beforehand from the landowner. Wilderness camping is still possible in much of this area, with many of the islands uninhabited. However, most are privately owned, and every year a few more get developed and become off-limits. Our plan to develop water trail campsites is twofold: we want to work in cooperation with landowners on private land and to approach government for access to Crown land.

We also learned a lesson in the differing needs of sailboaters and kayakers. Our friend in the sloop was able to motor through some narrow spots, but later had to go well out from shore. He also had some trouble staying at anchor on the island where the rest of us were pulled up.

The fog rolled in at sunset and was still thick the next morning. Using a marine chart and compass, we paddled from marker to marker past Sacrifice Island and around Bluff Head. The landscape changed from rocky slate islands to fertile drumlin hills. The fog lifted and we pulled up for lunch on a lovely crescent-shaped beach on Backman's Island, sharing the sheltered cove with a few cabin cruisers.

After lunch, the fog came back. Welcome to the Atlantic coast! From here, we had another few hours of follow-the-leader to Round Island, where to everyone's delight . . . the sun was blazing. After strolling the long beach, we got our first look at *Dorothy Louise*, a gorgeous 40-foot wooden turquoise schooner, here to join our cruise as a support and safety craft.

After a short stop, we paddled through — you guessed it — thick fog and past a few small islands to Oak Island Inn and Marina, our destination for the night. It was a real change for our group of hardcore wilderness campers to paddle ashore, soak in the hot tub and lounge in the pool . . . but we adjusted well. Then fourteen of us, including the crew of the schooner and friends, sat down to a spread in the dining room. It was a treat and a chance to experience some of the many amenities available to recreational boaters along the route. (This kind of information is available in our guidebook.)

## Nothing Bland about Blandford and Wreck Cove Is Safe

The next morning we hopped on the ferry to Big Tancook Island. This island, which has 250 residents, is a treasure to explore by foot, bike or boat. After lunch we paddled to Little Tancook Island, hiked the island trails, then made our way to Blandford on the mainland.

Contrary to its name, Blandford is a picturesque, unspoiled fishing village. Here we had a warm welcome at the Candle on the Water Bed and Breakfast, a century-old manse, complete with comfy beds with beautiful old quilts. There was room for the sailboats at the nearby government wharf. Following dinner, cooked in the backyard, we had a bonfire.

Day four started out very foggy as we headed out around the headlands of the Aspotogan Peninsula, which separates Mahone Bay from St. Margaret's Bay. Here, in exposed waters, we navigated using map and compass . . . and listening for the sound of breakers on ledges. A GPS position from the sloop skipper was also helpful. Along this headland, the landscape changes from slate to granite.

Since the open crossing at the mouth of St. Margaret's Bay can be treacherous, two kayakers paddled to shore and hitched a ride. Luckily for the rest of us, the fog lifted but big swells had to be negotiated. The group rendezvoused at a commercial campground for a rainy night of tenting. The schooner and sloop berthed at another government wharf, where we

encountered our first potato gun launcher. Some people from Ontario were hurling potatoes across the cove, with the goal of hitting their own RV!

Next day the paddlers set off in the fog, which was soon replaced by light winds and big swells for the trip past the famous Peggy's Cove light-house. This is a rugged stretch of coastline, so the four paddlers tackling this stretch took shelter behind some small islands along the way to High Island. Seals, who were hanging around the mackerel nets, followed them for a while.

The wind increased after lunch and the swells piled up. Big breakers crashed around the small, rocky islands and choppy waves were coming from all directions. One kayaker tipped in a cresting 10-foot (3 m) wave, but was able to get back in and pump out his boat.

In Prospect, we all stayed at Sue's house and enjoyed an evening sail on the schooner. The next day was calm and sunny, ideal conditions to paddle through the myriad of narrow channels and inshore islands to Lower Prospect. We camped on a private island close to shore. The owner is gener-ous in allowing boaters to use his property.

The following day, paddling to Sambro, we were treated to clear vistas of the granite cliffs and barrens of the Terence Bay Wilderness Area. We hope to develop our first campsites along this section of public land.

After a night at the home of another group member near Sambro, the remaining paddlers set off for MacNab's Island and our final campout. They had calm waters around the usually tricky Pennant Point and successfully completed a surf landing near Crystal Crescent Beach. Since the schooner had to sail far offshore to avoid shoals and ledges, it was not really a safety boat. However, it was useful for carrying gear and water, providing a phone and extra sleeping areas.

MacNab's Island, at the entrance to Halifax harbor, is a gem — 975 acres (395 hectares) of overgrown farmland and forest, crisscrossed by old trails and roads, with some lovely sand beaches and historic forts. Fortunately, it has not been developed into condos or theme parks, and the province has plans to make it a natural park.

We sailed into the shelter of Wreck Cove (much safer than the name implies), on the east side of the island, where many other boats were moored or beached. We arrived early enough to explore, then a fellow kayaker, from Halifax, showed up with wine and strawberries for the evening bonfire.

The final day was a short paddle to the Maritime Museum on the Halifax waterfront for a closing reception, where many curious tourists looked over our gear-laden kayaks and asked about the Water Trail.

The Nova Scotia Coastal Water Trail is a reality, with enhancements and improvements taking place when money is available.

*The Nova Scotia Coastal Water Trail (www.trails.gov.ns.ca) is a member of North American Water Trails Inc. (www.watertrails.org), a coalition of thirty-eight American and Canadian water trail groups. These trails are on both coastal and inland waters. Other Canadian members are the Canadian Heritage Rivers System, the Alexander Mackenzie Voyageur Route, Alberta Water Trails, the B.C. Marine Trail, the Saguenay Fiord and the St. Mary's Heritage Water Trail.*

# Tobeatic
## *Mystique and Mystery*

Andy Smith

WHEN I RETURNED TO NOVA SCOTIA THIRTY YEARS AGO I BECAME aware of something new . . . well, something not really new, of course, but new to me. Like many others, I was unaware of an incredible natural phenomenon in my own backyard — I was oblivious to the backcountry wilderness in southwestern Nova Scotia. I live on a ribbon of coastal, ocean-focused civilization based on the Atlantic fisheries. You can see this very clearly when looking at photographs taken from space — Nova Scotia is perfectly outlined by the lights from its coastal communities. The middle is dark.

The dark hole in the middle of the western end of the province is the home of the Tobeatic, or officially, the Tobeatic Wilderness Area. The Tobeatic is a vast hinterland, by Nova Scotia standards, of ancient Mi'kmaq migration routes, trout pools, bizarre balancing rocks deposited by retreating glaciers, bogs — lots of bogs — and mosquitoes, blackflies and other things appropriate to these dark regions. In time I came to learn of mysterious places: Jim Charles and his mythical gold mine and hideout. Awe-inspiring

old-growth hemlocks on Sporting Lake. The Shelburne River. Buckshot Lake. The Bingay Lakes. The Sanctuary. Wardens' cabins at Sand Beach, Irving and Spectacle Lakes. Junction Lake. House-sized erratics on House Lake. The upper Roseway River. And the Tobeatic.

"The" Tobeatic. This is how she is addressed locally by those who know her. To those who know her well she is sometimes referred to playfully, but affectionately, as simply the Tobi. Either way, the Tobeatic is addressed with profound reverence, in deference to all the ghosts she harbors, and to all who have ever paddled her caramel waters, walked her granite face and wizened vegetation, and felt her forbidding and sometimes inhospitable remoteness. But still it was the Tobeatic that I wanted to get to know. I was drawn to try to discover the inner Nova Scotia, as we each come to understand our own essence, and, I guess, ultimately our soul. This curiosity became my Tobeatic Wilderness Quest.

## Strong Pulse

Nova Scotia's Crown lands are a mere 28 percent of the province's land mass, and many would agree that the Tobeatic is the most significant block of Crown land and the most significant of the province's recently established thirteen wilderness areas. The Tobeatic, a web of interconnecting waterways, surrounds the political and geographic center of the western end of the province. It is dotted with shallow lakes and laced with small rivers. It is our only true wilderness and as such is the penultimate tripping experience in the province. It is our Northern Ontario, our Tatshenshini, Thelon and Nahanni, all in one.

For the most part, the Tobeatic's physical endowments are modest. Naturally acidic soils are thin and nutrient poor, plant cover is slow growing, and 250 years of European settlement have left a low-quality, generally unproductive, mixed forest only where there was sufficient soil and drainage for any forest. Land that can support a healthy forest is generally found around the margins of the Tobeatic, and much of the remaining land, primarily in the center of the wilderness area, either has always been bog or barren ground, or is no longer suitable for forest regeneration, in part because of deliberate burning for browse and berries in the 19th and early 20th centuries. However, the Tobeatic does still have a few small pockets of old-growth climax forest, and despite much of the interior being marginal, the now-protected Tobeatic will continue to recover from 250 years of exploitation and abuse. White pine, spruce and hemlock are reestablishing themselves, and the Shelburne-Roseway system of rivers, in its zigzag crossing of the Tobeatic, reflects the overall balance of forest, bog and barren.

Wildlife in the Tobeatic has, likewise, been affected by civilization and traditional forestry practices. Sport hunting in the late 19th and early 20th centuries decimated the moose, leaving only a threatened remnant population, and the woodland caribou were hunted to extinction by 1925. White-tailed deer, introduced in the 1940s to replace the moose and caribou, have thrived. Black bear and bobcat have maintained a reduced, though apparently sustainable, population base, and since the 1970s the coyote has spread into the Tobeatic to occupy the niche formerly occupied by the now-extinct gray wolf. Beaver are recovering well from over-trapping and are providing increased assistance in keeping water in the streams.

Despite the challenges it has faced, and still faces, the Tobeatic has a strong pulse. Its heart and soul are entwined with the meandering Shelburne and Roseway Rivers, which draw into themselves an extensive network of smaller streams that extend to all points of the compass — the Annapolis Valley and Bay of Fundy to the north, the Gulf of Maine to the west and south, and the open Atlantic Ocean to the east.

The Shelburne can be approached top to bottom, south to north and inside out. Over the past few years I have tried most of the routes, and luckily there are still more to draw me back into the Tobeatic's wilderness.

The core of the Tobeatic, the Shelburne-Roseway system of rivers, is composed of pieces of rivers that can be mixed and matched in a variety of ways, from longer trips of one to two weeks, or shorter trips of three to five days, and most can be done in either direction. However, there are three common routes in the Shelburne-Roseway system, each of which can be stacked on top of the others to produce the total cross-Tobeatic expedition. The three routes are these: the shorter Keji–Junction Lake route, the longer Whitesand route, and the longest, Sporting Lake–Buckshot route. Each requires a considerable shuttle, but this is often the price a tripper pays for wilderness.

## Kejimkujik–Junction Lake Route

The shorter trip, from three to five or more days, depending on the usual (fitness, knowledge of route and inclination), involves accessing the Shelburne River from the east through Kejimkujik National Park, or just Keji. From Keji you descend the Shelburne a short distance to Irving Lake, paddle and carry up streams through Siskech and House Lakes to Junction Lake on the Roseway River and again head downstream, this time to the southwestern boundary of the Tobeatic.

Kejimkujik is the central, and easiest, access and departure point on the Shelburne–Roseway system. Because of this, Keji is probably the most popular access for those not familiar with the Tobeatic. The national park has well-groomed carries, canoe rests, and campsites with cut firewood, outhouses and (usually) dry landings. There is a canoe outfitter in the park and a good park map of routes and carries, but it does not cover much of the Shelburne or Roseway Rivers. If planning to make the daylong cross-Keji trip to the Tobeatic you'll not only have to inform the park wardens at the check-in, but you'll also have to take along your own 1:50,000 topos.

One of my recent trips into the Tobeatic was over the Keji–Junction Lake route, and because we had only the long weekend in May, we traveled the route in 3.2 days and 3 nights (Friday evening is the 0.2). Yes, it was rushed, but the weather was good, the water sufficiently high and even the blackflies were not too bad. If you are going to squeeze the trip into a long weekend you'll also have to make sure you can launch from the put-in at the foot of Peskowesk Lake, which is usually only permitted in the park's off-season.

The Keji–Junction Lake route is a good introductory wilderness route through the Tobeatic. Although you do not get to experience the most remote portions of the upper Shelburne River, you do get most of the upper

Roseway and, if you plan well, your first night can even be in a cabin! Site 37 on Peskawa Lake in Keji is really a cabin, the Mason's Cabin, but it is not advertised as such. What more could you want as a transition site late afternoon Friday, after a long day's work and drive? Of course, enough other people know this to make it a prized location, so reserve it early in your planning. However, if Mason's Cabin is already booked, as it was last year when we went through, try site 38 or 40; although they are not cabins they still have, for better or worse, all the other amenities of camping in a national park. Another option is to camp on the Shelburne at the foot of the Granite Falls carry — a busy but excellent campsite.

From Pebbleloggitch Stillwater you'll drop down the Shelburne to Irving Lake before carrying and paddling up Siskech Brook to Siskech Lake. Sikech Lake has an aura of true wilderness — white pines windswept to the northeast, large glacier-deposited erratics and scattered, narrow sandy beaches dot the shoreline. The numerous islands and clumps of large erratics along the eastern shore create a surreal landscape worthy of a day's exploration. Although there are campsites in some of these clumps of rocks jutting into the lake, a convenient site is where House Lake Brook enters Siskech Lake at the beginning of a short carry. On our Victoria Day trip I would have been happy to settle for our second night on the shores of Siskech Lake, but I was easily outvoted.

House Lake, like Siskech, a glacial lake pockmarked with more immense erratics and lined with white pine wind vanes, leads to your exit from the Shelburne River watershed. The half-mile-long (1 km) carry into Junction Lake in the Roseway watershed can be very wet in places, but remember, "no wet, no water" — and you want water in the rivers.

Junction Lake has been a curious lure for those who lapse into two-dimensional thinking, me included. On its shores — or just off them, somewhere — is, we think, an iron rod in a rock known as Junction Rock, where the boundaries of four counties meet. So far it is still an abstraction, but on two different trips recently, armed with maps, notes and GPS instrumentation programed and in hand, nameless members of our group were unable to locate Junction Rock. Old-timers have described it, sworn they have seen it and can walk to it, but so far it has remained for me a figment of their imaginations. Still, you can be sure that every time I pass through Junction Lake I'll still spend a couple of hours looking.

We spent our second night near the foot of Junction Lake from which it is a short carry into the Roseway River and through a succession of smaller lakes, beaver dams and carries to Roseway Lake. From Roseway Lake, trippers can carry into the Jordan River watershed and paddle two days to the village of Jordan Falls, but we were staying focused on the Roseway and our objective, Upset Falls. However, we had gotten so far ahead of schedule on our first day that we stopped early on our second full day and spent the third night in the southwest arm of Roseway Lake. I had to use great restraint not to point out that we could have spent more time on Siskech and House Lakes.

Below Roseway Lake the river leads you through somewhat larger lakes between which there are well-marked carries, but the river often has sufficient volume in the spring to run the chutes — with scouting. Mink, Skudiak and Bluffhill Lakes were all at one time controlled for log driving by splash dams, structures designed to hold back a head of water until, when logs were needed downstream, they were opened and a surge of logs and water was sent down a sluice into the river below. In this way, spring run-off could be prolonged and controlled for downriver mills. Today some of the cribwork remains in various locations, but no longer do they restrict the Roseway's flow.

DeMoliter and McGill Lakes, surrounded as they are by a healthier forest, steep banks and numerous small arms and bays, are lovely lakes to paddle and explore. At Whetstone Lake the river bends to the southeast into Class II Horse Falls, which can be run, except in the highest and lowest water, into the still water above the Upset Falls take-out.

It is also possible to continue on through Upset Falls, with great caution, to Indian Fields, where you actually leave the Tobeatic, and from Indian Fields a lovely two-to-three-day moving-water route can be added to your journey by carrying into the Clyde River watershed, although its description will have to wait.

## Heart and Soul of the Tobeatic

The upper portion of the Shelburne-Roseway system joins the Keji–Junction Lake route below Granite Falls on the Shelburne River. Unlike the shorter three-to-five-day Keji–Junction Lake route, which crosses the eastern and southern portions of the Tobeatic, the two upper Shelburne River routes — the Whitesand and Sporting Lake–Buckshot routes and their approaches — cross the more remote northern and central portions of the Tobeatic, adding four to five days to the Shelburne-Roseway system of rivers. The additional days on the upper Shelburne River will allow you to experience the rest of the Tobeatic, the heart and soul of the Tobi. Together they are really the Tobeatic.

The upper Shelburne is the most challenging portion of the Shelburne-Roseway system and just to reach it takes two to three days. The paddling is across still waters and lakes, and the carries are uphill, frequent and long, up to 2 miles (3 km) long. But the reward is that you experience the most remote wilderness portion of the Tobeatic, its essence.

Both routes into the upper reaches of Shelburne River begin in the Sissiboo River watershed. The shorter Whitesand route joins the Shelburne at Sand Beach Lake, a day's paddle below the Shelburne's headwaters on Buckshot Lake. The longer Sporting Lake–Buckshot route joins the Shelburne at its headwaters, on Buckshot Lake.

As enjoyable and rewarding as it is, the Whitesand route has two drawbacks. The most significant is that it cuts off 25 percent of the upper Shelburne River, the most remote portion of the Shelburne-Roseway system. The second limiting factor is that the carry into Sand Beach Lake is a one-hour, 2-mile (3 km) trek, one way — not for the faint of heart. However, on the upside, there are fewer total miles of carrying required.

The Whitesand route leaves Fifth Lake through either Stovepipe or Burntland Carry, unless the flow is high, in which case you can paddle directly into Whitesand Stream, maybe the one advantage of a dam-controlled river. There is one modest portage, Wildcat Carry, above which there are a couple of beaver dams before you reach Whitesand Lake with its gorgeous beach-speckled shoreline. There are a couple of good campsites on Whitesand, but the most convenient is at the start of the carry into Rocky Stillwater on Moosehead Stream, which you'll have to take sooner or later anyway. Above Rocky Stream there are three more carries and three more beaver dams before you enter Moosehead Lake, from which the 2-mile (3 km) Moosehead, or Barrenlands, Carry leads across a hardwood ridge into Sand Beach Lake on the Shelburne.

Former Tobeatic Game Sanctuary warden Winston Hurlburt recently recounted that it was here, on Sand Beach Lake, in the late 1940s, that he saw, at one time and from one spot, twelve moose feeding in the rich shallows and marshlands of the lake.

From Sand Beach Lake, and the well-used Cofan (warden's) cabin on the still water just below the lake, it is about a six-hour paddle through small lakes, swifts and still waters to Granite Falls, a mandatory half-mile-long (1 km) portage that ends at the Granite Falls campsite at the head of Pebbleloggitch Stillwater. There are well-marked and well-used carries on this section of the river, but if water is moderate or high it is possible to run all but Granite Falls, though some of the chutes are rocky, narrow and prone to strainers.

The Sporting Lake–Buckshot route into the Shelburne, at least a day longer than the Whitesand route, begins with a paddle up a small portion of the Sissiboo flow into Sporting Lake Stream and a short carry before Rush Lake and from there a half-mile (1 km) carry into Sporting Lake. Because the three islands in Sporting Lake support one of the Tobeatic's best remaining examples of old-growth, climax stands of eastern hemlock, they are protected more stringently than the surrounding wilderness, though they are all part of the Tobeatic. Be sure to allow yourself sufficient time to experience the murmuring pines and the hemlocks of the islands.

There are several campsites along the southern arm of Sporting Lake, which is where you'll head to pick up the carry to Oakland Lake in the upper reaches of the Tusket River watershed. At the Oakland Lake narrows you veer off to the east and carry into two other lakes in the Tusket watershed, East Cranberry and Clearwater, before carrying into Buckshot Lake on Shelburne River.

Buckshot, the headwaters of the Shelburne River, is the spiritual and geographic center of the Tobeatic. It exudes an aura, a spirit, that cannot be duplicated or replaced. Tobeatic trippers have for decades, if not centuries, had their remains scattered to the Tobeatic gods on Buckshot Lake, and it is here in the heart of the Tobeatic that you are still most likely to see the lords of the forests, bogs and barrens, the moose and black bear.

From Buckshot, where another warden's cabin once stood against poachers, it's a day's paddling and carrying downstream to Sand Beach Lake, across much barren ground, through Stony Ditch Lake and into Pine Lake, where a set of old bedsprings still marks the site of yet another warden's cabin. Below Pine Lake you can take the half-mile (1 km) carry along the river if water is moderate or high, or the 1-mile (1.6 km) Esker Carry, each of which leads into Jim Charles Meadow and Sand Beach Lake where the two routes converge.

Whether you mesh the Sporting Lake–Buckshot route with the Whitesand route before leaving the Shelburne River at Keji, or combine these with the Roseway River, or just paddle the Kiji–Junction Lake route, your experience of the Tobeatic's wilderness will be indelibly etched in your memory, your heart and your soul. For you it, too, it will become *the* Tobeatic or, simply, the Tobi.

# Margaree River
## *The Hotfooters*

Lynn E. Noel

THE FIRST RIVER YOU PADDLE RUNS THROUGH THE REST OF YOUR LIFE. You discover your definition of a river, the journey where your subconscious learns the pattern for what a journey should be. You can be years or miles away from the physical river, and suddenly its reflecting pool will bubble up to the surface of your life to remind you who you are. My first river was the Margaree.

## Camp Discovery

I lean into the edge of the cliff, pressed into the wire fence that holds the meadow from its ragged plunge into the sea. I squint like a sailor, from Sight Point far out into the Gulf of St. Lawrence, where the capes of Inverness County billow down the western edge of the island. There to the north, hazy in the blue distance, floats an island, like a castle with a magic name. Margaree. My Avalon, my Bali Ha'i. Someday I will go. A voice hollers me out of reverie into adventure. "Yo, Hotfooter! Paddle time!" Michael and I race hotfoot through the daisies, tall grass whipping bare legs, down to the bleached bones of wooden steps to the cove.

Down to the rocks we skitter with the paddles, then clamber back with the canoe that clangs silver as a scratched and battered fish into the brown rockweedy swell. Solemnly we strap on life vests; earnestly we instruct each other in paddling technique as we back paddle into the slapping waves. Pry and draw, J and feather, ebb and flow goes the paddle talk. We are discovering our true selves.

We are the Hotfooters. Hotfoot is our canoe, our steed, our trusty Rosinante of the waves. We are in training, Hotfoot and her crew. Someday soon we will paddle to the sea.

## The Hotfooters

We are the Hotfooters — partners and best friends. We are so different. Michael is from Brooklyn, his black curly hair shaggy as a Puerto Rican bull. His animated hands are long-fingered, active, wrapped round a paddle or splayed akimbo as he talks. He is street-smart, savvy, wise-ass, pale olive skin tanned walnut under shirtless overalls.

My overalls have rainbow straps, with Camp Discovery embroidered in a rainbow arch of 1970s' balloon letters. Mouse-blond hair hangs braided behind proudly pierced ears that no longer stick out behind thick glasses. Contact lenses and braces are stigmata of the suburbs that set me far from Michael in the winter, but here in Nova Scotia we have found ourselves at home.

We are the Hotfooters — we are a team. We are workmates in the laundry room, where Michael once drilled a hole in the floor to drain an accidental flood. I keep his secret as teammates do. We are teammates at volleyball and on the construction crew for new cabins. We make awkward partners for the Virginia reel in the camp dining hall, where Dan Hughie MacIsaac saws away at his fiddle with the same handyman zip that sawed our floorboards that afternoon. Jigs and reels swirled us up out of our teenage gawkiness as surely as the swirl of a paddle in a pool. I yearned to discover that same sureness in myself about my place in the world. Founders of the Wave-watchers Club, we are its only steady members. For hours every day we crouch motionless on the rocks, memorizing the waves, hungrily absorbing every motion into our bodies. We time them, cheer them on, tag them out beyond the tide line in breathless counting on the thrill of the great one, the magic seventh.

We know these waves. We know this water. We have explored every cove along this coast for miles on either side of camp. We have gone as far as they will let us, and we are hungry for more. We want a real canoe trip. We want the Margaree. We are sure of our place and purpose in the world. We want to plunge to the source of it all and run with it as far as we can go. We want to paddle to the sea, to prove we are the Hotfooters. We are fifteen.

## Margaree to the Sea

At last the day arrives. We are the big kids on this trip, the year before we become counselors-in-training, and we pack food and haul boats and tighten down gear for the younger campers with a solemn sense of responsibility. We are the Hotfooters — the cargo canoe. We earn our pride of place at the head of the trip, and the privilege of not carrying a third passenger, by carrying tents and food while we scout for route hazards and lunch stops — a trust we take most seriously. Besides, it lets us go on ahead.

We are the Hotfooters — intrepid explorers on the watch for danger. Michael leans deftly around the bend as I keep lookout in the bow. And there, just ahead, we spy the wire strung low across the stream — a gaspereau weir. "Hey, Peter!" Our counselor pulls up the other canoes, and the Hotfooters scout safe passage as we line the boats safely through the knee-deep shallows that zigzag between the wire nets. Last year, we swung and bounced on the overhead wire, but this year we holler at the little kids who try to do the same. We have to set a good example or the fisherman will close his weirs to us. We are the Hotfooters and this is our river. We will take good care of it.

"I want to be a salmon," I tell Michael. We are bouncing on the ends of the canoe and laughing, barefoot legs hanging sunburnt in the low August rapids.

He scoffs at me. "Okay, gonna tip you!" There is a heave on Michael's end, and I splash and gasp in the current, laughing down the channel under the maples where the Northeast Margaree flows into the southwest up ahead towards Margaree Harbour.

Running the rapids is even more fun without the canoe, and we laugh and pant and splash upriver again and again, hurling ourselves into the stream, going with the flow. I reach out and grab a sweeper branch, hanging from it, bouncing, feeling the elastic tug of the tree in my arms, the river in my legs. If I let go I will be carried into the main channel, swept out to sea into a future too huge to know but where the horizons are limitless.

So I bounce — until Michael yanks the branch that throws me in. He swims upriver, laughing underwater.

Suddenly we are salmon, leaping and smacking upstream in the Northeast Margaree. I bury myself headfirst in the brown pools and fishtail upstream, hair streaming in the current, lungs burning, until I burst like a salmon into the foam below the falls. They say a salmon smells her way upriver by the press of the current against her nose. With blind eyes squinched tight against the gasping cold water, I know when I reach the rapids by the press of the roaring bubbles against my skin and the sudden lift of air within the water. You don't have to be a fisherman to play a fish. I know in that moment that I will always be able to find my way back here, no matter how far away the salmon swim.

We are the Hotfooters — we brave the unknown. We are running close up under the cutbank when we spot the cave. In the bow, Michael disappears into the shadow, and I brace on the gunwale and duck my head as I swing the stern in. Inside is dim and damp, where the river eats away at the scratchy, sulfur-yellow limestone walls. Our voices boom in the gurgling silence. "Wow, cool!" There is barely room to pry the canoe around the current's bend before we are swirled out again into sunlight, squinting and shouting with news of our intrepid discovery. We are the Hotfooters. We paddle through caves.

We are the Hotfooters — we go the distance. We have rounded the last bend in the valley, where the river flattens out into the hot, salty shimmer of the estuary. Far out on the blue tide is a lone canoe, pulling for the bridge that marks the river's mouth. "Come on, Michael!" We dig in, hating the flat-water, hating the brackish, back-aching taste of the final miles, but aching worse for the sea beyond the bridge.

And we're out ahead of them all, hotfooting it for the blue haze and blue waves and the first blue glimpse of Margaree Island at the river's mouth. Now the burning blue sky presses us down like the hot flat of a giant hand. "Feel the burn!" In another ten strokes we'll slide under the navy shadows of the bridge with its treacherous tidal rips. We have pleaded with the counselors for this privilege, and last year we had to pull out with the other canoes just above the bridge where the trailer waited to haul us back to camp. But we are the Hotfooters. With promises, pleas and practice, we have proven our worth. The bridge is ours, and the sea beyond.

A gasp and a rush and a rocketing, bucketing roar, and salt splashes the taste of sweat from our exultant faces. "Yee-hah! Hotfoot ho!" We have arrowed out beyond the current line into a new dimension of swells. We know these swells. It is swell. We swell with pride. And my eyes swell and swim in the salt spray until Margaree Island swims beyond my vision. It doesn't matter if I never get there. I know that I could. I am a Hotfooter. I have paddled to the sea.

## Margaree, Michael and Me

We are forty. Where is Michael? He went to college in Brooklyn, I heard, but I lost his address when I moved away. We vowed we'd come back, each of us, in our own time. I did return, though not to the Margaree, and spent a wild goose decade roving from Great Lakes to Pacific to Baffin and Newfoundland. Michael always said he'd grow up and work on a farm in Cape Breton, knowing it was a strange dream for a Brooklyn street kid. I believed him, though. Cape Breton is where he lives for me, and where I find him still.

I carry the map of Cape Breton in my mind, still and always. The mind's eye gazes through its grid like the wires of the old camp fence, leaning over the cliff into the blue distance. There in the Gulf haze floats Margaree Island, dream achieved yet goal forever. That's as it should be. It's enough that we remember who we are.

Somewhere up those billowing capes, perhaps in Inverness or Margaree Forks, I've always imagined I would someday spot a lanky, curly-headed farmer with a Brooklyn accent and overalls. I'd hand him this book, and watch his slow smile as he turns the pages. "Hey, Michael, it's me. And the Margaree."

# Notokwanon River
## Breathtaking, Bodacious and Buggy

Shawn Hodgins

It was Jacques Cartier, in 1535, who described Labrador as "the land God gave to Cain." In a way, he was right. The land is rugged and rivers untamed. But Labrador is full of contrasts. It has surreal beauty, stunning solitude and proud people. All in all, it's a perfect environment for physical renewal.

For over twenty-five years, I have been fortunate enough to travel by canoe on many rivers throughout the Canadian North. Asked to tell a story about a Labrador canoe trip, I was delighted, as it is one of the most impressive areas I have traveled. Given the historic conflicts between Newfoundland and Quebec over the Labrador border and the ongoing dispute over hydroelectric generation and its economic spin-offs, it is somewhat appropriate that this trip takes place in both provinces. For thirty days, we — a group of eight friends in the 1990s — traveled across northeastern Quebec to Labrador's Notokwanon River.

As you might expect, the easiest way to get to Labrador is from somewhere else — in our case, Schefferville in northern Quebec. The short story is this: we paddled east from Schefferville through several lakes to the De Pas River then descended to the George River. A day and a half on the George was followed by several days on the Du Mans River, and some further lake hopping, followed by a ten-day descent of the Notokwanon to the Labrador Sea. The trip ended in the Innu hamlet of Davis Inlet.

To begin the trip, we assembled in Quebec City and proceeded by car up the north shore of the St. Lawrence to Sept Isle, where we did the usual last-minute shopping and equipment rechecking. In an effort to ease the next day's early-morning train departure, canoes and equipment were checked onto a Quebec North Shore and Labrador Railway train that evening. This proved to be good planning. The next day was chaos: a lost credit card, fresh food (including lunch) left in the truck at the train station and a sprint to catch an already moving train. All a-b-o-a-r-d — barely! The ride on the QNSL is spectacular, but not a trip for the impatient. On a good day, it takes ten to twelve hours to travel the 250 miles (400 km). Many stops and delays

later, we reached Schefferville, just as the last vestiges of a northern sunset were disappearing. There was enough light to see how little remained of this once-prosperous northern mining town.

After more last-minute shopping (to replace the food left in our truck at Sept Isle), we were shuttled east to Lac Attikamigan and the start of our water journey. It is about a single day's paddle east through several lakes to the De Pas River. This height of land is fairly flat, with typical northern spruce forest and bog. My memories are of relatively warm weather, pretty lakes, calm waters, small shallow rapids, boggy portages and . . . *bugs*. After crossing and recrossing the Quebec-Labrador border, we were back in Quebec for a one-week descent of the beautiful De Pas, a delightful Class II–III river. The De Pas starts small and shallow, gradually building in size as it makes its way to the George. As it gradually drops into a spectacular wide valley, the surrounding rocky hills become more and more alluring, beckoning the would-be hiker. A few mother caribou and calves scattered the shore; we missed seeing the migrating George River herd by a few days.

After more than a week of paddling, we reached the mighty George River. It is here that many would say our sanity left us when, rather than continuing on downstream on the George, a spectacular trip in its own right, we began the slow grind of ascending the George. There is no question that upstream travel is hard work. However, it does have its own rewards and joys. There is a certain skill involved, and the more you do the better you get. Before long, you settle into a comfortable routine and forget you are traveling upriver — well, almost! Tracking with ropes and poling become important skills. Portaging, of course, is a big part of upstream travel; there are times when it is much more efficient to carry over a rapid than try to track up the shore. The relatively sparse forest helped. We were on the George River for just over a day before we reached the little known, hardly traveled Du Mans River.

We ascended the Du Mans, a stunningly beautiful Class II–III whitewater river, for about three days. Again, a combination of tracking and portaging was what it took. It was satisfying but exhausting, especially since we were starting to feel the time pressures of a prearranged food drop and plane exit for two members of our group who could not stay for the second half of our adventure. The arrival of a plane (a day late, as seems to be the norm) is always greeted with mixed feelings midway through a trip. It is an intrusion, though in this case the food and libations were both needed and welcome.

## Land of Contrasts

The journey from our plane rendezvous to the height of land and the Notokwanon River took five days. In many ways, this was the most memorable and spectacular part of the trip — a semi-barren, rugged landscape dotted with hundreds and hundreds of lakes of all sizes and shapes. The low-lying rocky hills surrounding many of the lakes, the foothills of the Torengat Mountains, make for great hiking. At times, navigation was easy, following small lakes and rivers. Other times, it was more challenging, as we moved between lakes or rivers, from one system to another. Numerous eskers provided great camping and occasionally good portage routes. Wildlife was sparse but fishing was good.

My memories are of spectacular lakes and hills, silent Innu hunt camps and ear-shattering NATO jet fighters (based in Goose Bay). On several occasions, screaming F-15s shattered our solitude, reminding us of the conflict between the Innu peoples of Labrador and the Canadian government over low-level training flights.

The place where we finally entered the North Notokwanon River was actually a long, narrow, unnamed lake, tucked in between high, barren hills. Descent of the Notokwanon took nine days. The river starts small and shallow and quickly builds in volume. There are three or four days of intense Class III and IV rapids. As we descended into the Notokwanon Valley, the forest became more dense and portaging more difficult.

At an unnamed but visually appealing waterfalls, the river is forced 90 degrees left into a half-mile-long (1 km) canyon. The carry around is about 1,200 yards through rough bush, but some of us elected to lower our canoes, with ropes, down below the falls and run out through the canyon. The intensity of the Notokwanon builds for several days, and then, in the midst of a big descent, it opens into a broad valley surrounded by high hills. There the current slows to a relaxed pace, and we sat back and enjoyed the sights.

From this peaceful valley, the river again rushes through a series of challenging Class III and IV rapids, dropping about 40 feet per mile (12 m/km). Over the final 15 miles (25 km), the current begins to slow. We saw bear and moose wading on the sandbars as we made our way to Merrifield Bay and the sea. Merrifield Bay enters the Labrador Sea (Atlantic) just south of Voisey Bay (a place that was beginning to make the news when we passed) and just north of the Innu community of Davis Inlet. Memories of the two-day coastal paddle are of wind and waves, whales and seals, and huge towering islands of rock along the coast.

Davis Inlet, like Labrador, is a place of contrasts. You see smiling friendly people, boarded windows, barred and vandalized buildings, spectacular landscape, garbage blowing through town from the dump, which is located just outside of town (upwind, 90 percent of the time). You see a caribou hunting culture settled on an island in the ocean, far from the herds, and youth out at summer encampments learning from their elders. And we saw plenty of substance abuse.

The Notokwanon was definitely a memorable trip and one that I would do again, even though Northern Quebec and Labrador, in midsummer, have some of the worst bugs anywhere in Canada. Some evenings while moving around the campsite (it was unpleasant to stay in one place), I remember saying to myself and others, "Why are we here? Never again!"

Canoe trips are like that, especially the challenging ones. They lead you to ask why. If I were talking to Jacques Cartier, I would tell him a Labrador experience is unparalleled and indescribable.

# Gros Morne National Park

*Knobby Seas, Slumping Mountains and Morris the Moose*

Kevin Redmond and Dan Murphy

"Alpha."
"Bravo."
"Charlie."
"Delta."
"Echo."
"Foxtrot."

Each paddling team called out in turn, reassuring the others they were okay and with the group. Thirty-knot headwinds confused the sea, challenging both body and mind. Waves smashed over the kayaks and lifted the fragile crafts, leaving them teetering on the breaking crests. Like whales, bows slapped down sending spray outward and upward. Gusting winds clawed at the waves, churning them into a salty mist that penetrated squinting eyes and the tiny cuts and abrasions collected from six days of paddling.

Then, without warning, the kayaks were attacked by waves rebounding from a 2,000-foot (600 m) vertical cliff. A quick brace and it was up into the next wave. The wave train seemed endless. We moved further offshore to avoid the confusion, but progress was negligible. The kayaks were dwarfed by the open water and towering cliffs, which plummet to the sea, limiting landing zones. There was no way but the paddle way — straight ahead. In the Atlantic Ocean's Gulf of St. Lawrence, we were committed.

"Alpha." "Bravo." "Charlie. "Echo." "Foxtrot." Where is the Delta boat? The call to raft up was given. Rafting up in these conditions was no easy task. A quick check found one of the two Delta paddlers was seasick. With some encouragement, they continued, with the lead boat setting the pace.

Dark clouds settled in and the sky let loose with a driving rain that drummed relentlessly on the decks of the kayaks. Strong winds forced the rains to the horizontal, and just when we thought it couldn't get any worse, the sky began to rumble and clap with thunder. We saw a lightning strike a

couple of miles ahead. The system was moving in our direction. We had to get off the water . . . but where?

Sea kayaking in Newfoundland and Labrador offers unique connections between past and present, rock and water — a rich, colorful living culture and natural history. Gros Morne National Park is no exception. Unlike canoeing wilderness rivers, where encounters with humans are rare, sea kayaking coastal Newfoundland means meeting local people and experiencing the rich history and hospitality of local communities.

For the first three days of our trip, we used Lomond, once the largest sawmill operation in Newfoundland, as a base camp. Like the adjacent mountains, this abandoned community is steeped in history. In the early 1900s, the logging industry flourished. Logs were driven down the Lomond River destined for Britain. The manicured grassy meadows of the nearby Lomond Campground and Killdevil Lodge are the same meadows that produced the hay that sustained the work horses so vital to the early logging industry. There are no horses today, but there are plenty of moose. Gros Morne National Park has perhaps the highest density of moose in the world. Morris the moose has been a familiar sight for more than ten years.

From the Lomond base camp, there's a wide variety of paddling and hiking possibilities. If you paddle when the bay is calm, you can explore the intertidal zone. Changing tides, light and seasonal cycles transform this unique part of the ocean into a thousand different experiences. Our first excursion was to the Lomond River estuary, where the tide is in charge, deciding who will enter and who will leave.

Two osprey caught our attention as they circled and plummeted to the sea, each surfacing with a fish in their talons. A bald eagle, nesting in a nearby pine, eyed an easy meal. Dropping out of its nest, the eagle glided towards one of the osprey hoping to harass it enough to part with its meal of fresh fish. But the osprey, with better speed and maneuverability, won the chase.

Our early morning walk through an intertidal zone was an enlightening experience. We found such animals as the common and smooth periwinkles, conical limpets, white barnacles, side swimmers, small shrimp and crabs. Plant life included lumpy and branched pink coraline algae, clumps of Irish moss, seaweeds and a wide variety of other interesting marine algae.

The Lomond peninsula, between the east and south arm of Bonne Bay, is primarily limestone. Cave systems and sinkholes along Newfoundland's west coast are evidence of this relatively soft rock. Approximately 3 miles (5 km) south of the Lomond River estuary is one of the largest known sinkholes. Measuring approximately 70 yards across and close to 75 yards deep, the sinkhole features a spectacular 82-foot-high (25 m) waterfall. Interestingly enough, this water then travels 2.5 miles (4 km) underground through limestone to a nearby pond, which eventually feeds the Lomond River.

Leaving the limestone cliffs of the Lomond peninsula, we paddled northeast. In the distance, Big Hill, Crow Cliff, Lookout Hills, Gros Morne and Killdevil Mountains reached skyward. Sculpted by the last glacial age of 11,000 years ago, they are at the mercy of time and the elements. Accumulated debris, or scree, at the base of these hills is evidence of the power of wind, water and the freeze-thaw cycle. According to Parks Canada, the Lookout Hills have slumped on such a massive scale that they are one of the largest examples of this kind of land movement known in North America.

## Going to the Fridge for a Drink

The sea kayak allows the paddler an intimate look at the coastal geology, but beware. On one occasion, Sheldon, our seasick paddler, paused in the still water to get a closer look at the rocks under his kayak. As the kayak drifted with the tide, Sheldon followed it under his kayak . . . literally! He proceeded to execute the first half of an Eskimo roll followed by a wet exit from his boat.

Any ensuing capsize became known as "going to the fridge for a drink." The east arm of Bonne Bay is called a natural refrigerator since its bottom temperature is 30° F (-1° C), yet the water remains unfrozen. Salinity prevents it from freezing, and winter chilling causes the water to become more dense and sink. This cool and deep water is home to a variety of marine organisms: arctic cod, which remain in the bay year-round, winged sea-star, arctic kelp, arctic jellyfish, snow crab and redfish.

As we wandered the beds of bladderwrack in the rocky outcrops of quartz, shales and gneiss along the north shore of the eastern arm, we found ourselves enveloped in a thick blanket of fog. Visibility was 50 to 65 feet (15–20 m) so we had to make the 2-mile (3 km) crossing back to camp in the fog. This first crossing became the genesis of our Alpha, Bravo, Charlie concept for keeping in voice contact while paddling in less than ideal conditions.

From Lomond, there are three developed hiking trails — Lomond River, Stuckless Pond and Stanleyville — one for each day's kayaking. Keeping an eye out for black bear and moose added to the excitement of each hike. While we were having evening dinner on the Stanleyville Trail, Morris the moose grazed for a half an hour, just 50 yards away.

The following morning we broke camp and packed our kayaks for the trip along the south shore of Bonne Bay's east arm. Paddling past abandoned communities, visions of once-vibrant bustling villages were reflected in the water between the shoreline and our passing kayaks. Along the way we encountered fishermen checking their lobster pots. Many fear the waning fishery, like the long-gone logging industry, may also become a thing of the past.

Heavy showers beat down on the decks of our kayaks. As we entered the tickle (narrow channel) between Norris Point and Gadds Harbour, the clouds were quickly whisked away by a driving headwind. Rounding the point, it was time for another check: Alpha, Bravo, Charlie . . . This was the first hard paddling we had experienced in four days and it seemed it was only beginning. We took a break at Gadds Harbour, surrounded by a flock of grazing sheep.

The clearing sky brought strong winds and whitecaps on the south arm of Bonne Bay, prompting us to move on. The paddle to Woody Point was a lateral crossing in the face of the oncoming wind. Rather than paddle broadside, we chose to do a wind ferry, making the crossing safer and reducing the effort.

Approaching Woody Point, the wind fell back and a group of curious local residents welcomed us to their gravel beach and quaint community. One of the welcoming party was eighty-five-year-old William Roberts, affectionately known as Uncle Bill. He smiled with pride as his granddaughter Alison beached her kayak. It was Uncle Bill who provided Alison with much of the encouragement to take up activities such as sea kayaking, and there was a part of him that would have liked to have been in that boat. Woody Point was our last opportunity to stock up on supplies before heading out in the unsettled shores of the Gulf of St. Lawrence. As we departed, Uncle Bill again offered kind words of support and good luck for Alison and our group.

A short paddle and we arrived at our camp for the night, the abandoned community of Curzon Village. As we sat around the campfire, we heard the blow of a whale. A single minke whale slipped silently away.

## Seasick Kayaker in Delta Boat

The following morning brought more clear skies and wind, enough wind to prevent us from venturing out in the unprotected Gulf of St. Lawrence. For the first time we used our weather radio, but knew the information might not be accurate — the reporting site is 125 miles (200 km) away and does not reflect the unique micro-climates in and around Bonne Bay. The most reliable water and weather conditions are from the fishermen out hauling their traps. Their accuracy can be uncanny.

Even though we were wind-bound, it was warm and sunny and everyone got to do what he or she pleased. Some hiked to the top of Lookout Hill while others paddled nearby, practicing surf landings and shore squirting (paddling between obstacles with a surging tidal run). Three probe boats ventured out near the mouth of the bay to check conditions in Gulf. That evening, while huddled around the campfire, we made plans for a five o'clock start the following morning.

Five o'clock became six. Along this stretch of the coast, it is important to avoid the wind as much as possible since landing zones are few and far between. When we rounded Eastern Head, the wind was beginning to blow. Rafting up, we discussed our options, realizing it was still early and we would not see the full force of the wind until around 10 A.M. The weather forecast called for 15-to-20-knot winds from the southwest, close to the limit of our comfort zone but manageable. But instead, we got 30-plus-knot winds and a seasick kayaker in Delta boat.

It took us over ten hours to cover the 10 miles (15 km) from Curzon Village to the Green Garden campsite. In the final couple of miles, the wind dropped and the sun began to shine. A flock of sheep shadowed us along the shore, nimbly traversing the steep cliffs.

As the evening sun and tide fell together, the late light reflected off the still waters of a large intertidal pool. A sheer cliff of ash and lava marked the eastern limit of our campsite. This naked cliff face was a striking contrast to the lush grassy terrace 115 feet (35 m) above.

Overnight, the wind changed from southwest to northwest. Strong southwest seas, still running from the previous day, collided with the overnight northwesterly winds, producing chaos on the water. Triangular surging wave peaks dotted the horizon. These knobby seas remained the last challenge between us and our destination — Trout River.

Paddling well offshore, we avoided rebounding waves. Once at the picturesque community of Trout River we were rewarded with stunning images — a vibrant fishing village in a flourishing river valley, the bare Tableland Mountains in the distant background and raised beaches in the foreground. The Tablelands represent one of two places in the world where the Earth's mantle is exposed; this uniqueness is why Gros Morne National Park was designated a UNESCO (United Nations Educational, Scientific and Cultural Organization) World Heritage Site in 1987.

In all, Gros Morne National Park has over 100 miles (160 km) of shoreline to challenge and engage paddlers of all abilities and interest. A diverse and spectacular range of marine and terrestrial features make paddling this coastline more than a paddling experience. It can become a life-forming experience.

*Section Two*

# 18 Profiles of 24 Trippers

# Wendy Grater
*Recipient of Many Black Feathers*

A_CCORDING TO AN OLD LEGEND, "IN BYGONE DAYS, WHEN THE LAND was only marked by footprints on narrow trails, the Voyageurs ventured by birchbark canoe and back-breaking portages across Canada's vast northland in search of furs and trade with the First Nations peoples. When a Voyageur returned from his first foray beyond the Arctic divide, he was awarded a black feather, or *plume noire*, to proudly wear in his hat."

This tradition of wilderness travel fosters an appreciation of nature and respect for the environment, and develops cooperation and teamwork, says Wendy Grater, a director, co-owner of and guide for Black Feather Adventure Company, Canada's largest paddling outfitter, since 1984.

In 2000, Wendy became the company owner by acquiring all the Black Feather shares. "I have personally paddled or hiked almost every destination that Black Feather offers," she explains. That's a lot of trips — from the Petawawa and French Rivers and Georgian Bay Islands in Ontario, the Dumoine River in Quebec and the Upper Stikine River in British Columbia to the Horton, Coppermine and Mountain Rivers in the Northwest Territories and the Hood and Burnside Rivers and Pond Inlet in Nunavut. In the late 1980s, Wendy pioneered sea kayak trips along the coasts of Greenland.

Wally Schaber, a veteran canoe-tripping guide and former next-door neighbor of canoeing icon Bill Mason, created Black Feather in 1971, and a lot of water has since passed under Black Feather canoes. The Parry Sound, Ontario, headquartered company now employs thirty people and offers eighty canoeing, sea kayaking and hiking trips a year.

Black Feather trips are built on four sturdy pillars: low impact on the land and water, the best equipment available, experienced and congenial guides, and outstanding food.

While no-trace camping is the goal, Black Feather trips tread softly (all garbage is packed out on every trip, even human waste on rivers such as the South Nahanni in the Northwest Territories). The best in canoes, paddles, splash covers, barrels, packs and wanigans are as much a trademark as is the black feather logo. "Our guides are highly experienced and trained. Each has specialized qualifications in canoeing, sea kayaking and or hiking, along with advanced wilderness first aid," Wendy explains. "All our guides go through an apprenticeship program to ensure their skills and leadership are top-notch. We provide financial incentives for them to upgrade their skills." Campfire cuisine includes baked breads, exotic dinner entrees and stick-to-your-ribs breakfasts.

The clientele, most of them from Canada and the United States, are usually repeat customers. "We have a core of people who consistently come on our trips. They like what we offer and know our guides," she says.

Wendy was born (1954) in Montreal and moved to Toronto at a young age. She and her family always camped. While studying outdoor education and physical education at the University of Toronto, she began working as a canoe tripper at Camp Kandalore, near Haliburton, Ontario, and continued for eight years. Her boss was Kirk Wipper, the dean of Canadian canoeing.

Another important person Wendy met at Kandalore was Fred Loosemore. They married in 1979.

Wendy knew Wally Schaber through canoeing and the creation of the Ontario Recreational Canoeing Association in 1979–1980. She and Fred joined Wally and Chris Harris as directors and part owners of Black Feather and the Trailhead group of outdoor stores in 1984. That same year, Wendy helped establish the Trailhead store in Toronto (and she is still involved, in a minority role).

In 1980, Wendy and Fred adopted a Vietnamese refugee. Their son Khoan soon became an accomplished paddler, graduating from Trent University in Peterborough and leading wilderness canoe trips for Black Feather. In the late 1980s, Wendy and Fred adopted Lisa and Alex, also of Vietnamese heritage, and they too are avid paddlers. In the summer of 2001, all three children paddled the South Nahanni River.

Wendy Grater finds many rewards in being at the helm of Black Feather. While there is lots of work and little downtime, she manages to lead one or two two-week trips a year and a number of clinics. In the summer of 2001, for example, she taught a whitewater course for Nahanni National Park wardens in June, led a women's French River trip in July, and led a Petawawa River canoe trip and Pond Inlet sea kayak trip in August. "We try to introduce a new trip every summer," she says. (Black Feather's winter program includes sea kayak trips in Baja, Mexico, and cross-country skiing and winter camping in Ontario.)

Why is paddling so fulfilling? "I feel most at home in the wilderness. . . . In a small, like-minded group you can witness natural team-building," she explains. "Ultimately, a paddling trip simplifies life."

# Ayalik
## *My First Arctic Canoe Trip*

Hi. My name is Ayalik. Or you can call me Eric — that's my Qallunaaq name. I'm five years old. I'd like to tell you other kids about my canoe trip last summer. We flew in from my home in Cambridge Bay — that's in Nunavut — in a float plane, which is one of my favorite things about living here. I get to fly in float planes every summer. After a long flight, maybe one hour or a hundred, the float plane left us beside a lake mostly covered with ice. Then we went for a walk — me and my Mum and Dad, but I call them Laurie and David.

If you ask me what the best part of the trip was, I say paddle, rapids and fish. I have my own paddle and sometimes I paddled. I'm really strong — wanna see my muscles? I caught lots of fish with my new orange fishing rod, but I especially remember the first one, my first ever. I could hardly believe I had a fish on my hook and it took a long time to bring it into the canoe. It was a really big trout. Good thing I was using a really strong hook.

Another really fun thing was skipping stones. Make sure, if you come here with your Dad or Mum, that you stop on beaches where there are good skipping stones. There's lots of them. At first I was lucky to get two or three bounces. But by the end of a couple of weeks I could sometimes get it to go for seven or eight. Still though, I get lots of sinkers that just go clunk. So did my Dad.

We saw musk oxen and caribou and lots of birds. Every night in the tent I looked through the bird book to pick out all the birds we saw. If you come up here, I can tell you which birds we have — I know them pretty

well now. My favorite is the peregrine falcon, because it's the fastest, and we saw one attack a duck in mid-air. Really cool. And I saw one of their nests too, with four eggs in it. One time, we found another kind of mother bird with three chicks running around on the tundra. My Mum said it was called a Baird's sandpiper. I got to pick up one of the babies for a minute, but then I had to let it go back to its mummy. That was one time when we were trapped by ice in a big lake. That was cool too, cause the ice makes a clinking sound and we got to pretend we were an ice-breaker.

One place where we camped there was a big hill. So I told David and Laurie that there was buried treasure up on the hill and we climbed up to look for it. Sure enough, we found some arrows scratched on great big boulders, pointing to the top, and there under some rocks I found a little box of pirate candy. That was the pirate's treasure. Long time ago, the pirates could sail their ship to that hill because it was an island in the sea. I saw all the seashells on the hill from that time. It was sometime just after something called the Ice Age, when the whole place was covered with ice right up to the sky. So that candy was really old, I guess, but it tasted good anyway. I wanted to go up other hills too after that.

One time we stopped at a place beside the river where some people just like my great-great-grandparents used to live. There were stone rings where they had their tents and big piles of rocks where they used to keep the meat or fish they caught. There was nobody there today. Most of the land we saw looked like nobody had ever been there.

There was lots to see. I saw big fish that had eaten little tiny fish. I saw some birds trying to catch little fish to eat. I saw where spiders had built their webs over some empty lemming holes. I didn't see a single lemming this year, but lots of old nests, though. I saw big and small lakes and rivers, and every day we marked on the map where we camped. I saw the wind blow the ice across the lake one way one day, so it piled up on the shore, then switch and blow it across the other way the next day. While I was learning all this cool stuff, I tried to teach my Dad about Pikachu, Bulbasaur, Pidgeotto and Squirtle, but it was hopeless. After three weeks, I was glad when the float plane came to get us again, to fly home, but for sure it was a really fun trip. If you can, get your Mum or Dad to take you on a canoe trip up here. Bye, now.

*To write this story down, Eric Ayalik Okalitana Pelly had a little help from his father in Cambridge Bay, Nunavut, David Pelly. During each summer since his first trip, Ayalik has participated in a three-week barrenlands canoe trip.*

# Scott Cunningham
*Circumnavigator Comes Home to Roost*

Scott Cunningham, born in 1949, didn't grow up in a canoe. He can't even remember paddling at all before age twenty-five, and from his late teens until early twenties, his destinations, in mindset and reality, were far from his native province.

He worked summers in Europe, where he pursued his passion for mountaineering. He even chose to study in France, where he could pursue his sport while learning another language and obtaining a Master's degree in science. When he returned to Nova Scotia to complete his doctoral studies in molecular biology at Dalhousie University, bouldering in Peggy's Cove seemed about all that was open to him — and that could scarcely compete with the rigors of the Matterhorn North Face.

However, the absence of the mountains and other vast tracks of wilderness couldn't suppress his desire for adventure. In seeking out something closer to home, he undertook a winter ski traverse of the Cape Breton Highlands and then a rugged fall hike up the Cheticamp River gorge. These were challenging journeys, but they were limiting in scope, and so he would have to look elsewhere.

What he found was right before his eyes. It literally surrounded him, and set Nova Scotia apart — over 4,350 miles (7,000 km) of rugged and diverse shoreline. He decided it was here that he should seek his challenge. He would circumnavigate the province in an open canoe.

In summer 1980, Scott and Paul Potter circumnavigated the entire province in an 18-foot Grumman canoe. During this epic trip, they viewed some of the most spectacular scenery in North America, as few have the chance to see it. The experience made Scott reassess his life goals and leave his research job at Laval University. He returned to the province of his birth, to a modest home on the Eastern Shore, with a desire to introduce others to the joy of exploring the Nova Scotia coastline from the unique perspective of a canoe. While building up his business (he had only one customer the first year), Scott made ends meet by creating hand-molded candles, which he sold at craft fairs and wholesaled across the county.

He acquired several canoes and spent free time (there was a lot in those early years) exploring other nooks and crannies that had eluded him during the circumnavigation. By 1986, it became apparent that, although coastal canoeing had stood the test of comfort, safety and practicality, the potential customer preferred this exploration with kayaks. The Coastal Adventures fleet was gradually transformed. Scott was fortunate that Harrie Tieken had just emigrated from Holland and brought his sea kayak manufacturing expertise (and his newly designed Sealution) with him to the Tangier area.

Since then, Scott, now joined by his partner, Gayle Wilson, has pioneered sea kayaking touring and instruction in Eastern Canada. He continued to explore the Atlantic Canada coastline and in 1996 compiled a detailed route guide to Nova Scotia (revised and updated in 2000). Similar guides are also in the works for New Brunswick, Prince Edward Island and Newfoundland. He has also paddled extensively in Europe (Britain, Wales, Germany, the Netherlands and France), where he obtained senior instructor status with the British Canoe Union.

Through his sea kayaking school, Scott has been instrumental in providing training for guides and outfitters, and brings in highly experienced sea kayaking coaches (many from Britain) to share their experience and expertise.

In fall 1998, Scott was contracted by the Canadian Recreational Canoeing Association to develop a national sea kayaking program. He developed course outlines and coordinated the implementation of the first national Canadian sea kayaking system. This ambitious project has united experienced instructors from British Columbia, the Great Lakes region, Quebec and Atlantic Canada.

Scott, who is a CRCA sea kayak instructor trainer and chair of the CRCA sea kayaking development committee, is back home with Gayle and their daughter, Sadie. There are now fifty kayaks in Coastal Adventure's fleet and 600 clients a year who participate in trips from one to eight days in length. Maybe soon there'll be a circumnavigation trip.

# Betty Pratt-Johnson
## *Just Say Yes, and the Energy Comes*

ENJOYING THE OUTDOORS, THEN WRITING ABOUT IT, IS WHAT BETTY Pratt-Johnson is all about. She started scuba diving at 37 years of age, white-water kayaking at 47, paragliding at 67, and then, at 70 . . . ice climbing.

"I just say yes to what I want to do, and the energy comes," Betty explains.

From 1978 through 1982, she expended a lot of energy paddling British Columbia's myriad rivers. Few people have paddled more rivers or more intensely. From 28 river runs and 12 hot springs in the West and East Kootenays to 17 river runs and 5 ocean-surfing sites on Vancouver Island, to 37 river runs and one tidal rapid in the Greater Vancouver, Whistler, Fraser Valley, Okanagan and Thompson River region, Betty has paddled them all, often more than once — and soaked in every hot spring she wrote about. You can read about them in her three bestselling *Whitewater Trips for Kayakers, Canoeists and Rafters* guidebooks.

Not bad for a paddler who was slow to learn the Eskimo roll and who, during her first year of kayaking, tipped and swam at least twice every trip.

"Early in my second season of paddling, I met 'Diesel' Dave Coles beside the Chilliwack (he later died on a river), and he encouraged me to go to a rolling session at the Capilano Kayak Club that night. At that session, two-time K-1 Canadian champion Eric Munshaw coached me, and more important, encouraged me by telling me how he learned to roll. He rented a motel pool and practiced for three months until he really got his roll down pat.

"In March, soon after that pool session, Brian Creer invited me to practice daily at the Lord Byng High School pool. Bev Ramey worked out there at the same time, and after that we paddled many rivers together. It took me three months of daily pool time to feel solid with my roll. And because of what Eric had told me, I was not embarrassed to keep trying until I got it.

"Then Bev and I and my former husband, John, practiced throwing ourselves over in the lower Seymour River and rolling up in a river situation but with two rescuers at the ready. We did that for three or four weekends. For a while my roll was 50 percent with accidental upsets on the river. After that my roll was 100 percent on the river for the next few years — until it fell apart on the Bull River. . . . We had a commemorative T-shirt made. On it was, in big letters, 'A Little Too Much Bull,' and a drawing of a bull tossing a kayak, and in small print beneath that, 'says Betty Pratt-Johnson.'"

Betty is quick to laugh at herself. She is also quick to credit others who helped her find her roll and her way. "Bill Ramey was a superb C-1 boater who encouraged me and gave me simple advice when he first took a group of us on the upper Thompson River from Goldpan Campground to the Nicoamen River," she says. "I had not learned to roll yet when he led us down this easy section. His advice: 'Head into the big stuff — that's safe. Avoid the side eddies.' I never forgot his words when paddling big water."

What's the biggest water Betty Pratt-Johnson has paddled? Lava Canyon on the Chilko, the Elaho at high water, Farwell Canyon on the Chilcotin, the Taseko and upper Fraser Rivers. As for her largest waterfall drop, that was on the Nimpkish River on Vancouver Island: "It was just 12 feet," she says with a chuckle.

Born in 1930 in Chicago, Illinois, Betty is a graduate of Purdue University. A successful freelance writer for more than thirty years, she has lived in British Columbia since 1961, moving from Vancouver to Kaslo, in the interior, in 1996. She married in 1957, and was divorced in 1999. She is mother of twin sons, Brian and Douglas, and has seven granddaughters.

Betty stopped paddling her kayak and her C-1 in 1983 because of an arthritic hip. Her paddling now is on top of a sit-on-top kayak en route to scuba diving locations. She has written three popular books on where to go scuba diving in Washington and British Columbia.

Big is not necessarily better. Betty says her main reason for paddling was to find out what was around the next bend. When running rivers, each moment is real and intense and challenging. After all, rivers change. "Whether exploring or repeating a favorite river run with friends, you must paddle every time as if it were a new river," she explains. "It is."

Her river philosophy is simple and succinct: "Paddling is for sheer fun."

Her Vancouver Island book is dedicated to "the very special people who fished me from many rivers, then paddled with me again." In particular, Ben Lemke, Willy Paffenholz, Mike Bohn, Colin Coe and many more from the Vancouver Kayak Club. "If they had not given me that kind of support throughout my first season paddling Class II rivers, I might never have developed as a paddler," she says now.

"I have lots of happy memories," Betty says. "But perhaps the most meaningful were those occasions when our group explored wilderness rivers, some of them probably first descents. Klaus Streckmann and the late Dane Wray taught us to use topographic maps; to climb from our boats and scout when we could not see around the next bend. No paddler should proceed downriver unless he or she can see two eddies ahead that are within his or her skill level to catch, so if you miss the first you can dart into the second and stop. . . . On some trips each paddler had the opportunity to lead. It was scary but rewarding.

"Willy (Paffenholz) was a seasoned old-time paddler who led me, and many others, down a lot of rivers and taught us informally as we went," Betty recalls. "The second time I kayaked the lower part of the Thompson River, from the Nicoamen River to Lytton, for some odd reason it was Willy's first time down that section. He laughed and said I was leading him.

"At the end of the run he handed me his homemade paddle and said, 'Your graduation present!' I treasure it."

# Rolf and Debra Kraiker
## *Teaching the Children Well*

By THE TIME KYLE KRAIKER AND HIS BROTHER BRENDAN WERE NINE AND six, respectively, they had pretty impressive canoe trip credentials. From the mouth of the Horton River on the shores of the Arctic Ocean to the island-dotted landscape of the Florida Everglades, to the fog-shrouded hills of Newfoundland to the mountain lakes of British Columbia, they had paddled through parts of this continent that most Canadians only dream about.

"Canoes are a great way to take children into the wilderness," says their mother, Debra. "Regardless of their age, kids will want to feel like they're part of the trip and parents need to be prepared to accommodate them."

Accommodation doesn't take much. Just a little more time to explain and instruct. Just a little more effort to demonstrate how to help out. And just a little more joy to explore and appreciate their surroundings.

"No other way of traveling through the wilderness makes it as easy to take children along as canoeing does," says father Rolf. "From our experience, I'd say the key to taking children into the wild is to start them as young as possible and never tackle trips that exceed your own abilities."

Debra and Rolf, both accomplished paddlers and instructors, are owners of Blazing Paddles, an Ontario canoe school near Barrie, Ontario (the website is www.blazingpaddles.ca). Rolf is a CRCA master canoe instructor and helped in preparing some of the Canadian Recreational Canoeing Association instructor's manuals.

The Kraikers have many skills and talents. They have served a number of terms on the Ontario Recreational Canoeing Association's board of directors, are longtime members and directors of the Barrie Canoe Club and volunteers for the CRCA.

They are authors of *From Cradle to Canoe*, a book described as the bible for canoeing with children, as well as many articles for outdoor and paddling magazines. Debra and Rolf are videographers of five nature documentaries, including *Arctic Sanctuary*, an account of their 1994 Thelon

River trip, for Discovery Channel. They also assisted with the production of a safe canoeing video for the CRCA and Canadian Coast Guard. In addition, they are designers of their own canoeing gear, from specialized clothing to reflector ovens. To relax, Rolf still enjoys designing, building and repairing wooden canoes and paddles.

Debra, who grew up on a farm near Beachburg, Ontario, is a high-school teacher who teaches and operates a teen-parent program in an alternative school for the Simcoe County Board of Education in Barrie. Rolf, who was born in Germany and came to Canada as an infant, is a full-time webmaster at Georgian College, a freelance book and magazine writer and photographer, and cameraman for TV nature documentaries.

Debra and Rolf met through canoeing and arrived at their wedding reception, on the shore of the Ottawa River, in a canoe that Rolf had built. "After dancing and laughing into the wee hours, we drove our old VW bus back to the shores of the Ottawa, packed up our canoe and headed out onto the river and spent the night on a favorite island," he remembers fondly. "Our honeymoon was a canoe trip down the White River to Lake Superior."

Like other veteran canoe trippers, the Kraikers have witnessed first-hand the evolution of canoes. "When we began canoe tripping, we used our old cedar-and-canvas canoe for everything — from a quiet day paddle in the nearby swamp to wilderness trips that spanned several weeks and included a lot of whitewater," he explains. "Today, we have two canoes that we use for most trips, but there's a collection of six other more specialized designs on racks in the backyard that we use regularly. We could still use a cedar-and-canvas canoe for all our paddling excursions, but the specialty canoes cut down on the worry we feel on some outings. This allows us to focus more on the trip. . . . We're still passionately in love with the feel of a wooden canoe paddled in the calm of a mist-filled morning."

In recent years the Kraikers started using folding canoes to ease logistical problems. Made from the same tough material as whitewater rafts, folding canoes have been popular in Europe for quite some time. "We have used folding Pakboat canoes on our Arctic trips and were pleased that we had. The canoes took a bit to get used to as they handled a little differently than we were accustomed to, but they were rugged enough and there were no problems being able to handle the heavy loads," he says. "We brought the canoes with us on commercial flights from Toronto to Inuvik as baggage, for example, and all our gear and canoes were inside a single-engine bush plane on the trip to the river. That meant we could reduce costs because we didn't have to charter the big twin-engine Otter."

Almost forty years ago, curiously, Rolf's first watercraft was an old Klepper folding kayak donated by a family friend. "While it was a great thrill to be independent on the water, it didn't quite fulfill my desire to have a canoe. I was never quite satisfied until my dad split the kayak paddle and put T-shaped canoe grips on the top of each half," he remembers. "It wasn't the most comfortable boat to kneel in, but I finally had a craft I could paddle like a canoe."

With all their trips combined, the Kraikers have easily paddled from the East Coast to the West Coast and back several times over. But in all those trips they've had very few mishaps. "We don't have any tales of narrow escapes or near disasters. With careful planning and preparation, there hasn't really been much go wrong on our canoe trips," Debra explains. "Instead, our favorite stories are some of the magical moments: the incredible rainbow that appears after a vicious storm, the many intriguing encounters we've had with animals, the interesting people you meet on a trip."

"Canoeing is the best way to become intimate with the land. You can cover so much more territory in a canoe. You don't need to concentrate on your feet, thereby allowing your eyes to soak up the landscape around you," Rolf says. "Travel by canoe is more about the journey than the destination."

It's obvious Kyle and Brendan Kraiker are in good hands. Soon they will teach their parents well.

# Jim Boyde
*Guide for Journeys Through Yukon Time*

In ORDER TO CONNECT THE OUTDOOR WORLD WITH THE INDOOR CLASS-room, there's an educational program in Yukon for high-school students called ACES — Achievement, Challenge, Environment and Service — with paddling playing a key role.

"Achievement can be academic, physical or psychological. As for challenge, program content challenges young people, helping to change their behavior and attitude patterns," explains Jim Boyde, a longtime canoe tripper, instructor and builder, who helped create ACES in 1989. "For environment, awareness of the natural, cultural and peer environments is important for reasonable classroom behavior, so everyone should know their roots and respect and develop lifestyles which are environmentally sensitive. For service, if they want full marks, students do fifteen hours of community service work."

As part of the ACES program, Jim takes two groups of students, in the spring and fall, on extended canoe expeditions. For a number of years, the fall group traveled on the Macmillan River, but lately it has followed the McQuesten–Beaver–Stewart Rivers. The spring group usually begins at Quiet

Lake and travels the Big Salmon and Yukon Rivers to Dawson City. These trips have three distinct purposes: to improve physical well-being, promote personal discovery and provide lifelong learning skills.

Jim is also involved with Journeys Through Yukon Time, a non-profit society that promotes active learning through building and renovating boats. "We engage youth, for the most part, from here and across Canada to do expeditions with these boats on Yukon rivers and learn something of how these boats connect to Yukon history," he says.

"In 2000, for example, we had a budget of $190,000, all of it from Yukon sources, and we built kayak-form canoes and hoe-handled paddles, renovated old wood-and-canvas canoes and built from scratch stitch-and-glue kayaks, cedar-strip canoes, lapstrake row boats . . . and a 22-foot-long canoe made of moose skin."

But these crafts are not just museum pieces; they were used by forty young Canadians on twelve-day trips on four different Yukon rivers.

Jim and his wife, Pam, who runs a business promoting wilderness tourism, know all about paddling Yukon rivers and expanding boundaries. In 1976, they canoed down the South Macmillan, Pelly and Yukon Rivers to Dawson City. In 1980, they went down the Wind and Peel Rivers to Fort McPherson. Two years later they returned to Fort McPherson, this time via the Bonnet Plume and Peel Rivers. In 1987, Jim, Pam and four others canoed from Porter Lake down the Hess and Stewart Rivers to Mayo, Yukon.

In the summer of 2001, Jim and Pam paddled the Snake River and, besides experiencing fabulous whitewater and hiking, and seeing Dall sheep, caribou, moose, grizzly bears, hawks and owls, they made sure they spent time at First Nation fish camps. "We sat around an outside stove drinking black tea and remembering the old days," he says. "Those experiences and images are now part of the ACES Yukon studies course."

Jim Boyde wasn't always so involved with canoes and canoeing. In fact, he didn't become interested until after high school. Born in 1943 in Williams Lake, British Columbia, he joined the navy in 1964 and was shipped to Inuvik, Northwest Territories, where he learned to cross-country ski. He combined his marksmanship and skiing skills in biathlon, representing Canada at the 1968 Winter Olympics in Grenoble, France. A year later he moved to Vancouver to attend Simon Fraser University, and with the guidance of paddling guru Brian Creer, became a master canoe instructor. In addition, he earned degrees in geography and teaching from SFU.

Yukon rivers didn't become destinations until Jim helped develop a wilderness leadership curriculum at Vancouver's Capilano College. Soon he was plying the waters of the Blackstone–Peel–Rat–Little Bell–Big Bell–Porcupine Rivers as well as the Ogilvie–Miner–Porcupine Rivers. Jim also started guiding raft trips on rivers such as the Firth and Alsek. With a teaching job waiting in Mayo, he moved permanently to Yukon in 1985 and immediately introduced canoe tripping as a means for students to better understand themselves and their environment.

Jim knows full well the benefits of computers and the Internet, but he feels there's too much sit-down-and-stare time. "Students need to rediscover how traditional First Nation travelers, European explorers, prospectors and contemporary recreational paddlers discovered themselves in the wilderness of Yukon," he explains. "With canoeing, there is no more fulfilling way to understand oneself and one's country."

# The Late Victoria Jason
## Kayaked Northwest Passage
## and Reintroduced Kayak to Inuit Village

THE PADDLING COMMUNITY LOST AN INFLUENTIAL AND IMPORTANT MEMBER on May 20, 2000. Victoria Jason, the first woman to kayak the Northwest Passage and responsible for reintroducing the kayak to the Inuit village of Kugaaruk, formerly Pelly Bay, in the late 1990s, died from a brain tumor. She was fifty-five.

Victoria first visited Kugaaruk, a hamlet of 520 denizens located 155 miles (250 km) north of the Arctic Circle, during her journey through the Northwest Passage. She completed the trip in four summers, from 1991 to 1994 (the last two summers she traveled solo). *Kabloona in the Yellow Kayak*, her account of that voyage, won the McNally Robinson Manitoba Book of the Year in 1996. (Kabloona means stranger in Inuit; her second book, *Kabloona Returns: Arctic Summers in Pelly Bay*, was published posthumously in the fall of 2002.)

Motorboats began to replace kayaks in Canada's North in the 1950s and 1960s. Victoria wanted the young Inuit to learn kayaking, not for hunting or sports, but to keep the tradition alive.

In 1997, the first year kayaks were brought to Kugaaruk, more than 330 residents, half of them school-age children, paddled kayaks. "Vicky was always patient and understanding," recalls Phil Hossack, a frequent paddling partner. "Standing thigh-deep in the frigid Arctic Ocean for hours at a time, she quickly focused beginners on paddling skills. Her most repeated lesson was: 'The kayak knows what to do.'"

An ecotourism business was born. "I never intended to start a tourist business," Victoria once said. "It probably started from selfish reasons. I wanted someone to kayak with, and it mushroomed from there." Today,

Kugaaruk attracts tourists who want to kayak in the region with Inuit guides. Victoria's enthusiasm lives on as a big part of that future.

"The best way to understand Victoria's way of thinking and her reasons for being in the Arctic was to paddle with her," Phil explains. "She loved the water, the land and the people. All the way out to the islands that shape Kugaaruk's harbor and back, Vicky's voice drifted across the bay as she sang 'You are My Sunshine.' Her kayak [a 16-foot-long fiberglass touring Bluewater Huron] was aptly named *Windsong*, and together they were one with the ocean."

Victoria was always a fighter. At forty-four, after recovering from two strokes, she left her job as a data entry operator with CN Rail in Winnipeg to try to kayak Canada's northern coast, from Churchill, Manitoba, to Tuktoyaktuk, Northwest Territories. That was the beginning of her long-distance paddling adventures.

Born in Durban, Manitoba, in 1945, she was twice married, the mother of three daughters, Angie, Debbie and Teresa, and grandmother of four children, Garrett, Keith, Denine and Aleia.

Victoria Jason was cremated and returned to the North she loved so much. The City of Winnipeg renamed a park near her former home.

"Vicky was a symbol of someone who threw off the shackles of the everyday world," Phil explains. "If you are kayaking anywhere in the world, you will meet people who'll remember her. Vicky showed all of us the lesson of discovering the vastness of one's own interior through the vastness of nature's exterior."

# Harry Collins
## From Wild River Surveyor to Miramichi Director

Back in the early 1970s, select paddlers from across Canada had dream jobs. They spent the summers paddling wild and remote rivers. And best of all, they got paid for the pleasure — approximately $8 an hour.

During the summers of 1971 to 1974, the Wild River Survey of Canada, initiated by Prime Minister Pierre Elliott Trudeau, himself an avid paddler, sent out teams of canoeists to survey, photograph and report on Canadian waterways — from the Yukon to Newfoundland and Labrador — for what eventually became the foundation for the Canadian Heritage Rivers System (CHRS).

Harry Collins, who was born in 1948 and raised in Huntsville, Ontario, learned to paddle on the Muskoka Lakes and in nearby Algonquin Park. He was one of the few wild river surveyors for all four years of the program; he then extended the survey into 1975. "I estimate, as a wild river rat, I paddled 5,000 miles (8,000 km) of the finest wilderness rivers in Canada during that time," he remembers fondly.

Harry Collins is cited eleven times in the seminal paddling book *Canoeing North Into the Unknown — A Record of River Travel: 1874 to 1974*. In 1971, he was a member of a crew who paddled the Sixty Mile and Yukon Rivers to Dawson City, Yukon. That same year he was also on the Macmillan River and down the Big Salmon to the Yukon River.

In 1972, Harry paddled extensively in Newfoundland and Labrador, on the Ugjoktuk River, including into Harp Lake; the Kanairiktok and Eagle Rivers; down the Petit Mécatina and the Natashquan River.

The following year he led a crew down the Frances and Liard Rivers in northern British Columbia and southern Northwest Territories. That year he also paddled the Stikine River in British Columbia. In 1974, he explored the east shore of Manitoba's Lake Winnipeg, including the Pigeon and Bloodvein Rivers.

Even though the Wild River Survey of Canada inventory was completed in 1974, Harry convinced administrators that the Notakwanon and other Newfoundland rivers should be included. He recruited three long-standing members of the program and together they had a rich summer of river travel.

Participation in the Wild River Survey presented Harry Collins with two other life-changing events: meeting his future wife and starting another love affair with Atlantic Canada. At the end of the trip down the Yukon River, he met Nicola McCleave, from Halifax, in Dawson City's Sourdough Saloon. She was in the Yukon as a participant in the Opportunities for Youth program. And after paddling in Newfoundland and Labrador in 1972, he knew he had to find a way back to live in the mysterious East.

After finishing his bachelor's degree in physical geography from Carleton University in Ottawa, Harry went on to study biology at Dalhousie University in Halifax. There he met Nicola again; they were married in 1976 in Newfoundland. After graduating, Harry worked briefly as a surficial geologist for the Newfoundland and Labrador government and after that as a planner for Parks Canada, principally in New Brunswick.

In 1993, he joined the Miramichi River Environment Assessment Committee in Newcastle, New Brunswick, as its executive director (the area of the Miramichi watershed is 5,200 square miles (13,000 square km), greater than 20 percent of the province). His committee is a community-based, multi-stakeholder organization dedicated to maintaining surface water quality.

Harry is the New Brunswick representative on the Canadian Heritage Rivers Board, a national program created in 1984 to recognize and protect the vital heritage role of rivers. For 2001–2002, he was the CHRB chairperson.

In June 2001, Fredericton was host for the 3rd Canadian River Heritage Conference. (Previous sites were Peterborough, Ontario, in 1995 and Victoria, B.C., in 1998, with Ontario's Grand River watershed on tap in 2004.) It was presented by the St. John River Society and sponsored in part by the CHRS, and the theme was Caring for the Waters that Connect Us. "It was a privilege hosting the Canadian Heritage Rivers Conference," says Harry, a member of the conference organizing team. "It was four days of special speakers, a river art exhibition, heritage and artifact displays, and all-day tours focusing on rivers and their importance in our lives."

Rivers have shaped Harry's life. He and Nicola have five children (three sons and two daughters) and they continue the paddling tradition in New Brunswick on coastal waterways and provincial rivers such as the Kennebecasis, Magaguadavic, Restigouche, Tobique and, of course, the Miramichi.

# Cathy Allooloo
## From City Kid to NARWAL Owner

SHE WENT ON TO PLACE THIRD AT THE NATIONAL WHITEWATER
Championships in Minden, Ontario, in 1981 and represent Canada at the
World Championships in Bala, Wales, that same year, but Cathy Allooloo's
first experience in a kayak was far from auspi-
cious. "Trying to make that stupid little boat
pass in between those hanging poles seemed
impossible," she remembers of her time in the
University of Alberta swimming pool. "I got out,
threw my paddle on the deck and left in disgust."

But Cathy is not a quitter. "The next day I
was back, intrigued by the challenge," she says.
"I learned how to roll in one session and then
went on to race at Alberta provincials for many
years, in both kayak and C-2, and placed in the top four at several national
championships between 1977 and 1981." Two outdoor education instructors
from the U of A — Mark Lund and Mors Kochanski — were instrumental
in developing her interest in paddling and the outdoors.

Born in 1957 in St. Catharines, Ontario, and growing up in Ottawa,
Mississauga and London, Cathy was an urban girl who didn't know much
about the wilderness and even less about paddling.

Today, however, she is owner and director of Northern And Remote
Wilderness Adventures (NARWAL), an outdoor adventure training school
incorporated in 1987 and based in Yellowknife, Northwest Territories. It
specializes in canoeing and kayaking instruction, tours and rentals. For more
than twenty years, Cathy has dedicated her summers to teaching paddling,
and she estimates she has personally instructed more than 3,000 clients.

NARWAL's paddling programs are held between early June and mid-
July. Then Cathy and family (husband Titus, daughters Kayley and Tiffany,
and sons Pauloosie and Devon) go touring. "Summers always include a family
canoe trip for at least a couple of weeks," she explains. "We figure this is
very important, otherwise the kids will grow up hating what we love."

In the summer of 2001, Cathy led a circumnavigation of Wilson Island on the east arm of Great Slave Lake. "On our return, the family came with us on a guided canoe-and-kayak tour from Yellowknife to Rae Edzo, along the north arm of Great Slave Lake. Almost immediately after that, we were off again with some Swedish clients for a two-week trip, which included eleven days of paddling on the Cameron River followed by four days of hiking around Greenstockings Lake on the tundra."

Cathy takes a breath and continues. "After our return, we had a two-week contract taking over 500 Yellowknife school kids on voyageur canoe rides. This was done in conjunction with the touring national exhibit, the Canadian Canoe, which was on display at the Northern Heritage Centre," she says. "By that point we were itching to get out of town again, so we took the kids out of school and headed north to the barrens to fish, pick berries and hunt caribou."

During the off-season, Cathy and Titus put food on the table by hunting or guiding hunts. The family also takes Japanese tourists ice fishing. "During these outings," she says, "we are often accompanied by the children."

Before heading north in 1981, Cathy participated in marathon paddling, often against men — and beating them; she helped develop Project Discovery, an outdoor adventure program for inner-city youth for the Edmonton Boys and Girls Club; led guided tours on B.C.'s Kootenay River; and was secretary of the Edmonton Whitewater Paddlers. After moving north, she held various positions for the City of Yellowknife, including recreation program manager and assistant director; and for the Government of the Northwest Territories, Cathy was assistant director for sport and recreation. During her summer holidays she continued to teach canoeing and kayaking.

But by 1996 she was tired and disillusioned. "I did some serious re-evaluating of my priorities," she says. "I wanted to have more time with my kids, so I took the plunge. I quit my job and decided to get back full-time to outdoor recreation. It was a big risk going from a cushy biweekly government paycheck to living hand to mouth."

Cathy has not looked back. "It was a bit of a struggle financially the first couple of years, especially with the birth of my son Devon, in 1996. But my life has been so rich. I've met so many amazing people and have been able to see so many beautiful and remote places — I do not have a single regret."

# Max Finkelstein
## *Downtown Mountain Man*

By Sheena Masson

V<small>ERY OCCASIONALLY YOU MEET SOMEONE WHO LIVES AN URBAN LIFE</small> but who is also comfortable spending months paddling wilderness rivers, portaging remote forest trails and camping wherever that day ends. Meet Max Finkelstein.

Ottawa is his home and Max, a canoeing wordsmith, works in a large office complex in nearby Hull, Quebec, for the Canadian Heritage Rivers System. But sometimes he paddles to work on the Ottawa River or even camps out on the river ice in winter. You get the picture.

"I'm most at home on a river, sleeping under the stars, whether in the wildest, remotest part of the barrenlands, or in some farmer's field — I just like to be outside."

Asked about his motivation to explore, Max explains: "I don't know why I have this urge, this overpowering urge, to see what's around the next bend, over the next hill, to follow every portage to its end. When I see a river, I always want to go up it, rather than down; I don't know why. Maybe because, as my friend Chris Taggart says, the greatest high is a height of land, and that's what you get to when you go upstream."

Through his work with the CHRS, Max (born 1952) has had the good fortune to paddle many of Canada's wild rivers, such as the Thelon in the Northwest Territories/Nunavut and the Soper on Baffin Island. Fortunately for the paddling community, he is a talented and creative writer and photographer. His articles appear regularly in paddling magazines and the CHRS website (www.chrs.ca). He is a well-known figure on the national paddling scene, speaking and showing his slides at conferences, symposiums and trade shows. Look for the inspiring guy with the unruly hair and massive shoulders. (Of course, that description could fit many long distance paddlers.)

Max's most challenging trip was to paddle and portage across Canada, retracing the 1793 voyage of explorer Alexander Mackenzie, the first European to reach the Pacific Ocean by land. Max did this over a three-year period, taking a few months off work each year and accompanied by a changing group of hardy friends.

He paddled the first and longest leg solo in 1997, heading west from Ottawa all the way to Cumberland House, Saskatchewan. The next year, Max and Chris Taggart, who had also undertaken his own cross-continental expedition in 1997, teamed up. They left Bella Coola on the British Columbia coast, hiking over the Coast Range, paddling down the Blackwater and *up!* the Fraser. This was followed by a lengthy trip down the Peace River, which flows north to Fort Chipewyan on Lake Athabasca. For the third leg, Max paddled the middle section of the route from northern Alberta east to The Pas to complete the journey in 1999.

He says, "That trip for me was a pilgrimage to being Canadian. To see the land from a canoe, to see the landscapes changing at the speed a canoe travels, to sleep on the land — it lets the land soak into you. I really feel Canadian now." His book on this epic trip, *Canoeing a Continent*, was published in 2002.

Max's newest paddling partner is son Isaac, born May 25, 1999, to Max and his wife, Connie. Connie was his partner on the Peace River portion of the trip. Isaac had his first canoe ride when he was three days old and was camping and paddling in the southwest United States a few months later. It was no surprise to hear that Max has had signed them all up for a trip down the Colorado River in eight years. Be assured there will be many family canoe trips before that.

# David Finch

## Combining Passions for History and Paddling

By John Geary

DAVID FINCH IS A HISTORIAN BY PROFESSION. WHILE HE BRINGS A REAL passion to that work, he has another abiding passion: canoes.

Born in 1956 in pre-revolutionary Cuba, and now based in Calgary, David grew up in South America, where he learned to love the water at an early age, snorkeling and scuba diving. He developed a love for canoeing at Canadian summer camps.

His canoeing passion expresses itself in many forms. One is his flotilla of canoes, each with its own interesting story.

"One guy literally showed up at my door one day and said, 'I hear you accept cedar-canvas boats; I'm taking a Chestnut to the dump. If you don't take it, that's where it'll end up,'" David recalls. Although the man did not want money, David paid him $200.

Of his current fleet of twelve, David acquired some as gifts, built some himself and purchased others, such as the birchbark canoe he found in the *Bargain Finder*, a publication he eventually stopped buying because, "every time I bought it, I ended up buying another canoe."

His canoe-building passion has also resulted in some interesting experiences — like the time he bought an entire tree in Quebec and had it transported to Alberta. "I wanted some long-length gunwales, as I was sick and tired of having them break on me or open up at the joints. So sight unseen, I bought a whole tree and had it shipped out by train."

David considers canoe building a hobby, just as supplying canoes for the film industry has become a regular sideline for him. About once or twice a year some producer calls, requesting canoes, stunt work or paddling instruction for an actor. His list of movie credits includes supplying canoes for the 1998 Anthony Hopkins movie *The Edge*; providing canoes and historical advice for the 1991 filming of a *Moment in History* segment about J. B. Tyrrell's discovery of dinosaurs in southern Alberta's Red Deer River region; and providing a pair of canoes for a 2000 Budweiser beer commercial.

His paddling and historical passions seem to feed one other. For instance, a canoe trip planted the seed for a twelve-year project that eventually germinated into the book *R. M. Patterson: Life of Great Adventure*.

"One day, while canoeing on the Bow River, I met Mike McBryan poling his canoe upstream. During our discussion, he told me I should read Patterson's book, *The Dangerous River*. Once I read it, I read all his books and discovered he had lived in this area. I realized there was no biography written about Patterson, so I started working on it."

One of David's favorite paddling experiences involved helping several handicapped individuals paddle a Voyageur canoe down the Bow River. One of the participants was a quadriplegic with limited movement in one arm. However, David and the trip outfitter rigged up an oar system on the side of the canoe for him. "He really felt like he was making a contribution. It was quite thrilling to watch these people experience such a beautiful environment. It was a very special day in my life."

Because paddling is so special to David, he has a hard time hanging up his paddle for the winter. He usually manages to paddle at least once every month of the year — Calgary chinooks often provide open water in winter months.

"It's pretty hard for me to go for more than a few days without getting a paddle wet somewhere," he says. "For me, that stepping into the canoe and pushing off is a very special spiritual and physical experience. Bill Mason had it right: it's like walking on water. It transports you to another way of being, another way of feeling — it restores my soul."

Paddling during winter does not always involve battling ice, however. David has dipped a paddle in some more southerly climes, such as Baja California, where he has sea kayaked. Although he loves paddling in the south as well as more northern waterways such as the South Nahanni, a river trip closer to home really holds some of his fondest paddling moments.

"An enduring favorite for me is the Kootenay River in the fall. By September, it's a very quiet wilderness river without many rafts and jet boats. We paddle it almost every year."

His wife, Jeannie, shares his passion for paddling, as does their daughter, Annie, who has been paddling solo since she was four years old.

It's a passion David Finch wishes more people could experience. "I like to encourage people to paddle because it gives them a different way to experience the river, the landscape and . . . life."

# Scott & Tanya MacGregor
## *Paddling Publishers*

THE PLACE: QUADEVILLE, IN ONTARIO'S MADAWASKA VALLEY.

The date: spring 1998.

The idea: to publish a whitewater magazine, written and produced by paddlers for paddlers.

Those involved: Scott MacGregor, Tanya Hamber and friends.

The atmosphere: good conversation over a few cool ones, of course; notes written on paper napkins.

Mission: to target the young growth market of freestyle and playboating while incorporating old-school river running and wilderness river tripping.

Focus: present lively stories and appealing photographs highlighting the latest in boats, paddles, events, techniques and personalities.

Personal background: Scott and Tanya both grew up near Hamilton,

Ontario (he was born in 1971; she in 1972). Both worked, but not at the same time, at Boundless Adventures in Ottawa Valley, taking disadvantaged people into the outdoors. They were employed as raft guides on the Ottawa River and enjoyed many canoe trips in classic Canadian Shield country. He attended Lakehead University to study outdoor recreation, then obtained a teaching degree; she earned a business degree from McMaster University. In 1996 they embarked on a three-and-a-half month-long sea kayak trip, called Stay Afloat Expedition, from Thunder Bay to Hamilton, and worked with the Canadian Coast Guard to promote safe boating. Scott and Tanya married in 1999.

Obstacles: little money and no publishing experience.

Funding: cashed in RRSPs, maxed out VISA cards.

Action: Scott and Tanya launch *Rapid* magazine, a full-color glossy, in early 1999.

Frequency: three times a year, increasing to four times in 2001. Completed successfully.

Major paddling locations: Ontario, Quebec, Alberta and British Columbia.

Demographics: of paddlers 21 to 40 years of age, 79 percent have a post-secondary education and 56 percent have a personal income of at least $40,000 a year.

Paddling season: more than 75 percent of paddlers stretch their paddling season from April to October, while an amazing 25 percent of these brave souls pick additional paddling days throughout the winter.

Limits: none; routes once considered unrunnable are simply a new challenge.

Future: whitewater paddling community is growing by 13 percent a year.

Progress report: in first three years, *Rapid* magazine has surpassed all expectations.

Comments: "The progress and growth of *Rapid* has been remarkable considering Scott and Tanya knew absolutely nothing about the publishing business," explains Matt Cruchet, who was at the original brainstorming meetings. "Their success is founded on an honest, upfront approach when dealing with people. Rather than trying to hide their lack of knowledge and muddle through, they embraced their ignorance and used their easygoing attitudes and sharp minds to figure things out."

Encore: Scott and Tanya launch *Adventure Kayak* magazine, a glossy, full-color quarterly, in 2001.

"I think *Adventure Kayak* magazine needs to capture the uniqueness of Canada's many different regions, blending the spirit of three spectacular ocean coastlines with the magic of the Great Lakes and secret pleasures of thousands of other lakes and waterways stretching across the country," Scott wrote in the first issue.

Market: an older readership, between 35 and 54; 91 percent have a college or university education; 63 percent work in professional or managerial jobs, making at least $65,000 a year.

Conclusion: "Through all the craziness of the magazines, Scott and Tanya remain true to who they are: paddlers," says Matt Cruchet. "Whether it's slipping out after work for a quick play session at the local hole or a weekend trip to Georgian Bay for a getaway sea kayak trip, their hearts always draw them to their paddles."

Postscript: *Canoeroots*, a Canadian canoeing magazine and annual buyer's guide, was launched in early 2002.

# David Mills
## Godfather of Prince Edward Island Paddling

Only 140 miles (224 km) long and between 2.5 and 37 miles (4–60 km) wide, Canada's smallest province might not have oodles of paddling opportunities, but it does have variety — scenic inland waterways and rollicking Gulf of St. Lawrence waves — all within easy access.

One paddler who has fostered and nurtured canoe awareness, skills development, whitewater appreciation, canoe building and power paddling on the Island for close to forty years is David Mills of Charlottetown, the birthplace of Confederation and 9 miles (15 km) from the Canadian mainland.

"Not only is David a skilled paddler, he is a student of paddling," explains John Hughes, who was a participant in David's first instructional course back in 1971 and later became a close friend and paddling companion. "David is a leader who thinks things through. He's also a very good organizer."

For the first fifteen years of his working career, David toiled for the Charlottetown YMCA. He was a provincial government civil servant for the next 26 years, 20 of those as recreation coordinator for provincial parks. He retired in 2000.

Music has always been a big part of his life. In fact, David was the drummer in P.E.I.'s first rock 'n' roll band; he's also an accomplished trumpet and trombone player.

Growing up near the waterfront in Charlottetown gave David (born in 1939) access to many water-related activities, yet his interest in canoeing didn't start until he was in his early teens. "I helped build a canvas-framed canoe using scrap materials acquired from building suppliers in the neighborhood," he remembers. "And when the canoe was finished, I paddled it about the waterfront."

With the Charlottetown YMCA, he was responsible for the aquatics program and directing the summer resident youth camp. Back then, in 1960, there was no boating program at the camp. "I introduced canoeing along with rowing and sailing," he says. "Canoeing and canoe tripping became a major activity for the camp in 1964."

The camp was at the entrance to the Charlottetown harbor, which provided access to three rivers: the Hillsborough, and the North and West Elliot. Canoe trips were from between one and three days long, depending on paddler experience, age and weather.

In the late 1960s, David attended a Red Cross seminar on small boating safety and heard Kirk Wipper, a Canadian canoeing legend, give an inspiring talk and instruction on paddling. David was hooked.

"That was the beginning of my formal training and involvement with the P.E.I. and national levels of the Canadian Recreational Canoeing Association. I served as P.E.I. president, national board member, instructor's certification committee member and many other positions," he explains. "The main purpose of my involvement with the CRCA was to acquire my national course conductor certification for flat water, canoe camping and moving water in order to instruct paddlers here on the Island."

With finely honed skills and exuberance to match, David expanded the YMCA camp's canoeing program by offering courses for adults and kids during the spring months. The first of these instructional courses, in 1971,

attracted John Hughes, who found self-propelled recreation appealing. "Since then, John and I worked together to develop canoeing and canoeing awareness at both the local and national levels," he says. They also organized and led many trips on rivers in Nova Scotia (Liscomb and St. Mary's), New Brunswick (St. Croix and Nepisguit), Maine (Allagash) and Prince Edward Island (West Elliot, North, Hillsborough, Montague, Brudenell, Morell and the Dunk).

As interest in canoeing mushroomed throughout the 1970s and 1980s, there was a need for increased and upgraded certification of canoeing instructors. "I developed an instructors level program and conducted, with John's assistance, courses for individuals and employees of the Red Cross, provincial parks, summer camps and other agencies," David explains.

And then in the 1990s, David ventured off into two different but symbiotic directions: he started teaching power paddling courses (making the best use of the push portion of the paddling cycle at sixty strokes per minute and higher) for participants in competitive paddling, and he renewed his interest in building canoes.

He designed and built a 16-and-a-half-foot-long fiberglass foam-core canoe, similar in style to a Mi'kmaq rough-water canoe. "I feel strongly that the birchbark and other canoes built by Native Canadians are so well designed that they need very little improvement," he says. The Island's earliest settlers, the Mi'kmaq, called Canada's seventh province Abegweit ("cradle in the waves").

As a retiree and cancer survivor, David has taken on an advisor role for paddlers, however, he can still be found paddling flat-water stretches as well as the Dunk River, a Class II during spring runoff, in the west-central part of the Island. Yes, he has dunked on the Dunk.

His family — wife, Gayle, sons Chris, Greg and Terry, and daughter, Cathy — are all enthusiastic paddlers.

David Mills knows, and has diligently imparted the value to others, about how important and fulfilling it is to get out on the water and paddle.

# Bill Jeffery
## *Saskatchewan's River Dog*

By Joan Jeffery

AFTER SPENDING EIGHTY DAYS IN A CANOE IN 2001, ON WATERWAYS IN Saskatchewan, Manitoba and the Northwest Territories, Bill Jeffery was ready for more. There was just one problem: freeze-up. He hung up his paddle for the year and kicked back at home, on the shores of the Sturgeon River, bordering Prince Albert National Park in north-central Saskatchewan. But as he collected the winter's supply of firewood and groomed the nearby cross-country ski trails, canoeing was never far from his thoughts. There are always lots of friends around to share photos and tall tales.

Bill, born in 1949, became enchanted with the canoe when he and I were first employed as teachers in northern Manitoba in the early 1970s. (He has a B.A. from the University of Winnipeg and an Education degree from the University of Manitoba.) Our first jobs took us to Leaf Rapids, a lovely northern community on the banks of the expansive Churchill River. Overnight canoe trips became weekend trips . . . became weeklong trips . . . became odysseys. Bill finally settled in the Prince Albert area after traveling in Australia, Asia, South America and Africa, where he managed to partake in many canoeing adventures.

With so many pristine waterways, northern Saskatchewan is a canoe tripper's paradise. While Bill can expound on the delights of numerous rivers, one of his most memorable was in the mid-1980s on the Dubawnt River system in the Northwest Territories. It was a thirty-five-day trip from Black Lake, in northern Saskatchewan, to Baker Lake, Northwest Territories (now in Nunavut). Bill and biologist friend Tim Trottier paddled a 16-foot-long cedar-strip canoe 900 miles (1,450 km). A few of the indelible moments included the 3-mile-long (5 km) Chipman portage, the frozen waters of Dubawnt Lake, migrating caribou herds and the merciless winds on the barrens.

An encounter with a polar bear on the shores of Hudson Bay, in the late 1980s, made a Seal River trip unforgettable. After paddling down the Bay to Churchill, Manitoba, on an earlier trip, Bill reasoned that the dangers of powerful tides and unpredictable weather far outweighed the joys of being escorted by beluga whales and harp seals. All went well until the end of the trip. While Bill and his paddling partner were waiting for pickup, an aggressive bruin approached and broke six ribs . . . cedar-strip canoe ribs.

Another favorite trip was on northern Saskatchewan's Grease River. In 1995, Bill and friends were unable to find any signs of travel by other recreational canoeists. Many rapids and waterfalls were unmarked on their topo-graphical maps, but spectacular Lefty Falls, which plunges 65 feet (20 m), making it the province's highest, was marked and had a definite portage.

A dream trip came true in the summer of 2001 when Bill participated in a three-week adventure with local Dene. They followed ancient Aboriginal hunting routes, starting in the Northwest Territories and finishing at the community of Black Lake, Saskatchewan. With the exception of a few food staples, caribou and fish were the mainstay of their diet. The elders provided a living history of ancient Dene names for every aspect of the land, and around the campfire, their stories and legends infused Bill with a new-found appreciation of their culture.

Although Bill has already lived some of his dreams, there are many more to ponder: putting his canoe on the Sturgeon River behind our home and paddling all the way to the Arctic Ocean; paddling into a remote lake at freeze-up, building a cabin and returning home at spring thaw; building a canoe on some isolated waterway and paddling it home. I share some of his dreams.

Every summer we spend two to three weeks exploring favorite rivers such as the Elk, Thelon, Clearwater, Bloodvein, Fond du Lac and William, to mention a few.

When Bill is not canoeing or thinking about canoeing, he occupies his time with other outdoor pursuits. His winter job, with Ski Fit North, keeps him busy teaching young people to cross-country ski. Over the past decade, thousands of kids learned lifelong skills thanks to Bill's efforts.

Once the rivers thaw, he is in great demand to give paddling instruction and guide canoe trips. What a grand existence for the 21st-century voyageur — my husband — a voyageur at heart.

# Ted Moores
## *Master Craftsman*

By Gwyneth Hoyle

In business since 1972, the Bear Mountain Boat Shop, renowned for pioneering the woodstrip epoxy canoe construction technique, has had a few homes, but the most recent is the most picturesque. In 2001, proprietor Ted Moores and partner, Joan Barrett, moved Bear Mountain to beside a 19th-century farmhouse, with a fine view of the Otonabee River and lights of Peterborough.

The move from Bancroft was made, in part, to be closer to the Canadian Canoe Museum, where Ted helped establish the workshop and Joan's energy and business sense were invaluable. The Museum regularly calls on Ted's encyclopedic knowledge of canoes and their builders to provide input for displays. And whenever Ted is in the shop, he's a magnet, attracting visitors and patiently answering their many questions. His weeklong canoe-building courses are always oversubscribed.

Ted, a self-taught graphic artist, was born in Oshawa, Ontario, but he credits his Newfoundland ancestry for his love of boats and water. In the early 1970s, he and Joan established Bear Mountain Boat Shop on a steep hill on the north edge of Algonquin Park, home of many bears. After much experimentation, Ted pioneered the woodstrip epoxy technique. The result: a ribless canoe, satin smooth inside and out, that is strong and light.

Also born during this time were daughters Daisy and Jenny. Despite the rugged charm of the Algonquin Park location, there were many drawbacks, so everyone packed up for the move to Oakville. But first Ted had to finish the canoe commissioned by Prime Minister Trudeau as a wedding gift to Prince Charles and Princess Diana.

In response to the overwhelming requests from people wanting to build their own strip canoes, Ted wrote and illustrated the book *Canoecraft*. Published in 1983, it has never been out of print. His second book, *Kayakcraft*, is just as popular. *Plywoodcraft* is in the planning stages.

In addition to his Canadian Canoe Museum work, Ted is busy building sprint racing canoes. In fact, all the four-man and half the war canoes now in competition in Canadian races were built in the Bear Mountain Boat Shop.

Looking to expand their horizons, Ted and Joan spent five weeks in the Central American country of Belize in late 2000 and early 2001. With fellow designer Steve Killing, they helped a group of locals build an expedition canoe for an important four-day competition. La Ruta Maya, held each March, is a 185-mile-long (300 km) race through the jungles of Guatemala and Belize. The three racers, who helped build their canoe using Ted's technique of cedar and epoxy, placed third in a field of seventy contestants.

Back home and part of the family enterprise since they were old enough to help in Bancroft, Daisy and Jenny are now grown up, with their own careers. They have made important contributions to the Bear Mountain Boat Shop and to paddling, after working many summers for the Madawaska Kanu Centre and Owl Rafting.

Canoes, kayaks and wooden boats are the lifeblood of this family.

# Kevin Redmond
*Newfoundland's Man on the Water*

H E IS AN ACCLAIMED PADDLING INSTRUCTOR. A PROLIFIC CANOE AND
sea kayak writer and photographer. He has paddled throughout most of
Canada, but most intimately in insular Newfoundland and Labrador and
along the Eastern Atlantic coast. Born in 1956, he knows the waterways of
his native province, and enjoys them, like few others.

Kevin Redmond of Portugal Cove, Newfoundland, 6 miles (10 km) north
of St. John's, was the second person in Canada to become a Master Canoe
Instructor with the Canadian Recreational Canoeing Association. Along the
way, he became a senior CRCA flat-water and moving water canoeing and
canoe touring instructor-trainer. He has put those skills to use by teaching
paddling at a variety of post-secondary institutions, including St. John's
Memorial University, Cabot Institute and College of the North Atlantic.
He is also the former chairperson of the CRCA's Technical and Program
Development Committee and for fifteen years served on the executive of
the Newfoundland Canoeing Association.

Long before it became popular, Kevin paddled the ocean in his canoe
— cod-jigging, exploring caves and visiting whales and icebergs.

Kevin has written numerous articles about canoeing and sea kayaking
in national and international magazines. He is co-author of *Canyons, Coves
and Coastal Waters: Choice Canoe and Kayak Routes of Newfoundland and
Labrador*, published in 1996, and is currently working on two books —
*Greatland Wildland: Journeys Through Newfoundland and Labrador*, and a
book that combines tall tales and descriptions of choice sea kayak routes.

Kevin has a good eye for detail, contrasts and the richness of color. His
award-winning photographs have graced the covers of many magazines and
books. He has won a number of categories in an annual Nikon-sponsored
photo contest and a collection of his photos was part of a 1999 exhibition in
Paris, France.

In a sea kayak, Kevin has paddled the north and south coasts of
Labrador, major portions of the Newfoundland coast, and in all regions of the
province such as Notre Dame Bay, Conception Bay, Avalon Peninsula,

Voisey's Bay, St. Lewis Sound, parts of the Labrador Sea, South Coast, Gros Morne, Hare Bare, White Bay and Bay of Islands. In a canoe, he has paddled the Main, Bay du Nord, Humber, Pinware (a first descent in a canoe), Gander, Terra Nova, Exploits, Churchill and Moisie Rivers, just to name a few.

A dedicated science and physical education teacher at St. John's Gonzaga High School, Kevin knows the importance of teaching new skills. One invaluable learning experience for him was in 1976 when he attended a ten-day woodsmanship school at Ontario's Camp Kandalore, hosted by Kirk Wipper and Mike Kettimer.

For all he has given to paddling, the CRCA honored Kevin with an award of merit. But he feels he still has much to learn and to offer. For him, the canoe is a vehicle to broad-based experiences.

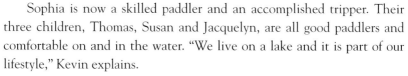

When Kevin and Sophia Fowler started going out, their third date was an ocean paddle. "As we were carrying gear to the beach, a kid looked at her and said, 'You're not going out there are you, missus?'" Kevin remembers with a chuckle. "And when Sophia said yes, the kid replied, 'You're going to die.'"

Since she wasn't a good swimmer and this was only her second time in a canoe, Sophia was quite trusting in Kevin's abilities. "It was a great evening on the water," he says. They married the following year, in 1984.

Sophia is now a skilled paddler and an accomplished tripper. Their three children, Thomas, Susan and Jacquelyn, are all good paddlers and comfortable on and in the water. "We live on a lake and it is part of our lifestyle," Kevin explains.

While the former nationally ranked lacrosse player participates in running and skiing marathons, paddling is his first love. "It is such a great way to take in a wide range of experiences," he says. "When we paddle, the experience of place moves from the brain to the heart, making it a life-forming experience."

And when it comes to choosing paddling partners, he says paddling skills are only one component. "I am thankful for the privilege of having paddled with so many different people and benefited from their special talents, enriching the experience for everyone."

# Anna Levesque, Tiffany Manchester, Saskia van Mourik, Jodee Dixon and Naomi Heffler

*Wonder Women: Paddling Rivers Around the World*

FIVE OF CANADA'S TOP-RATED COMPETITIVE FEMALE PADDLERS — ANNA Levesque, Tiffany Manchester, Saskia van Mourik, Jodee Dixon and Naomi Heffler — discuss their special paddling trips, why paddling is special and qualities needed to be a good paddler.

Anna Levesque (born 1974) of L'Orignal, Ontario, says two of her favorite paddling rivers are the Tule in California and the Ollin in Ecuador. "The Tule is

a Class IV–V drainage, about 45 miles (72 km) outside of Bakersfield. I was fortunate enough to be a part of the first descent of the south fork of the Tule. It is an incredible stretch lined with smooth bedrock, really fun slides and impressive drops. My favorite drop is a 45-foot (13.5 m) double that looks very intimidating, but is incredibly fun," she explains. "The Ollin is one of the most beautiful rivers I have ever paddled. Remote and surrounded by jungle, it is a two-day paddling trip. It is a Class III–IV run with lots of fun rapids and a few tight slots. The Cave rapid has an overhanging wall that extends from one side of the river to a boulder on the other side, forming a small cave. You paddle right through it!"

"Paddling is special because it challenges me and allows me to travel and experience places very few people see. It also introduces me to very special people," says Anna. "Every paddler is different, but the qualities I have are persistence, determination, focus, confidence, openness to suggestions and dedication."

Tiffany Manchester (born 1973) of Beachburg, Ontario, says New Zealand is her favorite place to paddle. "The Arahura, Class IV–V, enables you to practice your boof all day!" she explains. "Nepal is also great . . . it has every type of water. I paddled the Kali Gandaki, a five-day Class III–IV river, and went down with a raft support trip. Not only are the river features very challenging, but so is the attempt to stay healthy in water full of interesting creatures foreign to our immune systems.

"Paddling is such a challenging sport. I never feel satisfied with the level I'm at, because there is always so much more to learn. Second, it is a social sport that allows you to be outside with your friends, getting fit, having a good time and learning without even realizing it," Tiffany explains.

"To be a good paddler, you must be patient with yourself, driven to improve, happy, comfortable with showing your bare arse and not afraid to have greasy hair and stinky gear!"

Saskia van Mourik (born 1975) of Sundre, Alberta, likes the Slave River in the Northwest Territories — warm, large and uncrowded — and the Skoocumchuk in British Columbia. "It's crowded, but it is a sure way of running into friends you haven't seen in a long time," she says.

"Paddling has given me some of my most memorable experiences, but it has also taught me some harsh lessons."

To be a good paddler, "you need an open mind to try every discipline that whitewater paddling offers," Saskia explains. "It helps shape your technical abilities."

Jodee Dixon (born 1975) of the West Kootenays in British Columbia, favors the Mohaka River in New Zealand. "The river was challenging and

fun, with beautiful canyon walls and crazy rock formations," she says. "My paddling partners were great people, too, which always makes such a difference."

Jodee sees paddling as way to challenge herself. "A good paddler needs to focus, and be honest and confident in her abilities."

Naomi Heffler (born 1977) of Calgary, Alberta, Ottawa, Ontario, and Missinipe, Saskatchewan, says it's hard to pick favorites. However, two trips she has enjoyed are the Seal River in Manitoba and the Kipawa in Quebec. About the Seal, "As we moved down the river, it was neat to see the vegetation getting smaller as the sky got bigger than we thought possible,"

she explains. "The river has all the elements of a great wilderness canoe trip: big water, lots of wildlife including seals, caribou and polar bears, northern lights and good campsites."

As for the Kipawa, "the first drop is from the 20-foot [6 m] dam that holds the water in Lake Kipawa. . . . What a great start to the day! After the dam, there are a lot of rapids (up to Class III+ or IV) with big waves, big holes and some awesome play spots."

Why paddling is important: "Access to beautiful areas you couldn't otherwise get to, personal challenge and skill improvement, and spending time with friends," Naomi explains. "Most of all, I just love the water."

Qualities needed: confidence, reliability, determination, adaptability, focus.

# Pierre Elliott Trudeau (1919–2000)
## *Visionary, Adventurer*

By Jeff Jackson

"I WOULD NOT KNOW HOW TO INSTILL A TASTE FOR ADVENTURE IN those who have not acquired it."

So began a famous essay penned by Pierre Elliott Trudeau, Canada's long-standing prime minister, federalist, activist, intellectual, gunslinger and international irritant. While his name will live on in the story of our young nation, a certain group of Canadians will remember him because he paddled a canoe.

Introduced to the paddle at Taylor Statten's Camp Ahmek in Algonquin Park, Trudeau went on to travel rivers across Canada: an epic journey up the Ottawa, over the height of land and down the Harricanaw, across James Bay to Moose Factory (1941); on the Coppermine with the legendary Eric Morse (1966); and the rarely traveled South Nahanni River (1970). He was a regular on the Petawawa and Gatineau Rivers, just a few hours drive from Parliament Hill.

While in office, Trudeau commissioned the historic Canadian Wild River Survey — a cadre of canoe teams spread out across the North to inventory a most vital resource: wilderness rivers. This information resulted in the formation of the Canadian Heritage Rivers System (1984).

Not only did Trudeau take to his canoe for adventure and solitude, he made it okay to do so. He helped raise the act of canoeing from the realm of hunting and trapping to one of noble exploration, hearkening back to the days of the coureurs de bois. Furthermore, Trudeau happily expounded on the virtue of the canoe trip: "Canoeing gets you back close to nature, using a method of travel that does not even call for roads or paths. You are following nature's road; you are choosing the road less traveled by, as Robert Frost once wrote in another context, and that makes all the difference. . . . You discover a sort of simplifying of your values, a distinction between values artificially created and those that are necessary to your spiritual and human development."

In his 1944 essay *The Ascetic in a Canoe*, reproduced on page 271 of this book, Trudeau described his passion for paddling in the Canadian wilderness: "What sets a canoeing expedition apart is that it purifies you more rapidly and inescapably than any other. Travel a thousand miles by train and you are a brute; pedal five hundred on a bicycle and you remain basically a bourgeois; paddle a hundred in a canoe and you are already a child of nature."

In *Against the Current*, he said: "[A canoe expedition] involves a starting rather than a parting. Although it assumes the breaking of ties, its purpose is not to destroy the past, but to lay a foundation for the future."

It has been argued by political writers that Trudeau's time spent adventuring shaped his vision of nationhood. In *Right Honourable Men*, historian Michael Bliss claimed Trudeau had "an extraordinarily clear vision of the structure of the Canada he wanted to mould." And indeed, Trudeau himself concluded in *The Ascetic in a Canoe*, "I know a man whose school could never teach him patriotism, but who acquired that virtue when he felt in his bones the vastness of his land, and the greatness of those who founded it."

It is these sentiments Trudeau carried with him in his leadership, and returned to time and again when he took to his canoe.

# Vital Tips for Paddling and Protecting Canada's Waterways

# A Walking Tour of the Canadian Canoe Museum

Gwyneth Hoyle

MANY MUSEUMS HAVE CANOES AS PART OF THEIR COLLECTIONS. IN Canada, the Museum of Civilization in Ottawa, the Royal Ontario Museum in Toronto and the Glenbow in Calgary all have sizable collections of Aboriginal craft. In the northeastern United States, one of the nineteen buildings of the Adirondack Museum is devoted to portable boats, which include birchbark canoes as well as the famous Adirondack guide boats and lightweight Rushton canoes. At Clayton, New York, near the Thousand Islands, the Antique Boat Museum has a selection of carpentered canoes among its classic motor launches.

Only one museum, the Canadian Canoe Museum in Peterborough, Ontario, is devoted entirely to the collection of canoes, kayaks, allied water-craft and related artifacts. The latest extensive exhibit at this museum, spread over nine galleries, tells the story of the development of Canada through the medium of the canoe.

On entering the museum through the double pine doors, you are drawn to the portage past the waterfall, where you will find yourself in the Origins Gallery amid craft of the Aboriginal peoples. At the top of the portage is a huge whaling dugout from the north coast of Vancouver Island, carved from a single tree by the Nootka, or Nuu-chah-nulth people, at the end of the 19th century. Rigged with sails, it stands ready to go in pursuit of the whale that is depicted on both sides of the bow. Look up and you will see the Salish racing canoe, all 60 feet (18 m) of it, suspended in the air as though prepared for its next successful contest. It comes from the southeast coast of Vancouver Island and is reputed never to have lost a race. Surrounding you are dugouts from the West Coast, of different shapes and sizes, depending on who made them and the uses for which they were designed. The paddles that propelled them vary as much as the dugouts.

Move on now to the birchbarks, the canoes that came from a wide area of North America where large birch trees grow in abundance. Again you will notice that Aboriginal peoples from different parts of the country each used a unique bow-shape for their canoes, depending on the waters they were traveling. The G'wichin, from the area near the mouth of the Mackenzie River, shaped their canoes like the kayaks of their Inuit neighbors, but the decoration of Chinese trade beads indicates that they traded far and wide. Algonkian canoe-builders William and Mary Commanda, from Maniwaki, created pictures of wildlife from the Quebec hinterland in bas relief on the dark winter bark as their distinctive trademark. The shallow, sturgeon-nosed canoe of the Kootenai people from the interior of British Columbia was used for lake travel. Birch is not the only bark used for canoes. The Iroquois, from south of birch country, used elm bark and a replica is hanging in this gallery.

The kayaks, in racks around the wall, are arranged by geographical location and represent every part of the Arctic, from the Aleutians eastward to Greenland. With their skin coverings, they are the most delicate craft in the collection. On some can be seen carvings of bone, such as the oarlocks on the small umiak, or as toggles in the shape of animals on the front of some of the kayaks. There are also kayak frames, giving an insight into the mixture of art and practicality the Inuit people used to construct a working boat from the materials at hand, driftwood, bone, bits of string, wire and leather thongs.

Throughout the Origins Gallery audio-visual presentations of present-day canoe and kayak builders at work in their own communities are a reminder that these traditions are alive and healthy. As you leave the Origins Gallery, the reproduction of a full-size Mi'kmaq birchbark wigwam attests to

Aboriginal skill at using the bounty of the land to supply shelter as well as transportation. On the walls, examples of contemporary Aboriginal art portray the continuing importance of the canoe in the life of First Nations people. Cases containing a selection of models of Aboriginal craft from around the world complete this part of the museum.

Next you will come to a 19th-century canoe-builder's shed, the Traditional Skills Gallery, where Jeremy Ward is building a 36-foot bark canoe from materials that he has harvested. Rolls of birchbark are stored on shelves, and a large bundle of spruce root is waiting to be split and used for sewing the bark to the gunwales. From time to time other craftsmen are at work in this gallery, paddle-makers carving and sanding basswood or cherry, or basket-weavers pounding ash into splits to make portaging packs. Craft in need of conservation are sometimes brought into this shed and placed on supports for expert attention. In the future, when the large birchbark canoe is completed, it is hoped that a dugout or a kayak may be constructed here as well as carpentered canoes. The preservation of traditional skills is one of the objectives of the Canadian Canoe Museum.

When you reach the adjacent Trade and Alliance Gallery you notice that Europeans have arrived on the scene. A canot du nord, fully loaded with trade goods, stands at the canoe dock ready to leave for the hinterland. Further along, there is a voyageur encampment where a canot de maître is overturned to give shelter to the men while the bourgeois (the man in charge of the trip) sleeps in comfort in his tent. (The 24-foot-long canot du nord traveled west and north from Fort William, while the 36-foot-long canot de maître went from Montreal to Fort William.) This introduces you to the life of the fur trade before you descend to the ground floor to visit the trading post reconstructed from an authentic Hudson's Bay Company building that stood in Michipicoten on the north shore of Lake Superior in 1870. As the 20th century approached, the trading post outfitted people traveling north by canoe for many different reasons, surveyors of the Geological Survey, missionaries, prospectors and eventually recreational canoeists. Their story is told in the gallery called The Land Becomes Canada. In this gallery are some of the canoes and artifacts used by George Douglas from Lakefield, whose book, *Lands Forlorn*, about his exploration of the Coppermine River in 1911, is a classic of northern travel. Also in this gallery is the sectional canoe ordered by the National Geographic Society of Washington from the Peterborough Canoe Company for use in exploring the Chubb meteor crater in northern Ungava in 1951.

Carpentered canoes have already entered the picture, and in the gallery called "It Wasn't All Work," their use in regattas and other sports are featured. The tripping shed in the Summer Strokes Gallery revives memories of youth camps and the anticipation of the annual canoe trip. In the Peterborough Tradition, the wide range of craft that were built in the Peterborough–Lakefield–Rice Lake area are well represented. The variations in the canoes made by recognized builders using wide-boards, cedar strips and canvas covers are as subtly different as the variety of shapes seen in the Aboriginal craft.

Behind glass walls, a device incorporating the latest modern technology is at work measuring the timeless, simple perfection of design of individual craft. The SmartScan is a measuring apparatus that uses a synchronized light source, digital camera and robotic carriage all controlled by a computer with specialized software to document three-dimensional objects. The results are stored on disk for archival reference and conservation control, or they can be printed to show the cross-sections of particular craft at any given point to be used by a builder who wishes to construct a replica.

The last point of call is the Reflections Gallery, where you are prompted to think of the canoe as a spiritual vessel that transports you into the natural world. Here is the red Prospector that Bill Mason used to travel silently in harmony with his surroundings. His camping gear, underwater camera, paint box and unfinished sketches are arranged to give the impression of visiting his favorite campsite on Lake Superior. Artifacts of some of Canada's canoeists, no longer living, remind us that through the medium of the canoe and kayak the lives of ordinary people have been transformed into extraordinary adventures. The deerskin jacket and gloves of Pierre Trudeau, the trademark yellow visor worn by Victoria Jason, and packs and paddles belonging to Eric Morse are all here.

## From 1 to 600+

This priceless collection of canoes began with a simple dugout canoe. Professor M. G. Griffiths, head of the department of Physical Education at the University of Toronto, found it on his farm north of Lakefield. A member of his staff, Kirk Wipper, had recently acquired ownership of a boys' camp, Camp Kandalore, on Lake Kabakwa in the Haliburton Highlands of Ontario. Knowing Kirk's love of canoes and heritage, Professor Griffiths presented the dugout to the camp in 1959.

Patterned on the shape of the birchbark canoes used by the local Ojibwa, the dugout was carved out of a single basswood tree by Jacob and William Payne in 1895. The sleek lines and unadorned shape belie the rounded shape of the hull, which made the dugout a tippy craft to paddle. Kirk mounted it in the dining hall of the camp in a place of honor to remind the campers, who were in and out of canoes all day long, of the rich heritage of the craft they used.

Respect for pioneer heritage was part of the ethos at Camp Kandalore. Early logging implements and primitive farm equipment were strategically placed around the camp as reminders of this heritage, just as the voyageur and fur trade tradition was used by camp staff to instruct campers in nature lore and canoeing skills. Other canoes soon joined the Payne dugout, each with its own history. Peterborough freighter canoes that had once been used in the fur trade, canoes that had belonged to George Douglas, a birchbark from Maniwaki, Quebec, and early manufactured canoes of the Peterborough and Chestnut Canoe Companies were added to the heritage collection at Camp Kandalore. If the canoes were in good condition, campers were allowed to paddle them, carefully, to gain an appreciation of the skills of the past. The freighter canoes often served as floating platforms where performances were staged or as ferries to take campers to Chapel Island for Sunday services.

As the heritage group grew, it seemed that there were still hundreds more that would make superb additions to the collection. Kirk Wipper discovered that he had embarked on a never-ending search and he pursued

it with an insatiable passion. Some canoes came to Kandalore as gifts, but many more were sought out and acquired across the country and in the United States. By 1975 the collection numbered in the hundreds, and Kirk founded the Kanawa International Museum of Canoes, Kayaks and Rowing Craft as an entity separate from Camp Kandalore. The beautiful log building constructed to house the craft was soon outgrown as the collection continued to increase. The demands of such a huge collection became too much for one man, and a public board was appointed to administer the affairs of the Kanawa Museum in 1983. Housed in wooden buildings or, in the case of large craft, under shelters around the grounds of Camp Kandalore, this priceless collection could not be insured or protected against fire and theft. The need for a change of venue became imperative.

Peterborough and its surrounding area have a long history of canoe manufacture, beginning with John Stephenson's first plank canoes in the latter part of the 19th century. Accounts of exploration of northern Canada, such as that of the Tyrrell brothers in 1893, often began with the mention of the shipment of a canoe specially ordered from the Peterborough factory. With this background, it was natural for a group of historians from Trent University, led by John Jennings, Bruce Hodgins and Jamie Benidickson, who were also canoeing enthusiasts, to think about the possibilities of bringing the Kanawa collection to Peterborough. Negotiations were long and protracted, but in 1995 the Canadian Canoe Museum was incorporated, with a logo adopted from a pictograph found on Canoe Lake, north of Lake Superior.

In 1996, the Outboard Marine Corporation, one of Peterborough's major industries, had ceased operation and offered the Canadian Canoe Museum one of its factory buildings as storage space for the collection of canoes, now numbering close to 600. Next they gave the museum the large and imposing front office building that had been the corporation's Canadian headquarters. Bill Byrick, a man with a sterling record of success in the museum field at St. Marie-among-the-Hurons and at Discovery Harbour, and also a man who enjoys a challenge, accepted the invitation to become the new director of the fledgling museum. His task was to turn a warehouse full of canoes into a place that would lure visitors from around the world and give them a sense of the vital role of the canoe in the fabric of Canada.

There is a mystical quality inherent in the canoe that appeals to people. Whether it is the memory invoked by the pleasure of using a canoe or whether it is the historical connection of the canoe in the development of this country, canoes have a drawing power. Before the Canadian Canoe Museum became a place that could invite visitors, it attracted large numbers of volunteers with the skills to transform an office building into a living museum.

From the beginning, Aboriginal people were involved equally with members of the board and staff in planning how the story of the canoe would be told by the museum. One man in particular, Rick Beaver, Ojibwa biologist and artist, continues to connect Native communities from across the country in a dialogue with the museum. The Native people have emphasized to the museum that canoe-building traditions have not disappeared but remain an integral part of their lives today.

With the vision and imaginative direction of a small but dedicated staff, the story of the canoe, past and present, has come alive. In the wasteland between the exhibition building, named the Weston Centre, and the factory building where the bulk of the collection is housed, plans are under development for an outdoor learning center. A shallow pool, large enough for instructional paddling, is to be the centerpiece of this space.

The collection of over 600 craft, paddles and related artifacts is still growing as more and more people learn of the museum. Since it is never possible or desirable to exhibit more than a hundred or so at one time, future exhibits will be designed to showcase some of the myriad of fascinating craft that are in storage. There are exotic craft from the South Pacific and Europe; there are canoes that made incredible journeys, such as the Orellana, which carried Don Starkell and his son from Winnipeg to the mouth of the Amazon; and there are molds from which many different canoes were built. Volunteers continue to build specially fitted storage racks so that eventually visitors who wish to see canoes not currently on display will be able to view them in the collection center.

While canoes in some form were a universal means of transportation for indigenous peoples around the world, the story of Canada, with its vast system of lakes and rivers, is more closely linked to the canoe than most. With its comprehensive education program, learners of all ages are now discovering the impact of the canoe on the life of this country.

The Canadian Canoe Museum brings Canada's heritage to life in a way that people of all ages can enjoy. In the few years since it opened its doors to the public, the Museum has welcomed more than 25,000 visitors a year from all corners of the globe.

# A Grand Comeback by the Grand River

Alister Thomas

I TURNED MY BACK ON THE GRAND RIVER.

When I was growing up in Kitchener-Waterloo, in southwestern Ontario, in the 1960s and early 1970s, I rarely visited the urban river with the grand name. And sadly, I didn't care about it.

I remember the Grand River, which makes its way for 185 miles (296 km) from near Georgian Bay to Lake Erie, being described as "an open sewer," so I stayed away.

The only time I paddled the Grand, two times actually, was in the Paris-to-Brantford Canoe Race in the mid-1970s. It was fun being part of the winning team twice, but what struck me was how clean the water was and the abundance of wildlife. Also appealing were the bits and pieces of 19th-century architecture dotting the shores, remnants of the Grand's past lives.

A few of those lives, unfortunately, were characterized by filth and abuse. The Grand River, southern Ontario's largest watershed, was badly mistreated in the late 1800s and early 1900s as industries and communities dumped their untreated wastes directly into the Grand. It was a despicable practice that went on far too long.

Slowly, attitudes and government legislation began to change. One organization, the Grand River Conservation Authority, established in 1934, worked to turn neglect into concern, inaction into action, and helped bring the river back to life. The GRCA is Canada's first and the third-oldest conservation authority in the world.

"The vision of the GRCA is one of a healthy and sustaining relationship between the natural environment of the Grand River watershed and the demands on this environment by all forms of life," explains Chairman Peter Krause. "The GRCA's mission is 'to conserve the natural processes and resources that support a safe and healthy environment for future generations in the Grand River watershed.'"

The GRCA established various initiatives to reduce flood damage, improve water quality, provide adequate water supply, protect natural areas, and institute watershed planning and recreation and environmental education.

Such activities included structural initiatives, such as building the first water-control reservoirs in Canada, and non-structural projects, such as major reforestation programs to reduce runoff and erosion.

After the Grand flooded its banks in Cambridge in 1974, the GRCA built the Living Levee, which is a system of dikes to keep the river in bounds. It has been used as a catalyst for major redevelopment of the downtown core — including walkways and parkland in what was otherwise a sterile "turn your back on the river" environment. Similar projects have now been completed in Brantford, the Breslau area of Kitchener and Caledonia.

On the basis of its outstanding human heritage features and values and its abundance and diversity of exceptional recreational opportunities, the Grand River was declared a Canadian Heritage River in 1994. All the GRCA's good works were finally recognized nationally. The GRCA's nomination stated: "Ours is a story of the recovery of the Grand River from years of degradation and industrialization and how we are working together to keep it healthy for future generations."

Six years later the GRCA received international recognition when it was awarded the Australian Thiess Riverprize, the world's most prestigious award for river management excellence, previously awarded to England's Mersey River. The Grand was in tough against rivers in Japan, Wales, New Zealand and Australia. "The combination of programs undertaken by the GRCA and its partners over the past sixty years has produced one of the healthiest river systems in North America in a heavily populated area," says Krause. "The sport fish are back and recreational use of the river has increased significantly."

## Grand Worth

When I lived in K-W, I used to hear the only fish in the Grand was carp, a derogatory reference to the bottom-feeder as a garbage fish. Today, many species — smallmouth bass, black crappie, bullhead, pike, pumpkinseed, rainbow and brown trout, salmon, steelhead, walleye, white sucker, yellow perch . . . and carp — are plentiful.

To get on and around the Grand, there are all sorts of canoe and kayak outfitters providing crafts for paddling the river; trails for walking and cycling along the river valley (four rail corridors have been converted to hiking trails between Cambridge and Paris, Elora and Cataract, Brantford and Hamilton, and Paris and Brantford); camping spots and accommodations (bed and breakfasts, hotels and inns) for spending the night near the river; and plenty of maps, books and videos from the GRCA to help you find favorite locations on and near the river.

GRCA staff are witnessing an awareness of the Grand's worth with growing numbers of watershed residents — close to one million — exploring and enjoying its many natural and cultural resources. There is also an increased level of concern for the way the river is treated.

## Grand Strategy

The Grand River Conservation Authority, headquartered on the eastern outskirts of Cambridge, near the banks of the Grand, is operated and partly funded by thirty-four watershed municipalities. As such, it is a partnership of all local governments, pooling resources to manage the river system on an integrated watershed basis — to the mutual benefit of all.

The GRCA has undertaken many programs and services. These are the major ones:

*Focus on Watershed Issues and Background Report on the State of the Watershed*: To identify areas of watershed restoration that will yield the "best bang for the buck."

*Grand River Fisheries Management Plan*: A two-year project of the GRCA, provincial Ministry of Natural Resources and more than sixty angling clubs to identify priority actions to improve the Grand River fishery even further.

*Rural Water Quality Program*: Whereby urban residents pay a little more on their water bills to help upstream farmers undertake environmental farm plans. This is followed by on-farm work to reduce pollution from rural sources, thereby protecting community water. This program is so successful it is now used as a model by the Province of Ontario.

*Groundwater Mapping and Studies*: There was no detailed mapping of the Grand's groundwater resources, and this has now been accomplished. It will help communities find new water supplies, and more importantly, protect existing supplies from pollution sources.

*Water Budget*: A dialogue between cities up and down the Grand River system, informing each other of their present and future water needs and projected use demands.

*Grand River Water Quality Model*: A computerized model developed by the GRCA to predict the impact of urban growth on water quality and supply (all communities get their water from either groundwater or the river itself).

*Grand River Scenic Parkway*: A tourism initiative to help local and regional tourists discover, and thereby further appreciate, the scenic Grand River watershed.

*Grand River Country*: To promote tourism using the river as a common theme in upstream and downstream communities.

*Grand Champions*: A project of the Grand River Foundation whereby donors to specific projects are part of a "Grand Champions" team, championing the river.

*Twinning* the Fraser (British Columbia) and Grand Rivers — which has led to a mutual exchange of information, research and so on.

*Memorandum of Understanding with the University of Guelph*: Work with local watershed universities of research relating to the health of the watershed.

The GRCA has 100 full-time staff and an army of volunteers. To assist in the GRCA's multitude of activities, the Grand River Foundation, a registered charity, was created in 1965. In addition to preserving wildlife habitat, constructing recreation facilities and conducting environmental improvement programs, the Foundation is in charge of the $89,000 that the GRCA was awarded with the Australian Thiess Riverprize. This money will be used to support GRCA initiatives that improve river health and build community partnerships. An annual Riverprize initiative will remind watershed residents and others of the international regard given to the GRCA for its excellence in river management for years to come.

## Slaked Our Thirst

When Barbara Veale, the GRCA's Co-ordinator of Strategic Planning & Partnerships, was in Fredericton, New Brunswick, in the spring of 2001 at the 3rd Canadian River Heritage Conference to give a presentation, she began by summarizing what had transpired earlier at the conference. "I think we have discovered that not only do rivers connect us — upstream and downstream, past and present, urban and rural, French, English and First Nations, Canadian and American — but they define our history, our heritage and indeed shape who we are. Rivers, in fact, are us — they reflect our values, our sense of stewardship and our sense of caring for each other."

Also making a presentation at the River Heritage Conference was former federal cabinet minister and at the time Chair of the Fraser River Basin Council Iona Campagnolo (she's now lieutenant governor of British Columbia). She succinctly expressed the gratitude we should have for the Grand and all rivers. "Rivers have slaked our thirst, fed our hunger, fueled our machines, cleansed our bodies, guided our travels, inspired our intellects, spirits and cultures, enriched our heritage, and from the beginning of time have generously poured their wealth into our pockets."

To that end, I have turned and embraced the Grand and all it has to offer.

# A Canoe Trip Down the Grand

Eric Thomlinson

THE GRAND RIVER VALLEY CONTAINS THE LARGEST INLAND WATER SYSTEM *in Southern Ontario, draining a watershed of 2,635 square miles (6,800 square km). It was French priest and geographer René de Galinee, in 1669, who was the first European to make mention of the Grand.*

*The Grand has four major tributaries: the Nith, Conestogo, Speed and Eramosa Rivers. Originating near the village of Dundalk, in the Luther Marsh, the Grand River begins its descent to Lake Erie, where it contributes 10 percent of the drainage to that Great Lake.*

*As an organization, the Grand River Conservation Authority has done lots to improve the quality and environment of the Grand. But there is one person, Eric Thomlinson, born in 1928 in England, who is the Grand's unofficial protector and advocate. Eric's love of canoeing began in his early teens, working for free as a boat boy for a canoe rental company in Peasholme Park. His reward was a chance to paddle during quiet periods and at day's end.*

*Eric immigrated to Canada in 1948, making a career in sales and marketing. The last 10 years of his working life were spent traveling across Canada, selling motorhomes for his company, Funcraft Vehicles.*

*"During his business travels, Eric frequently observed canoeists on various rivers and lakes throughout Canada. Dressed in a business suit and tied to demanding schedules, he watched with envy but promised himself 'one day, that will be me out there on the water,'" explains Barbara Veale of the GRCA. "True to his own promise, he sold his company, and at age fifty-one he retired. Eric promptly bought a canoe and has canoed at every opportunity."*

*Barbara continues, "Besides being an avid canoeist and promoter of the Grand River, Eric was the founder of the the Ancient Mariners, a canoe club for seniors. He has spearheaded many river cleanups conducted by members of the canoe club throughout the Cambridge area. Eric has extensive knowledge of the history of the river and the natural environment and has acted as an interpretive guide for one of the river touring companies on the Grand River," she says. "In short, Eric shows his respect and love of the river by passing on its rich heritage and his stewardship ethics to others."*

*No one is better qualified to describe what it's like to paddle the Grand than Eric Thomlinson.*

For over thirty years, I have lived near the beautiful Grand River, in Cambridge. As it is a mere quarter mile from my front door, I have easy access to explore at will this amazing river. I have delighted in frequently canoeing several scenic stretches and enjoyed every moment I have spent on the river. One spring morning, in 1997, when the water levels were rising, I decided to explore the entire river, from source to mouth.

With my trusty 16-foot Prospector on my car-top carrier, my bicycle on a front bumper-mounted carrier and my tent and tripping gear stowed in the trunk, I was all set to go. Driving north through Kitchener, Elora, Fergus, Belwood and Grand Valley, I had many preview sightings of the river I was about to challenge.

Arriving at Riverview, a small hamlet about 5 miles (8 km) south of Dundalk, at the source, I found my put-in on a stretch of river not more than 5 feet (1.5 m) wide and 4 feet (1.2 m) deep in the midst of broad, flat farm country. After lashing my bicycle to the front seat of the canoe, I was ready for my Grand Adventure.

Several hours later, after fast, smooth and sometimes tricky maneuvering through gravel and sandbars, I arrived at picturesque Grand Valley. As I passed swiftly through the center of the village, I waved to a few residents, navigated several rock gardens and some interesting swifts through rolling scenic riverbanks. I eventually arrived at Belwood Lake to find it still covered with slushy ice!

With one foot in the canoe and the other foot out on the ice, I skated the last mile (1.6 km) to my take-out point at a small trailer park. Untying my bicycle from the front of the canoe, I rode 21 miles (35 km) back to my car in Riverview and returned to Belwood Lake to camp overnight at the south end of the lake.

Launching early the next morning, below the Shand Dam, Canada's first multi-purpose dam built in 1942 for flood control and low-flow augmentation during dry summer months, I drifted with the flow. The open country slowly evolved into small limestone cliffs along the shore. After several difficult portages through Fergus and Elora, and navigating stretches of swift flowing waters through the scenic Elora Gorge, I launched my canoe once again at the south end of the park below the low level bridge.

Suddenly, I felt as if I were in Northern Ontario. Pine trees descended on both sides of the riverbank, marked with limestone outcroppings. Everything was completely quiet, except for the babbling water and the occasional plane overhead. Soon, however, the river meandered through the pastoral countryside. Nearing Kitchener-Waterloo, I passed beneath the longest covered bridge in Ontario, at West Montrose. Often called the Kissing Bridge, it is quite an attraction to tourists. I continued to paddle downriver as far as Cambridge, where I cheated and snuck home for the night — ahhh, such comfort!

A glorious sunrise coincided with my departure from Cambridge into possibly the most beautiful and historic part of this magnificent Canadian Heritage River. An unbroken stretch of Carolinian forest lines each bank with black willows (the Mohawk name for the river, O:se Kenhionhata:tie, means Willow River), towering over 90 feet (27 m) high, framing hickory, sassafras, walnut, tamarack and sycamore. I also spotted wildlife everywhere — deer, muskrat, beaver, blue herons and ospreys.

After negotiating some Class I rapids, in a stretch of standing waves with several visible large rocks, I encountered two wet canoeists sitting on the bank. They had lost everything. I retrieved their canoe and gear, and two hours later sent them on their way.

Overnight, in the Brant Conservation Area, was rather chilly and lonely at this time of year, but a campfire and early to bed prepared me for a slower, wider, deeper section of river the next day. As the Grand flows towards Lake Erie, I encountered the remains of many buildings, canals, locks and landings from the days when freighters, barges and ferries traveled the river from Brantford through Westport, Middleport, Caledonia, York, Cayuga and Dunnville to Port Maitland, at the mouth of the river.

While paddling through the Six Nations land south of Brantford, Canada's largest First Nation reserve, I landed at an unused rope-ferry dock on the east bank at Chiefswood, a national historic site and home of the renowned poet E. Pauline Johnson, who wrote the beautiful poem inspired by the Grand River, "The Song My Paddle Sings." Here's how it concludes: "We've raced the rapid, we're far ahead! / The river slips through its silent bed. / Sway, sway, / As bubbles spray / And fall in tinkling tunes away. / And up on the hills against the sky, / A fir tree rocking its lullaby, / Swings, swings, / Its emerald wings, / Swelling the song that my paddle sings."

At Dunnville, the Grand truly lives up to its name. It is now hundreds of feet wide and quite deep in many places. I paddled through the Dunnville

Marshes, a unique natural area full of tall bullrushes, water lilies and thousands of ducks, cormorants, herons and egrets.

When I rounded the last 90-degree turn to the south near the lake, I received a big surprise. Towering above my tiny canoe was a large 700-foot-long lake freighter — docked, rusted and waiting to be scrapped. The last run out to the mouth of the river, to the pier near the lighthouse, provided a thrilling grand finale. Large waves up to 6 feet (1.8 m) high greeted me at the mouth.

If you have never tried to step out of a canoe with both it and the landing rising and falling, you have a real thrill coming. But it could not match my personal thrill of having met, challenged, enjoyed and even loved my Grand River. Come share it with me.

# Exhaustion and Fulfilment
## *The Ascetic in a Canoe*

Pierre Elliott Trudeau

I WOULD NOT KNOW HOW TO INSTIL A TASTE FOR ADVENTURE IN THOSE who have not acquired it. (Anyway, who can ever prove the necessity for the gypsy life?) And yet there are people who suddenly tear themselves away from their comfortable existence and, using the energy of their bodies as an example to their brains, apply themselves to the discovery of unsuspected pleasures and places.

I would like to point out to these people a type of labor from which they are certain to profit: an expedition by canoe.

I do not just mean "canoeing." Not that I wish to disparage that pastime, which is worth more than many another. But, looked at closely, there is perhaps only a difference of money between canoeists of Lafontaine Park [in central Montreal] and those who dare to cross a lake, make a portage, spend a night in a tent and return exhausted, always in the care of a fatherly guide — a brief interlude momentarily interrupting the normal course of digestion.

A canoeing expedition, which demands much more than that, is also much more rewarding.

It involves a starting rather than a parting. Although it assumes the breaking of ties, its purpose is not to destroy the past, but lay a foundation for the future. From now on, every living act will be built on this step, which will serve as a base long after the return of the expedition . . . and until the next one.

What is essential at the beginning is the resolve to reach the saturation point. Ideally, the trip should end only when the members are making no further progress within themselves. They should not be fooled, though, by a period of boredom, weariness or disgust; that is not the end, but the last obstacle before it. Let saturation be serene!

So you must paddle for days, or weeks, or perhaps months on end. My friends and I were obliged, on pain of death, to do more than a thousand miles by canoe, from Montreal to Hudson Bay. But let no one be deterred by a shortage of time. A more intense pace can compensate for a shorter trip.

What sets a canoeing expedition apart is that it purifies you more rapidly and inescapably than any other. Travel a thousand miles by train and you are a brute; pedal five hundred on a bicycle and you remain basically a bourgeois; paddle a hundred in a canoe and you are already a child of nature.

For it is a condition of such a trip that you entrust yourself, stripped of your worldly goods, to nature. Canoe and paddle, blanket and knife, salt pork and flour, fishing rod and rifle; that is about the extent of your wealth. To remove all the useless material baggage from a man's heritage is, at the same time, to free his mind from petty preoccupations, calculations and memories.

On the other hand, what fabulous and underdeveloped mines are to be found in nature, friendship and oneself! The paddler has no choice but to draw everything from them. Later, forgetting that his habit was adopted under duress, he will be astonished to find so many resources within himself.

Nevertheless, he will have returned a more ardent believer from a time when religion, like everything else, became simple. The impossibility of scandal creates a new morality, and prayer becomes a friendly chiding of the divinity, who has again become part of our everyday affairs. (My friend Guy Viau could say about our adventure, "We got along very well with God, who is a damn good sport. Only once did we threaten to break off diplomatic relations if he continued to rain on us. But we were joking. We would never have done so, and well he knew it. So he continued to rain on us.")

The canoe is also a school of friendship. You learn that your best friend is not a rifle, but someone who shares a night's sleep with you after ten hours of paddling at the other end of a canoe. Let's say that you have to be lined up a rapid and it's your turn to stay in the canoe and guide it. You watch your friend stumbling over logs, sliding on rocks, sticking in gumbo, tearing the skin on his legs and drinking water for which he does not thirst, yet never letting go of the rope; meanwhile, safely in the middle of the cataract, you spray your hauler with a stream of derision. When this same man has also fed you exactly half his catch, and has made a double portage because of your injury, you can boast of having a friend for life, and one who knows you well.

How does the trip affect your personality? Allow me to make a fine distinction, and I would say that you return not so much a man who reasons more, but a more reasonable man. For, throughout this time, your mind has learned to exercise itself in the working conditions which nature intended. Its primordial role has been to sustain the body in the struggle against a powerful universe. A good camper knows that it is more important to be ingenious than to be a genius. And conversely, the body, by demonstrating the true meaning of sensual pleasure, has been of service to the mind. You feel the beauty of animal pleasure when you draw a deep breath of rich morning air right through your body, which has been carried by the cold night, curled up like an unborn child. How can you describe the feeling which wells up in the heart and stomach as the canoe finally rides up on the shore of the campsite after a long day of plunging your paddle into rain-swept waters? Purely physical is the joy which the fire spreads through the palms of your hands and the soles of your feet while your chattering mouth belches the poisonous cold. The pleasurable torpor of such a moment is perhaps not too different from what the mystics of the East are seeking. At least it has allowed me to taste what one respected gentleman used to call the joys of hard living.

Make no mistake, these joys are exclusively physical. They have nothing to do with the satisfaction of the mind when it imposes unwelcome work on the body, a satisfaction, moreover, which is often mixed with pride, and which the body never fails to avenge. During a very long and exhausting portage, I have sometimes felt my reason defeated, and shamefully fleeing, while my legs and shoulders carried bravely on. The mumbled verses which marked the rhythm of my steps at the beginning had become the brutal grunts of "uh! uh! uh!" There was nothing aesthetic in that animal search for the bright clearing which always marks the end of a portage.

I do not want you to think that the mind is subjected to a healthy discipline merely by worrying about simplistic problems. I only wish to remind you of that principle of logic which states that valid conclusions do not generally follow from false premises. Now, in a canoe, where these premises are based on nature in its original state (rather than on books, ideas and habits of uncertain value), the mind conforms to that higher wisdom which we call natural philosophy; later, that healthy methodology and acquired humility will be useful in confronting mystical and spiritual questions.

I know a man whose school could never teach him patriotism, but who acquired that virtue when he felt in his bones the vastness of his land, and the greatness of those who founded it.

*Originally published in French in* Journal JEC, *June 1944. From* Against the Current *by Pierre Elliott Trudeau. Published by McClelland & Stewart, The Canadian Publishers. Reprinted with permission of the publisher.*

# Raff's Maxims for Happy Paddling

James Raffan

Backwards is better than sideways
When in doubt, straighten out
Smoke rots clothes
White gas dries skin
Socks burn
Sing loudly and often
Skin is waterproof
Urine hardens hands
WD-40 on a hook attracts fish
Aluminum sticks to rocks
ABS = Always Bounces (off) Stuff
Water levels change
Don't argue in rapids
Lean downstream
Face your hazards
GPS, Goof Proof System
Borrowed canoes bend
Nylon is not soundproof
Wet food is better than no food
PFD, Perfected Flotation Device
Duct tape can save a marriage
Wash your socks
Don't grab the gunwales
Scout before you shoot
Wet rocks are slippery
Declination is not politics
Hurrying can hurt
Clean your teeth
UV light rots nylon
Dirt repels bugs

Real women portage
Real men cook
Sun moves 4 outstretched finger widths per hour
Never trust a kayaker
Swim naked
Close cover before striking
Bears like hot food
Hair dries matches
The map is not the landscape
Change your underwear
Porcupines can't throw quills
The only thing we really own is time
Right is a relative term
Boots do not a swimmer make
Pencil doesn't run
Ocean is anagram of canoe
Blackflies love blue jeans
Black cats never have white stripes
Big belt buckles confuse compasses
Leave word
Waves break when Length = 7 X height
HBC = Here Before Christ
Stay in touch
Stay in line

Canoe suffering is usually self-imposed

DEET eats rainsuits

Voyageurs died young

Canoe < 3 feet long, probably coffee table

Drink lots, but not from swamps

Heated tape sticks better

Bum down when swimming in current

Grey Owl paddled on both sides

Balsam gum heals cuts

Fancy gear, competence

Take a stitch awl

Raccoons can open anything

Jesus couldn't swim

Spray covers keep water in too

Don't pee or spit into the wind

Even Pierre Trudeau dumped

Jewelweed eases poison ivy rash

Balance = dried prunes + cheese

Red Smarties make quick trail rouge

Cameras can cause blindness

Jimmy Hoffa dragged his canoe

First Aid is not safety planning

Zippers leak
Gore-Tex sucks
Powdered juice burns like flash powder
Spruce beer cleans like a white tornado
Praise the Swiss Army
Tie your boat
Always keep the open side up

# Contributors

**Laurel Archer** and **Brad Koop** met as canoe guides on the Churchill River in northern Saskatchewan. After losing their log home on Lac La Ronge to a forest fire, they headed west to Vancouver Island for new adventures. They now experience the serious difficulty of deciding whether to go kayak surfing, whitewater paddling, sea kayaking or canoe tripping in a climate where one can paddle all year-round!

Since 1988, **Sheila Archer** has spent her summers guiding whitewater canoe trips and teaching canoeing in northern Saskatchewan. Recently she became an instructor for Lakeland College's Adventure Tourism and Outdoor Recreation program in Vermilion, Alberta. Summers have therefore become a time to enjoy her own holidays and work with her horses rather than guide and instruct, but she still travels up to the Churchill River to keep her teaching teeth sharp, offering her services through Churchill River Canoe Outfitter's summer programs.

**Ksenia Barton** lives in Vancouver, British Columbia, and works as a professional biologist. Her love of nature and the outdoors was kindled by a summer tree-planting job during her university years. That experience prompted her to change her undergraduate major to biology and start venturing out into wilderness. As a field ecologist, she studies the interactions between flora, fauna and landforms in remote locations. In her leisure time, she enjoys nature on foot or by paddle.

**Dunnery Best** is a native of Winnipeg. He has never stopped tripping, and now mostly concentrates on long trips in inland waters with his wife, Francoise, and three children, all trippers. In the real world, Dunnery works with Merrill Lynch Canada. His particular friend Sandy Hart lives in the Chilcotin, where he operates an environmental consulting business.

**Sue Browne** is an environmental planner with over ten years' experience coordinating projects in Nova Scotia. She revised the two-volume *Natural History of Nova Scotia* and developed the award-winning Frogwatch program for the Nova Scotia Museum of Natural History. She recently opened the first official water trail for recreational boaters along the coast of Nova Scotia and chairs the N.S. Coastal Water Trail Association. She also has a keen interest in coastal conservation, illustrated by her work to protect the granite coastal barrens near her home in Prospect and her position on the Coastal Issues Committee of the Ecology Action Centre. Sue paddles kayaks and canoes, sails schooners and generally messes about in boats.

**Kevin Callan** is the bestselling author of *Killarney*; *A Paddler's Guide to Ontario's Cottage Country*; *Ways of the Wild: A Practical Guide to the Outdoors*; *Brook Trout and Blackflies: A Paddler's Guide to Algonquin Park*; *A Paddler's Guide to Ontario*; *A Paddler's Guide to the Rivers of Ontario and Quebec*; *Gone Canoeing: Weekend Wilderness Adventures in Southern Ontario* and *Ontario's Lost Canoe Routes*. He is a field editor for various outdoor magazines, including *Outdoor Canada, Explore* and *Kanawa*.

Kevin is a well-traveled canoe guide, averaging over a dozen wilderness trips a year, and has become a popular speaker as well as a frequent guest on radio and television. His latest film, documenting Wabakimi Provincial Park and the eccentric hermit Wendell Beckwith, was the overall winner in the 6th biennial Waterwalker Film Festival. For the past ten years, Kevin has worked as a part-time Environmental Issues instructor at Sir Sanford Fleming College. He lives in Peterborough, Ontario, the birthplace of the modern-day canoe.

**James Cullingham** is a documentary filmmaker and writer based in Toronto. His company, Tamarack Productions, has produced many award-winning documentaries about Canadian history, the North and aboriginal rights. He is currently a supervising producer with the current affairs program *VisionTV Insight* and an instructor with Seneca College at York University School of Communication Arts in Toronto.

**Geoffrey Danysk** has traveled widely and is proficient in rock climbing, mountain biking, whitewater kayaking and canoeing, rafting, backpacking, scrambling, snowboarding, telemark skiing, ice climbing, ski touring and ice canoeing. He is enrolled in the Southern Alberta Institute of Technology's Emergency Medical Responder program.

**C. E. S. Franks**, the author of *The Canoe and White Water*, is emeritus professor of Political Studies and Physical and Health Education at Queen's University in Kingston. Besides writing about canoeing, he has published widely on sport and government in Canada, and on Canadian politics and government. He is a fellow of the Royal Canadian Geographical Society and the Royal Society of Canada.

**John Geary** is a professional freelance writer and photographer who got his first taste of paddling as an eight-year-old at Camp Richildaca in Southern Ontario. He really fell in love with canoeing during his first overnight canoe trip at the age of twelve, while attending camp at Ontario's Haliburton Scout Reserve. Since then, he has canoed in Algonquin Park, Northern Ontario, Alberta, British Columbia, Saskatchewan and Nova Scotia, and has paddled a sea kayak in the Bay of Fundy, the Queen Charlotte Islands and the cays of Belize, Central America. He has written articles about canoeing and kayaking for *Canoe & Kayak Magazine*, *Canoe Journal*, *Nature Canada*, *Coast Magazine*, *Ski Canada Magazine's Outside Guide*, *Fast Forward Weekly*, *Synchronicity*, *Odyssey*, the *Prince Rupert Daily News* and the *Alaska Highway News*. He lives in Calgary with his wife, Ann, and their two African gray parrots, Nikki and Coco.

**Jim Graham** is the sales manager and resident cartoonist at *The Roughneck* magazine, based in Calgary.

**Faye Hallett** and John Vlchek have been doing annual canoe trips for over twenty-seven years, mainly in Western Canada and the Yukon. The Nahanni was paddled after going "overland" from the Yukon to reach its source. In 1985 they paddled from Rocky Mountain House, Alberta, to Montreal. When not tripping they spend their time teaching canoeing, and training for marathon canoe races in Prince George, British Columbia.

**Howard Heffler** lives with his wife and two daughters in Calgary, where he works as an environmental manager in the oil patch as a way of supporting his outdoor recreation addiction. Therapy sessions revolve around hiking, canoe tripping and whitewater canoeing in the summer and backcountry skiing in the winter.

**Bob Henderson** teaches Outdoor Education at McMaster University in Hamilton, Ontario, and writes a heritage travel column in *Kanawa*, the magazine of the Canadian Recreational Canoe Association.

**Bruce W. Hodgins** is a professor emeritus of History and Canadian Studies at Trent University, Peterborough, where he taught from 1965 to 1996. He has been president of Camp Wanapitei, Temagami, since 1971. He and his wife, Carol, have probably co-led more near North and Far North wilderness canoe trips, youth and adult, beginning in 1957, than any other couple.

Bruce has written widely on our canoeing heritage and on refigured wilderness. He co-authored with Jamie Benidickson *The Temagami Experience*, co-authored with Gwyneth Hoyle *Canoeing North into the Unknown: A Record of River Travel, 1874–1974*, authored *Wanapitei on Temagami*, co-edited and contributed to *Nastawgan: The Canadian North by Canoe and Snowshoe, Using Wilderness: Essays on the Evolution of Youth Camping in Ontario, On the Land: Aboriginal Self-determination in Northern Quebec and Labrador, Canada's River Heritage, Changing Parks: The History, Future and Cultural Content of Parks and Heritage Landscape, The Canoe in Canadian Cultures* (with John Jennings and Doreen Small) as well as numerous articles.

Since 1981 Bruce has been heavily involved, in varying capacities, with the relocation to Peterborough, the refounding and the development of the Canadian Canoe Museum. He is a past-president of the Ontario Recreational Association. He's also a son, father, brother, uncle or cousin to members of a very significant canoe-tripping family.

**Glenn Hodgins** is the touring and outreach officer at the Ontario Arts Council. He oversees the Touring and Collaborations Program, a granting program for Ontario-based artists, presenters and exhibitors. His responsibilities include running the annual OAC conferences.

Before joining the OAC, Glenn worked with Tafelmusik for twelve years. Glenn is a graduate of the Faculty of Music at the University of Toronto where he received his Bachelor of Music in Piano Performance. He has also been awarded the ARCT in Piano Performance from the Royal Conservatory of Music in Toronto. In his spare time, he is a canoe-trip leader and instructor with Wanapitei CANOE, leading extensive trips in many remote regions of Canada usually involving summer expeditions to the Arctic.

For more than twenty-five years, **Shawn Hodgins** has paddled extensively throughout the Canadian North. He is a co-owner and guide of Wanapitei CANOE, an adventure trip company based on Lake Temagami in Northern Ontario.

**Bert Horwood** thinks he was likely conceived in a canoe. Whatever the truth, he is a lifelong paddler and canoe-tripper. Bert worked as a high-school teacher and professor of education until his retirement from the Outdoor and Experiential Education unit at Queen's University, in 1992. Since then, he has contributed time and energy to several professional educational organizations and to the Religious Society of Friends (Quakers), while always being ready to drop everything for a canoe trip.

**Bryon Howard**'s interest in sustainable travel and starting an adventure travel company led him on a world odyssey, beginning in 1985. He has traveled and worked in New Zealand, India, Bangladesh, Nepal, Europe, Northern Africa, Central and South America and both the Pacific and Atlantic coasts of North America. He studied recreation at Acadia University and has an MBA from Athabasca University. Bryon and his wife, Shirley, operate Outside Expeditions and a bed and breakfast, Osprey Outlook, at Rustico Bay, Prince Edward Island.

**Gwyneth Hoyle**'s life seems to revolve around the canoe. She paddles with grandchildren and friends in season, and is on the board of directors and an active volunteer at the Canadian Canoe Museum year-round. Her independent research on subjects related to northern travel and the fur trade has produced two books: *Canoeing North into the Unknown*, with co-author Bruce Hodgins, and most recently, *Flowers in the Snow*, the biography of an intrepid Scottish woman, botanist and solo arctic traveler in the 1930s.

**Jeff Jackson** is a writer, paddler and professor at Algonquin College in the Ottawa Valley.

**Joan Jeffery** is an elementary-school principal who describes her husband, Bill, as an outdoor fanatic. Both enjoy wilderness tripping, cross-country skiing, cycling and running. Bill completed an ironman in 2000, and in fall 2001, Joan qualified for the Boston Marathon. The Jefferys have enjoyed many adventures in far-off reaches of the world.

**Stephan Kesting** has a background in botany and ecology, and works as a firefighter in Delta, British Columbia. He has worked as a canoe guide and instructor for Churchill River Canoe Outfitters/Horizons Unlimited in northern Saskatchewan and as a raft guide on the Tatshenshini. He is a "cross-boater," using kayaks and canoes to explore lakes, rivers and creeks wherever he goes.

**Sheena Masson** lives in the seaside village of Hubbards, on the South Shore of Nova Scotia. She writes about paddling, teaches paddling and sometimes even gets to go paddling. She is still trying to learn the Eskimo roll and teach her cat to sit on command.

**Gary and Joanie McGuffin** are known worldwide for their expeditions and conservation efforts to protect wild places. They are the authors of three bestselling books — *Where Rivers Run*, the tale of their 6,000-mile (10,000 km) honeymoon canoe trip from the Atlantic to the Arctic Ocean; *Superior: Journeys on an Inland Sea*, which won the Great Lakes Booksellers Award; and their internationally acclaimed canoe instruction book, *Paddle Your Own Canoe*. Their photographic exhibitions based on their journeys travel to galleries across North America. The McGuffins tour worldwide with their presentations speaking on behalf of preserving ancient forests and wild waterways. Gary and Joanie make their home in the Algoma Highlands near the shores of Lake Superior with their daughter, Sila, and their Alaskan malamute, Kalija. To find out more, see their website, www.adventurers.org.

**Keith Morton** is a longtime paddler, hiker and backcountry skier who lives in Calgary. He instructs on a range of outdoor subjects and is the equipment and new products editor for *Explore* magazine. He is also the author of *Planning a Wilderness Trip in Canada and Alaska*, published by Rocky Mountain Books.

**Lynn Noel** is the author and editor of *Voyages: Canada's Heritage Rivers*. Her great-grandfather, master of a Lunenburg schooner, immigrated to "the Boston states" in the 1890s from the Annapolis Valley.

**David Pelly**, who organized and led the 1988 Kazan expedition, has been writing about the North for twenty years, often on wilderness themes derived from thousands of miles traveled by canoe and foot in summer, snowmobile and dog sled in winter. He is widely published and a frequent lecturer on the Arctic, its history, the land and its people. He is the author of *Thelon: A River Sanctuary*, a biography of the largest and oldest wilderness preserve anywhere in North America. His most recent book, *Sacred Hunt*, examines the traditional relationship between Inuit and seals.

**James Raffan** is an experienced paddler whom friends and family consider a dubious source of free advice.

**Teen Sivell**, her husband, Joe Ferri, and their two sons live on an Ontario apple orchard overlooking Georgian Bay. According to Joe, Teen avoids farm work by riding her horses and putting the canoe in the water whenever possible. In Teen's opinion, giving Joe a chance to swat deerflies from a canoe on local rivers in the heat of summer is enough of a change from swatting deerflies in the orchard.

**Andy Smith**, who spent much of his youth in New Hampshire, began canoeing as a teenager at the summer home of his extended family in Central Argyle, Nova Scotia, and it was early family trips down Nova Scotia's Tusket River that inspired him to a lifelong love of canoeing. After living for a short time in Old Chelsea in Quebec and in Ottawa, Andy moved back to Nova Scotia to attend Dalhousie University and has lived, paddled and taught in the public schools of southwestern Nova Scotia ever since. Over the past thirty-five years Andy has paddled a diverse collection of rivers in the eastern United States and Canada, from the Potomac in Virginia and Maryland, to the St. Croix in Maine and New Brunswick, and the Gatineau and Dumoine Rivers in Quebec, however, the preponderance of his paddling time has been spent exploring the rivers and wilderness areas of Nova Scotia's Digby, Yarmouth and Shelburne Counties. Since recently retiring from teaching, Andy Smith has written a number of articles on local rivers and has finished a paddling guide to the rivers of southwestern Nova Scotia.

**Alister Thomas**, a Calgary-based magazine editor, lives half a block from the Bow River.

**Hap Wilson** has been guiding wilderness canoeing expeditions for over thirty years. Artist, photographer, former park ranger, environmental activist, Hap has authored six bestselling canoe route guidebooks, revered for accuracy and detail. His original maps and illustrations were featured in *Voyages: Canada's Heritage Rivers*, which won the Natural Resources Council of America Award for best environmental book in 1995. Hap acted as Pierce Brosnan's personal canoe trainer in the *Grey Owl* film. He and his wife, Stephanie, run an outdoor retreat in Lady Evelyn-Smoothwater Wilderness Park in Temagami, Ontario. They have two children, Christopher and Alexa.

# Photo Credits

# Topographical Maps

Information was gathered from resources of the Canada Centre for Topographic Information, Natural Resources Canada, including three index maps and this website: http://maps.nrcan.gc.ca.

**Paddling BC's Inside Passage, British Columbia (Bella Coola to Prince Rupert)**
1:250,000 - Bella Coola: 93 D; Laredo Sound: 103 A; Douglas Channel: 103 H; Prince Rupert: 103 J.
1:50,000 - Bella Coola: 93 D/7; Labouchere Channel: 93 D/6; Ocean Falls: 93 D/5; Spiller Channel: 103 A/8; Roderick Island: 103 A/9; Laredo Sound: 103 A/10; Laredo Inlet: 103 A/15; Butedale: 103 H/2; Ursula Channel: 103 H/7; Hartley Bay: 103 H/6; Port Stephens: 103 H/5; Lowe Inlet: 103 H/12; Kumealon Lake: 103 H/13; Kildala Arm: 103 H/16; Port Edward: 103 J/1; Prince Rupert: 103 J/8.

**Nitinat Triangle Canoe Route, British Columbia**
1:250,000 - Cape Flattery: 92 C.
1:50,000 - Carmanah Creek: 92 C/10; Little Nitinat River: 92 C/15.

**Vision Quest, British Columbia (Telegraph Cove to Bella Bella)**
1:50,000 - Alert Bay: 92 L; Rivers Inlet: 92 M; Bella Coola: 93 D; Laredo Sound: 103 A.
1:250,000 - Alert Bay: 92 L/10; Broughton Island: 92 L/15; Bradley Lagoon: 92 L/14; Shushartie: 92 L/13; Cape Caution: 92 M/4; Goose Bay: 92 M/5; Fish Egg Inlet: 92 M/12; Namu: 92 M/13; Fisher Channel: 93 D/4; Bella Bella: 103 A/1.
Marine Charts - 3546; 3547; 3574; 3597; 3598; 3778; 3727; 3728; 3729.

**Alsek River, Yukon & British Columbia**
1:250,000 - Dezadesh Range: 115 A; Mount St. Elias: 115 B; Tatsheshini River: 114 P; Yakutat: 114 O.
1:50,000 - Range Lake: 114 P/13 (Turnback Canyon).

**Rat-Peel-Porcupine Rivers, Yukon & Northwest Territories**
1:250,000 - Ogilivie River: 116 G & 116 F (E1/2); Hart River: 116 H; Wind River: 106 E; Trail River: 106 L; Martin House: 106 K; Fort McPherson: 106 M; Bell River: 116 P; Old Crow: 116 O (E1/2).
1:50,000 - Mount Fairborn: 116 G/4; Mount Gale: 116 G/5; Mount Chief Isaac: 116 G/6; Mount Bouvette: 116 G/7; Mount Jeckell: 116 G/8;

Churchward Hill: 116 G/9; Mount Cronkhite: 116 H/12; Scriver Creek: 116 H/13; Enterprise Creek: 116 H/14; Pothole Lake: 116 H/15; Canyon Creek: 116 H/16; Aberdeen Canyon: 106 E/13; 106 E/14; Chappie Lake: 106 E/15; Solo Lake: 106 E/16; 106 L/1; Hogan Lake: 106 L/8; 106 K/5; Seguin Lakes: 106 L/9; Trail River: 106 L/10; Tabor Lakes: 106 L/15; Tidigeh Lake: 106 L/14; 106 M/2; 106 M/3; Fort McPherson: 106 M/7; Peel River Mouth: 106 M/10; Moses Hill: 116 P/7; Lapierre House: 116 P/6; Mason Hill:116 P/5; Mount Millen: Cranberry Hill: 116 O/8; Rat Indian Creek: 116 O/9; Cadzow Lake: 116 O/10; Nothla Hill: 116 O/11; Old Crow: 116 O/12.

**Little Nahanni, Northwest Territories**
1:250,000 - Little Nahanni: 105 I.
1:50,000 - Shelf Lake: 105 I/1; Upper Hyland Lake: 105 I/2; Dozer Lake: 105 I/7.

**Grease River, Saskatchewan**
1:250,000 - Fond-Du-Lac: 74 O
1:50,000 - Fontaine Lake: 74 O/9; Wiley Lake: 74 O/8.

**Peace River, British Columbia & Alberta**
1:250,000 - Charlie Lake: 94 A; Grande Prairie: 83 M; Clear Hills: 84 D; Peace River: 84 C; Bison Lake: 84 F, Mount Watt: 84 K; John D'Or Prairie: 84 J; Lake Claire: 84 I; Peace Point: 84 P; Fort Chipewyan: 74 L.
1:50,000 - Hudson Hope: 94 A/4; Moberly River: 94 A/3; Fort St John: 94 A/2; Shearer Dale: 94 A/1; Cherry Point: 84 D/4; Josephine Creek: 84 D/3; Many Islands: 84 D/6; Hines Creek: 84 D/2; Rycroft: 83 M/15; Codesa: 83 M16; Grimshaw: 84 C/4; Peace River: 84 C/3; Weberville: 84 C/6; Seal Lake: 84 C/1: Buchanan Creek: 84 C/14; Crummy Lake: 84 F/3; Nina Lake: 84 F/6; Scully Creek: 84 F/11; Wolverine River: 84 F/10; Paddle Prairie: 84 F/14; Metis: 84 K/3; Moose Island: 84 K/2; Child Lake: 84 K/7; Fort Vermilion: 84 K/8; Sled Island: 84 J/5; Adams Landing: 84 J/6, Vermilion Chutes: 84 J/7; Wentzel River: 84 J/10; Fifth Meridian: 84 J/9; Buchanan Lake: 84 I/12; Stovel Lake: 84 I/11; Big Slough: 84I/14; Jackfish Lake: 84 I/15; Boyer Rapids: 84 P/2; Square Lake: 84 P/1; Point Providence: 84 I/16 Baril River: 74 L/13; Rivière Des Rochers: 74 L/14; Fort Chipwyan: 74 L/11.

**Poling, Alberta**
**(from Gorge Creek to Sandy McNabb)**
1:250,000 - Kananaskis Lakes: 82 J
1:50,000 - Mount Rae: 82 J/10.

**Ice Canoeing, Alberta & Quebec**
1:250,000 - Calgary: 82 O; Quebec: 21 L.
1:50,000 - Calgary: 82 O/1; Quebec: 21 L/14.

## Kazan River, Northwest Territories & Nunavut
1:250,000 - Fort Smith: 75 D; Ennadai Lake: 65 C; Ennadai: 65 F;
Kamilukuak Lake: 65 K; Tulemalu Lake: 65 J; Thirty Mile Lake: 65 P;
Macquoid Lake: 55 M; Baker Lake: 56 D.
1:50,000 - Soulier Lake: 75 D/9; Tabane Lake: 65 C/12; Rochon Lake:
65 C/13; Halfway Bluff: 65 C/14; 65 F/3; 65 F/2; North End Lake: 65 F/7;
Dimma Lake: 65 F/10; 65 F/15; 65 K/2; 65 K/8; 65 J/5; 65 J/3; 65 J/2; 65
J/7; 65 J/1; 65 J/8; 65 J/9; 65 J/16; 65 JI13; 65 P/4; 65 P/3; Tattanniq Lake:
65 P/6; 65 P/11; 65 P/10; 65 P/9; Kazan Falls: 55 M/12; 55 M/13;
Tanataluk Island: 56 D/3.

## Prince Albert National Park, Saskatchewan
1:250,000 - Green Lake: 73 J.
1:50,000 - Crean Lake: 73 J/1; Strange Lake: 73 J/2.

## Clearwater River, Saskatchewan
1:250,000 - Lloyd Lake: 74 F; La Loche: 74 C; Fort McMurray: 74 D; .
1:50,000 - Neff Lake: 74 F/1; McArter Lake: 74 C/16; Mackie Rapids: 74
C/15; Tocker Lake: 74 C/14; Heise Lake: 74 C/13; Wallis Bay: 74 C/12;
Bunting Bay: 74 D/9; High Hill River: 74 D/16; 74 D/15; Hollies Creek:
74 D/ 10; Fort McMurray: 74 D/11.

## Seal River, Manitoba
1:250,000 - Tadoule Lake: 64 J; Shethanei Lake: 64 I; Churchill: 54 L;
Caribou River: 54 M.
1:50,000 - Seaman Island: 64 J/15; Dawes Lake: 64 I/13; Steel River:
64 I/14; Wither Lake: 64 I/15; Meades Lake: 64 I/16; Eppler Lake: 54
L/13; Warner Lake: 54 M/4; Sothe Lake: 54 M/3; Tambanay Rapids: 54
L/14; Sothe Lake: 54 M/3 Point of the Woods: 54 M/2.

## Bloodvein River, Ontario & Manitoba
1:250,000 - Trout Lake: 52 N; Carroll Lake: 52 M; Hecla: 62 P.
1:50,000 - Red Lake: 52 N/4; Pipestone Bay: 52 M/1; Murdock Lake: 52
M/2; Sabourne Lake: 52 M/7; Artery Lake: 52 M/6; North Eagle Lake: 52
M/5; Murdoch Lake: 52 M/2; Minango Lake: 62 P/9; Pine Dock: 62 P/10;
Princess Harbour: 62 P/15.

## 5 Northern Rivers
*(1) Coppermine, Northwest Territories & Nunavut*
1:250,000 - Redrock Lake: 86 G; Hepburn Lake: 86 J; Sloan River: 86 K;
Dismal Lake: 86 N; Coppermine: 86 O.
1:50,000 - Rocknest Lake: 86 G/9; 86 G/16; Fairy Lake River: 86 J/1;
86J/8; Fontano Lake: 86 J/7; 86 J/10; Muskox Lakes: 86 J/11; Stanbridge
Lake: 86 J/14; 86 J/13; Qingaluk Lake: 86 K/16; Rocky Defile Rapids:
86 N/1; 86 O/4; Burnt Creek: 86 O/5; 86 O/12; Escape Rapids: 86 O/11;
Ricardson Bay: 86 O/14.

*(2) Nanook, Northwest Territories & Nunavut*
1:250,000 - Kagloryuak River: 77 F; Burns Lake: 77 G; Cape Stang: 77 H.
1:50,000 - 77 F/16; 77 G/1; 77 H/4; 77 H/5; 77H/12.

*(3) Horton, Northwest Territories*
1:250,000 - Franklin Bay: 97 C; Simpson Lake: 97 B; Erly Lake: 97 A;
Horton Lake: 96 O.
1:50,000 - Old Horton Creek: 97 C/14; 97 C/11; Coal Creek: 97 C/6; 97
C/3; 97 C/2; Gilmore Lake: 97 B/15; Granet Lake: 97 B/10; 97 B/9; 97
A/12; 97 A/15; 97 A/4; 96 O/14; 96 O/15; 96 O/10; 96 O/9.

*(4) Ellice, Nunavut*
1:250,000 - Brichta Lake: 76 P; Overby Lake: 76 I; Duggan Lake: 76 H;
Beechey Lake: 76 G.
1:50,000 - Whitebear Point: 67 B/4; 66 M/13; 76 P/13; 76 P/9; 76 P/8;
76 P/1; 76 P/2; 76 I/15; 76 I/16; 76 I/10; 76 I/7; 76 I/6; 76 I/4; 76 H/14;
76 H/13; 76 H/12; 76 H/5; 76 G/9; 76 G/8.

*(5) Kuujjua, Northwest Territories & Nunavut*
1:250,000 - Walker Bay: 87 G; Saneraun Hills: 87 H; Burns Lake: 77 G.
1:50,000 - Kuujjua River: 87 G/8; 87 G/1; 87 H/4; 87 H/3; 87 H/2; 87
H/7; 87 H/8; 87 H/9; 77 G/12; 77 G/8; 77 G/11; 77 G/10; 77 G/5.

**Lake Superior, Ontario, Minnesota, Wisconsin & Michigan**
1:250,000 - Schreiber: 42 D; Thunder Bay: 52 A; Thunder Bay: 48088-A1
(U.S.); Two Harbours: 47090-A1 (U.S.); Ashland: A6090-A1 (U.S.);
Hancock: 47087-A1 (U.S.); Iron River: 46088-A1 (U.S.); Marquette:
46086-A1 (U.S.); Sault Saint Marie: 46084-A1 (U.S.); Saute Ste Marie:
41 K; Michipicoten: 41 N; White River: 42 C.
1:50,000 - Marathon: 42 D/9; Goodchild Lake: 42 D/16; Coldwell: 42
D/15; Pic Island: 42 D/10; Schreiber: 42 D/14; Slate Islands: 42 D/11;
Rossport: 42 D/13; Grebe Point: 42 D/12; Red Rock: 52 A/16; Shesheeb
Bay: 52 A/9; Loon: 52 A/10; Thunder Bay: 52 A/6; Jarvis River: 52A/3;
Œle Parisienne: 41 K/10; Pancake Bay: 41 K/15; Mamainse Point: 41 N/2;
Agawa Bay: 41 N/7; Old Woman Lake: 41 N/10; Michipicoten River: 41
N/15; Dog Harbour: 41 N/14; Bonner Head: 41 N/13; Pukaskwa: 42 C/4;
Otter Island: 42 D/1; Oiseau Bay: 42 D/8.

**Winisk River, Ontario**
1:250,000 - Winiskisis Channel: 43 E; Clendenning River: 43 L; Sutton
Lake: 43 K; Winisk: 43 N.
1:50,000 - Lastcedar Lake: 43 E/3; 43 E/6; Tashkarapids: 43 E/11; Meggisi
Creek: 43 E/14; 43 L/3; 43 L/6; Banipatau Creek: 43 L/11; Winino Creek:
43 L/15; 43 L/10; 43 L/9; 43 K/13; 43 K/14; Peawanuck: 43 N/3.

**Wabakimi Provincial Park, Ontario**
1:250,000 - Armstrong: 52 I; Fawn River: 53 I.

1:50,000 - Armstrong: 52 I/6; Goldsborough Lake: 52 I/11; Wabakimi Lake; 52 I/12; Burntrock Lake: 52 I/14; 53 I/5.

## Chiniguichi River and Laura Creek Circuit, Ontario
1:250,000 - Sudbury: 41 I.
1:50,000 - Lake Temagami: 41 I/16; Milnet: 41 I/15.

## Madawaska River, Ontario
1:250,000 - Pembroke: 31 F.
1:50,000 - Barry's Bay: 31 F/5; Brudenell: 31 F/6; Denbigh: 31 F/3.

## No-NameTrent-Peterborough Canoe Group, Ontario
1:250,000 - Lake Simcoe: 31 D.
1:50,000 - Peterborough: 31D/8.

## Rupert River, Quebec
1:250,000 - Baie Abatagouche: 32 I, Lac Baudeau: 32 P; Lac Mesgouez: 32 O; Lac Nemiscau: 32 N; Fort-Rupert: 32 M.
1:50,000 - Île Guillaume-Couture: 32 I/13; Île Peuvereau: 32 P/4; Lac Miskittenau: 32 O/1; Lac La Bardelière: 32 O/7; Lac Bellinger: 32 O/8; Lac Goulde: 32 O/11; Lac Des Montagnes: 32 O/12; Lac De La Sicotière: 32 N/8; Lac Nemiscau: 32 N/7, Lac Mizières: 32 N/6; Ruisseau Gaulier: 32 N/5; Colline Jaray: 32 M/8; Fort-Rupert: 32 M/7.

## Offshore New Brunswick
1:250,000 - Eastport: 21B; Fredericton: 21 G.
1:50,000 - Grand Manan Island: 21B/10; Campobello Island: 21B/15; McDougall Lake: 21G/7.
Marine Charts - 4331; 4373; 4340.

## Saint John River, New Brunswick
1:250,000 - Fredericton: 21 G.
1:50,000 - Federicton: 21 G/15; Grand Lake: 21 G/16.

## PEI's East Side, Prince Edward Island
1:250,000 - Charlottetown: 11 L.
1:50,000 - Montaue: 11 L/2; Boughton Island: 11 L/1.

## Nova Scotia's Coastal Water Trail
Marine Charts: Lunenburg Harbour: 4328; Mahone Bay: 4381; Chebucto Head to Betty Island: 4385; Halifax Habour: 4237.

## Tobeatic River, Nova Scotia
1:250,000 - Annapolis Royal: 21 A.
1:50,000 - Lake Rossignol: 21 A/3; Wentworth Lake: 21 A/4, Weymouth: 21 A/5; Kejimkujik Lake: 21 A/6.

## Margaree River, Nova Scotia
1:250,000 - Sydney: 11 K.
1:50,000 - Chéticamp River: 11K/10; St Annis Harbour: 11K/7;
Margaree: 11K/6.

## Notokwanon River, Newfoundland and Labrador
1:250,000 - Mistastin Lake: 13 M; Nain: 14 C; Hopedale: 13 N.
1:50,000 - Lac Ramusio: 13 M/5; Lac Machault: 13 M/12; 13 M/11;
13 M/10; 13 M/15; 13 M/16; 13 N/13; Garland Bight: 14 C4; Akpiktok
Island: 14 C/3; Sango Bay: 13 N/14; Davis Inlet: 13 N/15.

## Gros Morne National Park, Newfoundland and Labrador
1:250,000 - Sandy Lake: 12 H.
1:50,000 - St. Paul Inlet: 12 H/13; Gros Morne: 12 H/12; King's Point:
12 H/9; Springdale: 12 H/8.